89644

89644

558.012.31

D0364032

INSTITUTE

IMI *information service*
Sandyford, Dublin 16
Telephone 2078513 Fax 295 9479
email library@imi.ie
Internet http://www.imi.ie

2 6 OCT 2000		
2 4 JUN 2002		
2 9 MAR 2006		

STRATEGY OF THE DOLPHIN

STRATEGY OF THE DOLPHIN

Winning Elegantly by Coping Powerfully in a World of Turbulent Change

DUDLEY LYNCH AND
PAUL L. KORDIS

HUTCHINSON BUSINESS BOOKS

COPYRIGHT © 1988 by BRAIN TECHNOLOGIES CORP.

First trade edition published in the United States of America
by William Morrow and Company, Inc., New York

First published in Great Britain by
Hutchinson Business Books
An imprint of Century Hutchinson Limited
62-65 Chandos Place, London WC2N 4NW

Century Hutchinson Australia (Pty) Limited
89-91 Albion Street, Surry Hills,
New South Wales 2010, Australia

Century Hutchinson New Zealand Limited
PO Box 40-085, 32-34 View Road, Glenfield,
Auckland 10, New Zealand

Century Hutchinson South Africa (Pty) Limited
PO Box 337, Bergylai 2012, South Africa

British Library Cataloguing in Publication Data
Lynch, Dudley.
The Strategy of the Dolphin: winning elegantly by
coping powerfully in a world of turbulent change.
1. Organisational change. Management aspects
I. Title   II. Kordis, Paul L.
658.4'06

ISBN 0-09-174208-0

Brain Technologies Corporation is active throughout the world helping corporate clients benefit from the concepts and principles outlined in Strategy of the Dolphin. *For a copy of BTC's catalogue of dolphin-based learning materials, audio-visual aids and educational testing inventories, or for more information on BTC's consulting and management development services, contact Brain Technologies Corporation direct.*

Dudley Lynch, President
Brain Technologies Corporation
2290 East Prospect Road
Suite Two
Fort Collins
Colorado 80525 USA
Tel: 303 493 9210
Fax: 303 493 9243

Printed in the United States of America
BOOK DESIGN BY JAYE ZIMET

To Delphinus Delphis
Patience

ACKNOWLEDGMENTS

Conceptually and intellectually, there are three separate "seas" of ideas that have been harvested to produce *Strategy of the Dolphin*.

One is the viewpoint that biology is intricately connected to human outcomes—that is, that when we are studying the development of human values and behavior, it is a *psychobiosocial* task we are addressing. For us, the key figure here is the late Dr. Clare W. Graves, who spent much of his career at Union College. A scholar-provocateur, Clare Graves was, as Australians are wont to say, "a tall poppy" who stood head and shoulders above his colleagues in the field of developmental structuralism in psychology. Even now, he's little known because a devastating period of spiraling ill health struck him down as he neared the peak of his creative powers. I am indebted to Don Beck and Christopher Cowan of the National Values Center for introducing me both personally and intellectually to Graves and for a genuinely selfless sharing of Graves's materials, models, and observations. Thanks also to Vince Flowers and Charles Hughes of The Center for Values Research, to the late Arnold Mitchell of the Values and Lifestyles (VALS) Program at SRI International, and to more than sixty-five other "developmental structuralists" in academic psychology whose work we tapped to create the values code discussed in Chapter 4.

Another major figure whose ideas permeate this work is the late Buckminster Fuller, "Bucky" to the millions worldwide who will always feel kinship with this brilliantly strange little savant with the "sci-fi" mind. I knew him—know him—only through his writings, his art, and his network of admirers, including David G. Neenan and Marshall Thurber, who have aided my personal understanding of Fuller's concepts.

Finally, there are those insightful minds who added to my understanding of open systems, in particular the brain, both human and dolphin varieties: Michael Hutchison, author of *Megabrain;* Frank Robson, the "dolphin man" of Taradale, New Zealand, who dug through a lifetime's collection of notes and photographs to provide me with a graduate education on dolphin capabilities; the ever-imaginative Doug Michels, designer of the futuristic Bluestar space station for housing both man and dolphin; and Kenneth L. Adams, appreciated once again for that uncanny ability to provide key insights at key times.

I know my family loves me, or else they'd never tolerate the disruption this kind of project brings to our lives together. To my life partner, Sherry Ann Lynch, and daughters Kimberly Lynn and Mendy Suzanne, I can only say one more time how fortunate I feel to have discovered you in my very personal ocean.

My intellectual partner in this enterprise, Paul L. Kordis, came up on my personal horizon like a sunrise, and I'll spend the rest of my career working out the implications and consequences of what I've learned from him. I thank you, Paul, for your courage, imagination, intelligence, and, most of all, for your forbearing spirit.

The selflessness, camaraderie, and instrumental support of a number of persons have been critical in times past and near: my parents, Mabel and Mardell Lynch; my longtime mentor, John Ludtka; Stan and Barbara Levenson, Gary John, Dave Terrell, Fred Janisch, Paul Gilbertson, Lee Sneath, Pam Deutsch, John A. Jackson, Larry and Linda Hahn, Foy Richey, and Lorrie Hart.

My thanks to my agent, John Brockman, and my editor, Adrian Zackheim, who understood immediately what this project is about and who helped make it happen with amazing speed and an astonishing minimum of fuss.

And to dolphins of both kinds, land and sea, simply know that

I'm committed to building on what we've begun here together. I'll be in touch.

Dudley Lynch
Fort Collins
October 11, 1988

The paradox of acknowledgment is that it is nearly impossible to be completely inclusive and acceptably brief. Therefore, I thank my parents, family, and friends for enduring a writer in their midst and for their continued inspiration—and Pauline Elson, Rich Vliet, Gary Young, and Wayne Viney, who at critical points in my life gave me the support I needed when I least deserved it. These people should be cloned and scattered throughout the universe.

Paul L. Kordis
Fort Collins
October 11, 1988

CONTENTS _____

12 Contents

INTRODUCTION ____

At the boundary, life blossoms.
—James Gleick, Chaos

For at least forty thousand years, and probably much longer, people, their families, and their organizations, commercial and social alike, have typically pursued two kinds of strategies for coping with the world.

The *strategy of the carp.*

And the *strategy of the shark.*

This book is about a powerful new strategy: one that has sprung full blown of late from a brain that understands that the world has changed and therefore so must we. *What must change is the quality and quantity of our awareness of complexity and our skills and comfort level in working with it.*

In their domination of human history, the carp and shark strategies of information processing have posted severe limitations on what humans can notice and how much freedom they will be permitted in response to a changing world.

Persons who utilize only the strategy of the carp suffer from a blinding *hypnosis*—an inability to acknowledge and accept as real very crucial aspects of the world at large.

And people who are habituated to the strategy of the shark are addicts. Their *addictions* and *compulsions* doom them to be perennial "bulls in the china closets"—or worse—of our societies, organizations, and families. Originally motivated by

The future ain't what it used to be. ARTHUR C. CLARKE, *THE ADVENTURE OF TOMORROW*

Ideas have consequences. RICHARD WEAVER

I don't think we are ever going to see those halcyon days again. JUDITH LARSEN, *SILICON VALLEY FEVER*

The strategies of the carp and the shark are "hard-wired" into us.

13

pleasure, sharks in the long run become motivated by the avoidance of pain. Living and doing business as we do in environments with closer and closer tolerances, we find their excessive adrenaline and intolerance of comity and flexibility to be increasingly irritable if not outright dangerous.

Both the strategies of the carp and the shark remain with us because to be basic about it, both strategies are "hard-wired" into us. Specifically, they are hard-wired into our "old," isolated, nonverbal brain structures. We can no more totally eliminate their influences and do things like run an accounting firm, operate a beauty shop, manufacture computers, command an army, or coach an athletic team than we can throw away our heads and still call ourselves living creatures capable of being overdrawn at the bank. You'll recognize these strategies right away unless you choose not to, which is a bit of a Catch-22 situation, since choosing not to recognize something of value is, in itself, the use of one of the strategies. The strategy of the carp.

The "old" brain offers us the proverbial "three Fs" as behavioral choices for responding to external events: *fight, flight,* or *freeze*. A carp (that is, a person using the carp strategy) typically uses only two of these choices, flight or freeze. Obviously, carps get eaten a lot, although if one takes pains to stay in carp waters amid plenty of carp friends and do mostly carp work, at certain times one may be able to make a relatively safe life of it. If they have a choice, carps usually go along. However, if they can, they avoid choices entirely. George Bernard Shaw recognized the signature dynamics of the carp's strategy. "Liberty [the freedom to exercise choice] means responsibility," he wrote. "That's why most men [and women*] dread it."

You cannot take a single breath unless God wills it. SIXTY-YEAR-OLD LANDOWNER/ FARMER FROM GURHA, INDIA

The pride of our nation is in our cemeteries. AFRICAN HYMN

Je me debrouille. (I get by, I manage, I improvise.) POPULAR PHRASE IN ZAIRE

---

* Shaw refused to take responsibility for acknowledging in his use of the English language that slightly more than half the human race is female. Carping out, so to speak, he used the literary "men" to connote the generic "human." That's the easy way. Frankly, we're uncomfortable with the need to address this issue in a footnote and thoroughly dissatisfied with the fact that literary English has as yet found no solution to this or to the he/she conundrum. In *Strategy of the Dolphin,* we're going to use whichever pronoun strikes our fancy at the moment. As we say in our distributor contracts at Brain Technologies Corporation, "Any reference to the masculine gender is equally applicable to the feminine gender, and vice versa."

*T*here are times when it makes sense in the organization to be a carp, and later on we'll discuss these at some length. And times when it makes sense to be a shark, which we will also discuss with genuine enthusiasm. Usually the strategy of the shark is viewed as a strategy intended to produce a personal win, whatever the cost. When you must swim in the vicinity of sharks, the rules are pretty clear:

- Discover what the sharks look like and who they are (''the ones with the sharp teeth'').
- Don't thrash around and make a lot of noise.
- Don't hang around with the bait fish (''the carps'').
- Don't be afraid to scare off a shark when one comes sniffing around (''sometimes all it takes is a good clout on the nose'').
- If you get bitten, don't bleed.
- Don't tire yourself out swimming against the tide.
- And, most importantly, find some other dolphins to swim around with.[1]

''Real'' dolphins are some of the most prized creatures of the deep. We can suspect that they are very intelligent, perhaps in their own way more intelligent than we *Homo sapiens*. Certainly, their brains are large enough—about fifteen hundred grams, somewhat larger on average than the typical human brain—and the dolphin's associational cortex, the part of the brain specialized for abstract and conceptual thinking, is larger than ours. And it is a brain, as those fervent enthusiasts devoted to strengthening ties between our large-brained species and theirs are quick to point out, that has been as large as or larger than ours for at least thirty million years.

Dolphin behavior around sharks is legendary, and probably deservedly so. Using their intelligence and their wiles, they can be deadly to sharks. Bite them to death? Oh, no. Dolphins circle and ram, circle and ram. Using their bulbous noses as amphibious bludgeons, they methodically crush the shark's ''rib cage'' until the murderous creature sinks helplessly to the bottom. But rather

Any real good businessman has a streak of barracuda in him. . . .
U.S. MERCHANDISING EXECUTIVE QUOTED IN *THE WALL STREET JOURNAL*

Many an investor or hot-to-trot manager has been victimized by the *Look of a Winner* con. They are seduced into a venture that glows with the sheen of success. Gleaming new Ferraris. Palatial offices. Custom-tailored silk suits. Ostrich-skin boots with matching briefcase. Diamond pinky rings. Extravagant entertainment, wining and dining. ''Business meetings'' at exotic locations. The superficial logic is: ''They must be doing awfully well if they can afford to spread all that money around,'' and ''After all, nothing succeeds like success.'' G. RAY FUNK-HOUSER AND ROBERT R. ROTHBERG, *THE PURSUIT OF GROWTH*

We are in an age that assumes the narrowing trends of specialization to be logical, natural, and desirable. Consequently, society expects all earnestly responsible communication to be crisply brief. Advancing science has now discovered that all the known cases of biological extinction have been caused by overspecialization, whose concentration of only selected genes sacrifices general adaptability. Thus the specialist's brief for pinpoint brevity is dubious. In the meantime, humanity has been deprived of comprehensive understanding. Specialization has bred feelings of isolation, futility, and confusion in individuals. It has also resulted in the individual's leaving responsibility for thinking and social action to others. Specialization breeds biases that ultimately aggregate as international and ideological discord, which, in turn, leads to war. BUCKMINSTER FULLER, SYNERGETICS

than its skill at shark combat, we have chosen the dolphin to symbolize our thoughts on coping and choice-making in rapid-change times because of the mammal's natural abilities to think constructively and creatively. Do dolphins think? Without question. When they don't get what they want, they quickly and precisely alter their behaviors in sometimes ingenious ways in pursuit of what they are after.

If dolphins can do it, why can't we?

We think we can.

The strategy of the dolphin requires that we think about how we think. This raises the human coping and change capabilities available by an order of magnitude. With a twist of the mental and emotional kaleidoscope, the dolphin (human variety) changes the nature, the rules, perhaps even the playing surface and the players themselves. Dolphins enjoy, exploit, explore, and experience to the fullest of their faculties the ability of the integrated, highly social (internally), fully involved human brain to second-guess itself and other brains in advance. The result is often an ocean of ideas. A maelstrom of possibilities. An awakening of potential. A suddenly visible way out of the shark pool so stunning that it is the mental equal to a punch in the solar plexus.

You might have thought that the dawning of the Atomic Age signaled the need for a drastic new thought process for managing human affairs. But that watershed event wasn't quite drastic enough. Instead, it required something like the oil embargo—a *global* event—to etch indelibly on our minds that we had crossed a Rubicon so momentous that the strategies of the carp and the shark were obsolete when you are managing and maneuvering on the cutting edges of change. So the world that has made this kind of thinking so necessary and appealing dates realistically only from the early 1970s.

Our hope: that we can learn to quit interpreting our failures as successes.

Our hope in writing *Strategy of the Dolphin* is that such an effort can help you avoid, regularly and with a minimum of effort, the core entrapments both of the strategy of the carp and the strategy of the shark: *the maddening ability of contemporary brains to "characteristically interpret their behavior as successful even if it leads eventually and inevitably to failure."* [2]

The ease with which categories of individuals and their organizations can achieve "dolphinization" will vary. It is obvious that some will have to contend with "natural barriers of the soul" to make it happen. For example, users of our traditional authoritarian belief systems—and that includes most of our corporations and other bureaucracies—are going to be challenged to the hilt by the idea of empowering a new dimension of personal abundance. To cite another example, "New Age" thinkers, for all their exciting potential, must summon the courage to confront yet another truth about themselves: that they are closer than ever to a quantum jump in personal power but are still leaving it unappropriated and unappreciated and in doing so are still personally deprived and diminished. And *everyone* who aspires to be a winner in the 1990s and beyond must take seriously the overriding theme that underlies *Strategy of the Dolphin*, the book and the power: to succeed in the kind of world that is preshadowing the 21st Century, you must develop *a new kind of mind.*

*I*n choosing to name that new mind after the world's oldest symbol for thinking smarter—*delphinus delphis*—we aren't borrowing so much on the actual behavior of the sea's most brainy performer as we are being inspired by its toughness, its charm, its intuitiveness and its intelligence. Yet, we have to admit that there are very appealing similarities between the dolphin of the sea and the new thinking sub-species, *homo sapiens delphinus,* we are describing.

The reasonable man adapts himself to the world: the unreasonable one persists in trying to adapt the world to himself. Therefore all progress depends on the unreasonable man.
GEORGE BERNARD SHAW

Life spirals laboriously upward to higher and higher levels paying for every step. . . . It passes into levels of higher differentiation and centralization and pays for this by loss of regulability after disturbances. It invents a highly developed nervous system and therewith pain. It adds to the primeval parts of the nervous system a brain which allows consciousness that by means of a world of symbols grants foresight and control of the future.
LUDWIG VON BERTALANFFY, *PROBLEMS OF LIFE*

A human being should be able to change a diaper, plan an invasion, butcher a hog, conn a ship, design a building, write a sonnet, balance accounts, build a wall, set a bone, comfort the dying, take orders, give orders, cooperate, act alone, solve equations, analyze a new problem, pitch manure, program a computer, cook a tasty meal, fight efficiently, die gallantly. Specialization is for insects. ROBERT A. HEINLEIN, *THE NOTEBOOKS OF LAZARUS LONG*

Life happens too fast for you ever to think about it. If you could just persuade people of this, but they insist on amassing information.
KURT VONNEGUT, JR.

- Dolphins of both varieties—the sea's and the seashore's—thrive in a tough environment.
- They both are ever-vigilant, reading the currents, searching for clues, monitoring developments.
- They both swim well in any ocean, float in any current, dive in any pool.
- They take action well together—or act competently alone.
- If things aren't working, they often ruthlessly pursue something different, something that *does* work.
- And, as we have already noted, if necessary they can be deadly to a shark.

We would argue that for us humans, the "strategy of the dolphin" is the first truly new system for winning in almost half a century. During that 50 years, approaches to success have offered little more than a variation on one basic theme: think positively. Because there are many other ways to think and other ways you need to think in a world with a lot of changes going on—and a lot of challenges to work through—we want to replace that venerable but aging idea with a better one: *think powerfully*.

But in a way that helps *everyone* get his or her needs met.

And helps everyone succeed to the fullest range of his or her personal competencies.

And makes this world a better place.

That's going to require a new kind of player, with a new kind of mind. Those individuals and those organizations willing to develop that kind of mind are going to be the participants of choice in a new kind of game. And the people and organizations making it possible for all of us to take home the marbles when the world is changing rapidly.

1
GOING FOR THE ELEGANT OUTCOME: DOLPHINS ARE AS DOLPHINS DO

*T*he strategy of the dolphin is a diamond-bit-ended search for *what works*. For what makes sense. For what will get the job done, get our goals met, and get our future delivered with some credible assurance that the planet, the race, and as many other species as we can bring along will survive and, if possible, thrive.

The strategy of the dolphin has a way of spooking other people's sacred cows.

Dolphins don't give in or give up easily until it makes a difference. Then they are capable of surrender.

Dolphins are not very ideological, but if it matters, they can be intensely political.

Dolphins are unyielding on principle unless the principle no longer makes any sense.

Dolphins like to win. But they don't need for you to lose unless you insist on it.

Dolphins tell the truth and thus avoid wasting time, energy, and resources on useless, unproductive drama.

Dolphins have a vision of the way they want the corporation, the organization, the world to be—but they aren't kamikazes about it.

Dolphins almost always act on "the big picture," but they are

I've been trying for some time to develop a life-style that doesn't require my presence. GARY TRUDEAU

Loyalty to a petrified opinion never yet broke a chain or freed a human soul. MARK TWAIN

19

also capable of focusing on the smallest detail. Dolphins are quick to retaliate if the situation calls for it, but they'll instantly forgive you, knowing that a grudge is an artificial and ultimately insupportable barrier in a fluid, creative universe.

Dolphins make superb managers and leaders, and in a world where they are putting their superior strategic and tactical thinking capabilities to work, they are destined to keep carps and sharks increasingly off balance and disadvantaged when challenged.

*E*ven if you are determined to remain a carp or a shark, you may find it of interest to expand your knowledge of dolphins and dolphin thinking. Otherwise, much of the world of management and the world in general in the coming years may not make a lot of sense.

When sharks encounter a dolphin, they often erroneously assume that they are dealing with a carp. Carps, on the other hand, typically mistake dolphins for sharks. In addition, many people in organizations *think* they know what dolphins *are* but fail to appreciate many subtle—and vital—distinctions and find still others totally illusive. An even greater number of people remain ignorant that there are such creatures as dolphins in organizations and thus have never considered becoming one, whatever *it* is and whatever the benefits.

Obviously, here is a bit of confusion asking to be cleared up.

First, a word about what dolphins aren't.

They are not platinum-plated "superfish" swimming haughtily around the shop or the front office or the boardroom or the computer center awaiting the right moment to impart superior wisdom, stunning ideals, or awe-inspiring breakthrough solutions. About the only time you can be sure that you have a dolphin in your midst is if progress is being

The average man, who does not know what to do with his life, wants another one which will last forever.   ANATOLE FRANCE

You know dolphins are near if you are making progress when it long since should have ceased.

made at times when, by any sensible standard, progress long since should have ceased.

Dolphins aren't creatures who live by the book, even if that book is called *Strategy of the Dolphin*. Much of the time, in fact, they look like, act like, and may not resist being treated like sharks or carps.

Dolphins, in fact, may resist using their dolphin knowledge and powers on many occasions, copping out for strategic or tactical reasons in the manner of a carp or going for the jugular with the intensity of a shark. Dolphins aren't—heaven forbid!—gurus or really very inclined at all toward the fringe-tinged, ''touchy-feely,'' left-field approaches of mysticism, the occult, or the unscientific, although they are typically open to anything that works.

Dolphins may be ''big cheeses'' in their organizations, but then again they are just as likely to be ''worker bees,'' particularly in high-tech or other information age kinds of organizations.

Dolphins are not opposed to winning. If there is little at stake or if they can learn something significant, they aren't opposed to losing, either. They aren't reluctant to give in, aren't hesitant to compromise, and don't mind the heat in the kitchen of conflict and tough going—if it *genuinely* makes sense. If it makes *elegant* sense!

It would seem, then, that when we focus on elegant sense-making, we are defining something that is central to dolphinhood in the organization. Where we find thoughts, feelings, actions, and intuitions that bring together people and resources *elegantly,* we find circumstances and situations that are attractive to dolphins. To understand the value and power of developing our skills as dolphins, let's look—as a dolphin looks—at what our options are for ''making elegant sense'' in a rapidly changing world.

Never underestimate the power of human stupidity.

Stupidity is the only universal capital crime; the sentence is death, there is no appeal, and the execution is carried out automatically and without pity. ROBERT A. HEINLEIN, *THE NOTEBOOKS OF LAZARUS LONG*

What do we mean by ''elegant''? Looking in our *Webster's Third New International Dictionary,* we discover the meaning we are after in definition 1(d):

"characterized by [scientific] precision, neatness, and simplicity." Elegant solutions do not emerge with the needed frequency in today's business world because of the invariability, inflexibility, and insensibility of carp and shark thinking.

Elegant solutions escape us in too many instances of negotiating because, in reality, given our deeply inbred feelings about the supposed value of competition and about winning and losing in our organizational cultures, neither party ever gets its needs fully met. And the popular "win/win" concept that has emerged out of the humanistic psychology movement is also too frequently a chimera—a trade-off kind of enterprise calculated more to produce good feelings than outstandingly good results. To say it again, the tendency is deep within us to grow self-congratulatory even when, for the long term and for the widest interest, we have failed.

As cavemen and cavewomen, believing that the gods had so decreed, we could shrug off the fact that the target of the hunt had escaped. Raising grains on the world's savannas, even if our ingrained stubbornness blinded us to elegant solutions, we usually still had our land and the next season to wrestle with the consequences. Even in the Industrial Age, flexibility and elegance in thinking weren't overly needed or valued, not by Frederick Taylor, the nineteenth-century genius who more than anyone else created the organizational blueprint for the times, nor by most of his managerial descendants-in-spirit.

Fast responses can be advantageous but they are by no means the total answer.

[The] great leader is one for whom his men will CHEERFULLY give up their lives. That is the real test of leadership.   REAR ADMIRAL CHESTER WARD

I have not been able to find a single person in my organization who would die for me, much less CHEERFULLY die for me. This definitely shows I am not a leader in accordance with Admiral Ward's definition.

Now, though, it matters.

Realizing this, some opinion-shapers and management theorists argue for faster and faster response times. As a model, some of them look to the so-called O.O.D.A. loop—the cycle of observation, orientation, decision, and then action described by the Air Force after studying why some pilots were better in wartime dogfights than others. Certainly, there are times when fast responses are advantages, or critical. In times like these, dolphins may revert to sharklike thinking. But O.O.D.A. isn't the answer when the challenge is to weld difficult new alliances, wield power in radically new fashion, or wrench loose from limiting perspectives.

For the late 1980s and the 1990s, we believe the most successful organizations are going to be those capable of solving their most fundamental challenges and problems with elegance. *Dolphin*like elegance.

So believing this, let's now jump into the pool, recognizing that there are times to act like a carp, times to act like a shark, and times to think like a dolphin. The power comes from knowing, and acting on the knowledge of, which is which and what is what.

Incidentally, when Admiral Ward's article came out I telephoned him and asked him how many people in his office had volunteered cheerfully to die for him, whereupon he hung up on me. ADMIRAL H. G. RICK-OVER

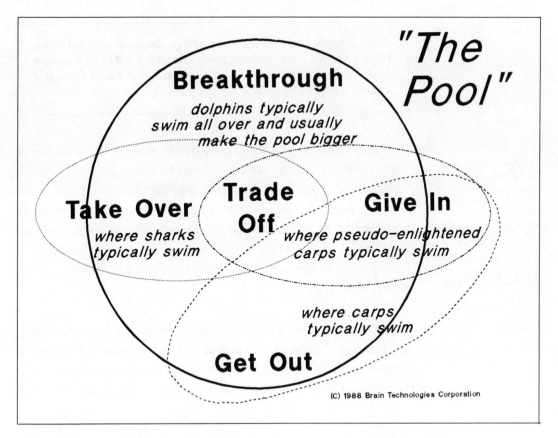

Figure 1.1. Where Carps, Sharks, and Dolphins Swim

What's "the pool"? Easy. The pool is *what is possible*. In the whole wide universe? No, what's possible in *your* personal universe, and in ours, and in our organizations' universe.

For this reason, our personal and organizational universes can be very different, depending on what we believe.

Carps and sharks believe that we *live in a world of scarcity*—that there is only so much to go around and since we are always in danger of running out, what we have and how much of it we can have very much depend on our behaving in structured, predictable ways.

Essentially, carps repeat to themselves unconsciously for the most part and usually for a lifetime this kind of "belief methodology":

> **"I am a carp, and I believe in scarcity. Because of this belief, I don't expect ever to do or have enough. So *if I can't escape from learning and responsibility by staying away from it, I usually sacrifice myself.*"**

I cannot help myself at all, for he [the demon] uses my limbs and organs, my neck, my tongue, and my lungs. . . . THE MALLEUS MALEFICARUM

If it was so, it might be; and if it were so, it would be; but as it isn't, it ain't. That's logic. LEWIS CARROLL, *THROUGH THE LOOKING GLASS*

The making of a carp typically begins early in life with one or more traumatic events strong enough to cause an individual to make, deep within the psyche, that crippling decision: *I can't win; not now, not later, not ever.* So believing, the focus now becomes not losing. The reasoning and its consequences become cyclical, reinforcing, and usually self-fulfilling. As counselor Stewart Emery notes in *Actualizations: You Don't Have to Rehearse to Be Yourself:*

We can see, if we look, that most of the planet is playing the game from "I can't win, but how do I avoid losing?" Once we have made that decision, the best we can get out of life is nothing. Once we have gotten to the point where we decide, "I can't win, how do I avoid losing?" happiness is when it doesn't hurt. Not bad is the best it gets. We no longer expect it to be good; we just hope it won't be too bad.[1]

S o believing, nothing threatens—or enrages—a carp more than the possibility of abundance. The carp's belief in limits is nothing short of the hypnotic. In the "self-hate" triad (of persecutor, rescuer, and victim) that psychologists often call the Drama Triangle (first identified by Dr. Stephen Karpman), our carp perennially reside at the victims' corner, jammed as it always is with the cracker barrels of losers and the miseries of caretaking unrequited. A permanent house number at the victims' corner entitles carps to all the roles—and the agonies—now fashionably described in an era increasingly sensitive to the ills of addiction as "the codependents'." Codependent on what? On the opportunity to avoid being personally responsible for their actions and doing something positively different by forever being in thrall to someone else: a "persecutor" (that is, a shark) or other victims "who can't help themselves." The hypnosis cutting the carp off from acknowledging the possibility of change, of abundance, is little short of extraordinary to observe and analyze, as Anne Wilson Schaef and Diane Fassel have done. In *The Addictive Organization,* they note:

Carps reside permanently at the victims' corner in the Drama Triangle.

> Co-dependents [our carps] . . . spend most of their time understanding the needs of others and picking up subtle cues about what others want from them. At the same time they are astute observers. They intuitively know what responses are required in most situations, and they give them. Their impression management disguises a wide-ranging dishonesty that is experienced by others as niceness,

One who had been threatened by the gangs with reprisals for calling the police was asked why she did not go to stay with her parents farther out on the West Side. "That just brings the trouble on them too. You got to take what comes with your own life." ADAM WALINSKY

If it's a major accident that gets broad coverage, there may be some degree of avoidance factor over the short-term which tends to taper off because I guess people have short memories. AIRLINE STOCKS ANALYST righteousness, and an unlimited capacity for understanding and listening. Co-dependents will rarely come right out and tell you what they want. They are experts at vagueness, manipulation, rumor and gossip. . . . Culturally, the co-dependent looks like the loving, giving person, yet as we work with co-dependents we find that underneath their composed exterior, they are frequently angry, depressed, and extremely controlling and manipulative.[2]

In their trancelike avoidance of the possibility of abundance, carps often actually see themselves as residing elsewhere on the Drama Triangle. It is easy for carps to think they are "born to rescue." At the rescuer's corner, carps hang out a sign that says, in effect, "We fix feelings, do others' thinking, and suffer *your* consequences for you." Such one-stop service for life's victims can generate nice feelings, feelings of being needed and "doing good"—for a while. Until we notice that despite our seeming good works and intentions we have Rodney Dangerfield's disease: no respect. Our beneficiaries aren't following our advice and are showing no

Playing rescuer all the time brings on Rodney Danger-field's disease: no respect

gratitude. At that point, the carp-*née*-rescuer feels betrayed in that no one is willing to take care of her, especially those she is caring for. That in turn offers the person she has supposedly been "rescuing" an opportunity to be the persecutor—to show indignation at having been thought to be incompetent to begin with— and suddenly the carp is back in familiar turf, the victims' corner, which is actually home.

To keep at bay the opportunity to enjoy abundance and the possibilities of real change, the carp becomes adept at self-prescribing solutions intended to thwart breakthrough situations. Again, Stewart Emery is a shrewd observer. He has identified the six primary solutions carps prescribe for themselves to avoid having to take personal responsibility for achieving abundance and change:

Airline passengers may be angrier than ever about terrible service, yet their actions appear to provide little incentive for carriers to change their ways. Travelers frequently return to fly the same airline after bad experiences. And only in the most extreme cases have carriers actually lost business in reaction to service foul-ups. *THE WALL STREET JOURNAL*

- Don't play.
- Keep others from winning.
- Don't complete anything.
- Destroy the game.
- Play the nice-guy routine.
- Become a problem.[3]

In Figure 1.1, the pool for carps is circumscribed at the lower right, a narrow, elongated area anchored on one end by a way of thinking we call Get-out and on the other end by a way of thinking we call Give-in. Using the Get-out strategy consistently doesn't do much for your chances of survival. Eventually, each of the other strategies named in Figure 1.1 will bypass this one. Why's that? Because as we shall soon see, each of the other strategies at least produces a result or creates some kind of bond, tie, or relationship with others. People who consistently take their baseball bats and go home are hermits, whatever their age or their game. *Hermits.* Hermetical. Sealed off. Cut off. Isolated. In most cases, the carp who consistently plays Get-out lives with scarcities of one kind or another. In this instance, belief is indeed the precursor of reality: carp reality, with carp scarcity.

In the long term, playing Give-in isn't much better. In fact, it can be much worse. Play Give-in consistently and you risk extinction. Why's that? For two reasons that register mightily on the Richter Scale of dilemma resolution.

*F*irst, the players you are most likely to give in *to* are usually sharks, and if you continue to do nothing but give in—to surrender—you eventually will have nothing left. (Neither, for that matter, will the shark, which will eventually be forced to cannibalize his own ranks after eating all the carps.) The other choice is to play with dolphins, and dolphins will quickly discover you have no stomach for dealing with challenging issues and little to nothing to contribute to elegant solutions, and they'll

To tell you the truth, it doesn't bother me a bit. I really don't care about it. I'm fifty-five years old, I've had a good life, and I guess I've got to go one way or another. GEORGIA RESIDENT ON RADON GAS DANGER

When people are free to do as they please, they usually imitate each other. ERIC HOFFER

Get-out renders you incapable of making a positive contribution—of leveraging.

come to prefer other swimming partners. Frustrated at being ignored, put down, or left out, you may *then* attempt to retaliate passively, trying forms of covert manipulation or sabotage. And in doing so, you run the risk that your dolphin will revert to shark behavior. Suddenly, the one thing you thought was a "given"—the safeness and sanctity of your bonds to other players—is under attack. Carp that you are, you are now likely to scurry to Get-out, and in doing so to remove yourself completely as a factor in the equations we variously call "the organization," "the team," "the family," "the group," or "the relationship." In every case, you are no longer capable of contributing or receiving positively. The grave danger of playing Get-out is that you must make all your mistakes by yourself. It doesn't allow you to leverage off the experiences of others.

Sharks respond much differently. They tell themselves repeatedly and again unconsciously for the most part:

If you can't do the time, don't do the crime.
MOBSTER SAYING

A swift and vigorous assumption of the offensive, the flashing sword of vengeance, is the most brilliant point in the defensive.   KARL VON CLAUSEWITZ

All warfare is based on deception. . . . When near, make it appear that you are far away; when far away, that you are near.
SUN TZU

"I am a shark, and I believe in scarcity. Because of this belief, I intend to get as much as I can no matter what. First, I try to lick them, and if I don't succeed, I try to join them."

Sharks believe there must be a loser and are determined that it is to be anyone but them. Thus rather than migrate to the victims' corner of the Drama Triangle, sharks lay claim to the persecutors' corner. There they become addicts to "the scarcity game," and there they create addictive systems and addictive organizations as their legacy to those they hire, sell to, buy from, and otherwise associate with. You can know that you are in the danger zone of the sharks' feeding waters if you are constantly confronted with:

■ **The "con."** If you are not in any immediate danger and understand what is happening, it can be fascinating to watch the lengths to which an accomplished shark will go to avoid the spotlight of responsibility. Whoever the eventual victim, the inner intent is always the same: to minimize the risk (and thus the likelihood of pain) of not being a winner, however small the issue or the outcome.

- **The fog.** Confusion is a natural cover for sharks. And the person or group causing the confusion is seldom an object of scrutiny because everyone else is caught up trying to assess what is going on. Roiling the waters is as conventional a shark tactic as gliding silently in the shadows.

- **The denial.** What will not be acknowledged cannot be confronted, contained, altered, or felt. And sharks have an eel's touch for avoiding the realness of events. Thus perhaps the gravest danger to the shark becomes believing his own fabrications as a way of warding off unwanted and unpleasant truths.

- **The "fix."** Sharks are like alternating current in their narcissism. In their warped view, everything they are willing to acknowledge flows either in their favor or against them. Constitutionally, they are unable to forgo for very long a renewing injection of the drug called "self." Since this "self" is unconnected to a larger humanity or purpose, it feeds the sense that only scarcity is real.

- **The assumption.** Visit any exhibition hall for a major industry trade convention and you will find yourself surrounded by "the assumption." Booth after booth is manned by sharks insisting that their product or approach is the only possible *right* answer. The assumption is based on the shark's need to believe that if all else and everyone else fails, his won't and he won't. It's a terrible burden: the shark's need to be right 100 percent of the time and the steely vigilance required to cover up the inevitable failures.

- **The crisis and the grip.** Being in the grip of something means being held in control. Sharks desperately want you to be in their control and are therefore constantly creating crises that force you to play it their way. To be in *con*trol requires that you constantly be on *pa*trol. Because sharks must spend so much

You've got to recognize that you're greedy. I want more than what my neighbor has. I want a better car, better clothes; I want my kids to go to a better school. I want better food in the house. Those are the basics. Beyond that, I want the respect of my community—I want them to know I'm an achiever. I want control. I want to make decisions. Then I want the ultimate. I want the power.   QUOTED BY JIM WALL IN *BOSSES*

He was an emotional player who took losses harder than most. Marv had gone out with Freddy, Pete, and me a number of times. When we won, he always had a good time. When we lost, he was liable to give anyone he met a bad time. If he fumbled and we lost, it was worse. He would get real deep into bourbon whiskey, and at some point in the evening you knew he was going to break something. Glass, a bottle, a window—something had to shatter.   KEN STABLER AND BERRY STAINBACK, *SNAKE*

Eventually with Takeover, you run out of suitable victims.

time on the perimeter of their feelings and the surface of events seeking to maintain control, they eventually lose touch with their inner processes: their intuitions, their emotions, their deeper purposes. Much in life *can* be controlled, but it is one of the paradoxes of existence that you must be capable of surrender to pull it off. Sharks prefer even the illusion of control to doing anything that might make things better.

This being the case, we shouldn't be surprised that the two major strategies in the elliptical space in Figure 1.1 denoted as "shark waters" are Takeover and Trade-off.

These two strategies are overwhelming favorites for executives, managers, owners, supervisors, business school faculty members, lawyers, accountants, bankers, investors, and the other myriad players for power in business.

*I*n 1976, playwright Tom Stoppard had the protagonist in his work *Travesties* say, "War is capitalism with the gloves off." Every generation of modern management to now has behaved in sufficient fashion to provide a living marketplace endorsement of Stoppard's view of capitalism. In the executive suite, few players have ever suffered from having a copy of the works of the great war thinkers in sight—Sun Tzu, Niccolò Machiavelli, Karl von Clausewitz, Ferdinand Foch. For all the world to see, the Takeover strategy so literally dominated the attention of major corporations in the 1970s and 1980s that "corporate raiders" were making almost as many headlines as the president. In *The Corporate Warriors*, business writer Douglas K. Ramsey listed nine "principles" of military strategy he believed were equally applicable to corporate conflict such as that personified by "the raiders":

1. Maneuver: the need for flexibility, keeping options open to deploy troops, expand manufacturing, cut prices, and so on.
2. Objective: clearly defining the goal of combat [which is always to dominate], targeting where the company should be at the end of it.
3. Offense: attacking the enemy or competition.
4. Surprise [of the enemy or opponent]: Clausewitz called it "the foundation of all military undertakings."
5. Economy of force: mobilizing the fewest resources and personnel necessary to achieve the objective.
6. Mass: "Concentrate your strength" is the way Sun Tzu put it.
7. Unity of command: clear lines of authority extending from the commanding—or chief executive—officer.
8. Simplicity: what military offices summarize with the acronym KISS: *K*eep *I*t *S*imple, *S*tupid.
9. Security: maintaining secrecy and loyalty inside the military or corporate unit.[4]

Machiavelli was a wimp.

The mainstay of training here is confidence. That's why we show them how to let a tank run over them. It gets their confidence up. OFFICER IN CHARGE OF U.S. SPECIAL OPERATIONS COMMAND

Greed is all right, by the way. I think greed is healthy. You can be greedy and still feel good about yourself. IVAN F. BOESKY

Toward the end of the 1980s, some of the largest individual raiders helped illustrate the downside of the Takeover strategy just as a few years earlier they had been some of its most vocal, visible, and viable examples of the technique's efficacy.

Instead of visiting sleepless nights on top executives at industry giants like Gulf, Unocal, Phillips Petroleum, Diamond Shamrock, and Amerada Hess, as they had earlier, some of the key raiders had been reduced to only occasional capers in their efforts to capture control of corporations other than their own. Oh, they were still around, still making occasional headlines, and since the supply of carps and sharks in American business was by no means depleted, still proving worrisome to vulnerable companies. No doubt they would have other triumphs. But some of the corporate raiders who had proven virtually unassailable in the previous decade when they were routinely making millions even when they lost, were discovering what could have been principle No. 10 in Douglas Ramsey's list: *It isn't easy to kill what ain't there, what won't sit still, or what will kill you first.* They were running low on easy targets. Those targets that remained were increasingly on to the raider and his ilk and had become increasingly skilled in recruiting powerful allies in "white knights," buyers of junk (high-paying, high-risk) bonds, lenders, state legislators, regulators, and the press.

For nothing can seem foul to those that win.—
SHAKESPEARE, *HENRY IV, PART I,*
ACT V, SCENE 1

From the Little League ballplayer who bursts into tears after his team loses, to the college student in the football stadium chanting "We're number one!"; from Lyndon Johnson, whose judgment was almost certainly distorted by his oft-stated desire not to be the first American president to lose a war, to the third grader who despises his classmate for a superior performance on an arithmetic test; we manifest a staggering cultural obsession with victory.   PSYCHOLOGIST ELLIOT ARONSON

A shark—as the corporate raider is often called in news headlines—can enjoy high payoff potential in terms of power, influence, and control when using the Takeover strategy, but only for a time. In actuality, the life expectancy of the shark is not much greater than that of a carp, a factor overwhelmingly ignored in business. Eventually, the easy supply of victims—carps and other sharks—begins to diminish. And eventually, because one's list of enemies grows, one's opponents grow wiser and more wily, and the supply of ready victims wanes, this strategy usually collapses on itself, driving survival chances to extinction as it is bypassed by the two remaining strategies, Trade-off and Breakthrough. The reason why there is not wider acknowledgment and recognition of this phenomenon is that the supply of human sharks appears endless. There are always sharks bloodying the water, but the chances of any individual shark surviving are alarmingly slim. Those who do make it frequently do so because of their savvy in migrating to the Trade-off strategy. Failing at licking them, they will now try to join them.

In *Dealmaking: All the Negotiating Skills and Secrets You Need*, investment banker Robert Lawrence Kuhn says:

> Compromise is the art of getting both sides to agree to a resolution that neither side likes. As long as everybody is unhappy, goes one adage, the deal is a fair one.[5]

A fair deal. That's one way—the shark's way—of looking at the strategy we are calling Trade-off.

Alfie Kohn in *No Contest: The Case Against Competition* offers another perspective on Trade-off:

> A wealth of advice is available on how to become successful— what to wear, how to negotiate, and so forth—and virtually all of it proceeds from the premise that you should adjust yourself to conditions as you find them. Adaptation is a critical part of the self-help model: You must succeed within the institutions and according to the rules that already exist. To do well is to fit in, and to fit in is to fortify the structures into which you are being fit.[6]

To do well (enough). To fit in. To fortify the structures into which you are being fit. To *adapt*. Those are other ways of describing Trade-off.

In terms of outcome, one word characterizes nearly everything that happens in Trade-off: moderate.

There is a *moderate* gain of some kind for all players.

There is a *moderate* personal access to power, influence, and control for all players.

There is a *moderate* amount of choice for coping for all players, although this diminishes over time.

There is only a *moderate* amount of time-consuming, resource-depleting drama generated as a "compromise" is forged.

A *moderate* degree of self-esteem is preserved because the players lose only a part of what they want.

That trophy is the truth, the only truth. I told him to get mean, punish some people, put some fear into them, you have to hate to win. I didn't tell him to break anybody's ribs. . . . I told him there is no such thing as second place. THE COACH IN JASON MILLER'S *THAT CHAMPIONSHIP SEASON*

Three outstanding attitudes—obliviousness to the growing disaffection of constituents, primacy of self-aggrandizement, [and the] illusion of invulnerable status—are persistent aspects of folly. BARBARA TUCHMAN, *THE MARCH OF FOLLY*

There is usually a *moderate* amount of survival value in Trade-off, at least for the short term.

So why, with progress created on such a variety of fronts, should we be so cautious as to attach a warning label to the Trade-off strategy? After all, in some ways it resembles what people today call a win/win outcome, in this case one where everybody gets something, perhaps even enough to move on to bigger and greater things.

In times of rapid change, Trade-off doesn't cut it because it is essentially a defensive strategy. It doesn't play to strengths; it seeks to minimize vulnerability from weakness. Trade-off isn't a genuine "win" because it, too, is a focus on "not losing" by at least getting *something*. Trade-off enervates because when it is finished and the payoffs are distributed, no one feels totally fulfilled. Emotions get expressed externally with sighs and shrugs, and the beverages of choice in postmortem celebrations are not bubbly champagnes but fortifying hard liquors.

In *Dealmaker,* Robert Kuhn's instructions for forging compromises are all negative, sharklike instructions:

- Don't be the first to concede a major issue.
- Suggest only minor compromises first.
- Don't compromise near deadlines.
- Concede the right way.
- Milk concessions.
- Skew the split.

A competitive culture endures by tearing people down. JULES HENRY

Whenever I hear the word "culture," I reach for my revolver. HERMANN GÖRING

If used consistently, Trade-off can diminish the quality of your life in the best of times and can jeopardize the very survival of your enterprise, your self-esteem, and your future. Why? Because each time a Trade-off occurs, what you hoped to gain is, in effect, cut in half. That is why we style a Trade-off as not a win/win but as half a win/win. A win/win over 2. It is possible, in fact, to "adapt" yourself right into extinction. Every frog ever boiled in a lidless pan serves as evidence. The creature has instincts sufficient for motivating the muscle power needed to propel itself immediately from a pan of boiling water. But if the frog is placed in the soup when it is still cool or only lukewarm and the heat is increased gradually, then more than the heat is up—the jig is up for the frog. So it can be for sharks and anyone else who plays Trade-off too many times, over time.

Adapting is something a frog does when the heat is turned up slowly.

And when it is dolphins that they are up against, Trade-off–playing sharks don't stand much of a chance. Dolphins are dolphins because they are accustomed to using win/win,[2] win/win,[3] win/win,[4] and, on occasion, strategies with the potential of even greater geometric outcomes.

Let's look at the part of the pool where only dolphins swim, with an eye to identifying, if we can, the defining nature of what it is—at the core—that distinguishes a dolphin from a carp or a shark.

Recall that both carps and sharks believe in scarcity. Because they believe in scarcity, they believe that their survival is a result of their behaviors—of how they act. And they usually act characteristically: Carps play Get-out and Give-in, sharks play Takeover and Trade-off. In slower times, in smaller pools, one could often get by as a believer in scarcity, but in advanced economies, that choice is fast receding. It's not there when we face increasing complexity and have fewer and fewer simple answers. It's not there when we have increasing interaction in a global economy. It's not there with the information glut and the need to accelerate the learning curve. In such a world, carps and sharks are at increasingly severe risk because they are *locked into* their behaviors, mistakenly thinking that they *are* their behaviors. When confronted with the need to change, they characteristically ''burrow'' deeper into those behaviors; they

attempt to do more of the same *harder*. Dolphins don't. Dolphins believe they have self-worth independent of their behaviors. Dolphins possess this psychological preamble:

> **I am a dolphin, and I believe in potential scarcity and potential abundance. Since I believe that we can have either—that it is *our choice*—and that we can learn to leverage what we have and utilize our resources elegantly, I make flexibility and doing more with less the cornerstones of how I create my world.**

So believing, dolphins do not view "the pool" in a conventional way. Seen through a dolphin's eyes, the way the pool appears is captured in Figure 1.2.

W e spoke earlier of the critical need in times of rapid change to *think about how we think* regularly, consistently, and strategically. Dolphins do. Rather than let *behaviors* determine who they are, dolphins *are*—at any given moment and in any given situation—whatever selected behavior permits them, first, to do more with less, and, second, to work toward elegant (that is, precise, clean, simple) outcomes.

The difference, then, between the strategy of the dolphin and most other "survival" strategies currently in use or jockeying for a tryout is this: the dolphin's strategy is a *sustainable* and *comprehensive* approach designed to benefit from playing finite games from an infinite perspective. That is to say, the difference between the strategy of the dolphin and the strategies of the shark and the carp is the difference in what each of them does with the element of surprise.

You may find this sudden gossamer of an idea confusing, even discouragingly disengaging. What are finite games? And what is to be gained in a world of hard realities from discussing such a foreign germ as "an infinite perspective"? Admittedly, it sounds

The world stands aside to let anyone pass who knows where he is going. DAVID STARR JORDAN

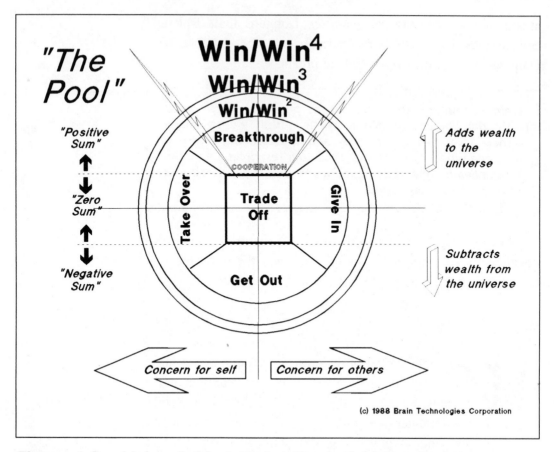

Figure 1.2.   Value Added, Value Traded, Value Lost

as if we have unexpectedly veered a long way from where, in business and organizations, the rubber meets the road.

But untangling matters won't require but a moment, and where these ideas intersect with dolphinhood, we will find more than rubber and roads; we'll find new answers to the chokeholds and bottlenecks currently plaguing our personal and institutional futures.

Carps and sharks play finite games only.

Carps and sharks seek to play finite games only. In a finite game, as philosopher James Carse noted so elegantly in *Finite and Infinite Games*, we seek to control every possible eventuality—to control, totally, the future *and* the past as a way of anesthetizing the present. We want to control the game, the players, the outcome, and the audience. Carps do it by repeatedly giving in or getting out. Sharks do it by relentlessly taking or pushing for the advantage in trade-offs. Currently, our brains are too often programmed this way, aberrantly, for reasons largely unknown.

In an infinite game, of which there is only one, the future reaches back, challenging the present and changing the past.

A t all times if so allowed, play in the infinite game offers the present the perspective of a new beginning and a new ending. Therefore, in every encounter, in every situation, the dolphin is always *thinking about how he and others are thinking,* knowing that nothing is more tellingly reflective of which kind of game we are playing.

Is someone in the game thinking that this is the only way the game can be played?

Is someone insisting that only certain players can participate?

Is someone claiming that there has to be winners *and* losers?

Is someone saying that time is running out?

Is someone strongly asserting that rules are rules—and can't be changed?

Has the game grown too serious—so serious that its players are seeking to cement their hold on power rather than arrange matters so that everyone involved can continue to play in strength?

Has the game degenerated merely to consuming time rather than generating options?

Is anyone trying to hide future moves as a way of keeping others unprepared and off guard?

Have what people are called (their titles, awards, degrees) and what they own (their property, their compensation, their perks) become more important to them than their names?

As Carse points out, ''Finite players play within boundaries; infinite players play with boundaries. . . . The rules of a finite

A key to self-management is the capacity for self-observation. It is important to realize that self-observation is not the same as overcriticism, judgmentalism, paralysis of analysis. It is rather a consistent monitoring of one's performance from a perspective significantly detached to allow for accurate evaluation.
CHARLES A. GARFIELD, *PEAK PERFORMERS: THE NEW HEROES OF AMERICAN BUSINESS*

Infinite players play with boundaries; finite players play within boundaries.

game may not change; the rules of an infinite game must change.''[7] And within the infinite game are played many, many finite games.

As dolphins, we always approach the pool out of strength and never from weakness, although dolphins do understand and as needed will utilize the paradoxical strength that resides in vulnerability. Later, we may *choose* to be vulnerable. But *never*—if it is at all within our strength and influence—until we have had time to assess and time to think about how others are thinking. If we are to survive playing with menacing, marauding sharks, we must *always* act to preserve our abilities to, if necessary, get out of the pool. Or if it is required to protect ourselves or to impress others with the benefits of taking us seriously and playing with integrity, to levy a hefty swat on the nose.

Of initial concern to a dolphin is the slice of reality represented by the segments of Figure 1.2 shown on the following page.

Takeover, Trade-off, and Give-in are all "zero-sum" games in which no new wealth is created. Instead, wealth is shifted around. You may—or we may—gain wealth, but it will be at the expense of others. Dolphins know that over time all zero-sum strategies tend to degenerate into "negative-sum," or lose/lose, strategies in which there are no winners, temporary or otherwise. Takeover players run out of victims—and friends. With each Trade-off, the players end up with less and less. Give-in players rob their colleagues of the opportunity to leverage off what they might bring to the table. And, too, Give-in players are prone to sabotage play in a desperate attempt to salvage a little bit of self-esteem.

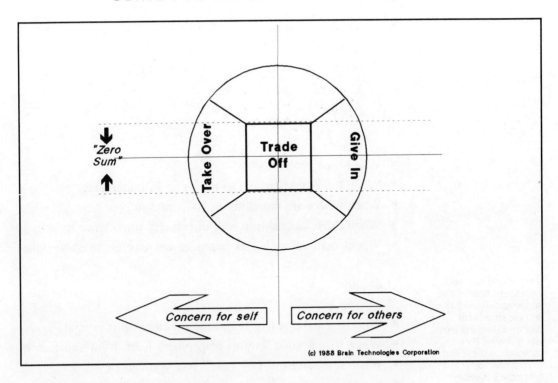

(c) 1988 Brain Technologies Corporation

Knowing this, why do dolphins ever play "zero-sum" games? For these reasons:

Dolphins aren't magicians. Possessing no magic wands, dolphins realize they must take the world as it is. As James Carse wrote, "A world must be its own spontaneous source."[8] In the midst of a finite carp or shark game, there may appear a chance to change the rules or the boundaries, but a dolphin never knows. She can often play along without her survival being endangered, so long as outcomes are acceptable, harmless, or keep things moving.

"Zero-sum" outcomes can be useful even as they consume time and resources. Dolphins deliberately use "win/lose" strategies on these occasions:

Takeover:

- When time is severely limited and a specific outcome is crucial.

- When the relationship is of little importance and a specific outcome is critical.
- When appropriate retaliation is necessary.

Trade-off:

- When time is short.
- When the issue is trivial to moderate in importance.
- When others are unwilling to cooperate fully.
- When the relationship is still of primary importance to you.
- When positions are highly polarized but progress must be made.

Give-in:

- When the issue is trivial and the relationship is crucial.
- When it is a good way to help others learn from experience.
- When it is wise to "buy time" and you cannot get out.
- In an emergency when compliance is critical.
- When you discover you are wrong.

[People who deal well with stress] believe that an increase in the pain and the strain must happen before the pain will go away. Their approach to stress and life is similar to Nietzsche's statement: "Whatever doesn't kill me makes me stronger."
SALVATORE MADDI

On occasion, "zero-sum" strategies can be very powerful. If healing is needed in a situation or relationship, it may make sense to use a Give-in strategy in which the user knowingly accepts limits and suffers the consequences. On the other hand, a medical or other emergency can create a situation where Takeover is the only strategy that makes any sense. For example, no paramedic or physician is going to tolerate interference by other parties in a life-or-death matter. Relationships can be ironed out later; what matters is the payoff; getting the patient stabilized and so forth. Trade-off, however, may be just what the doctor ordered if a path needs to be cleared to more vital concerns. Dolphins may choose to accept some loss so the parties can then go to work on issues and opportunities capable of "breakthrough" outcomes.

When a dolphin can see no advantage to staying in a "zero-sum" game, there is another option: to get out.

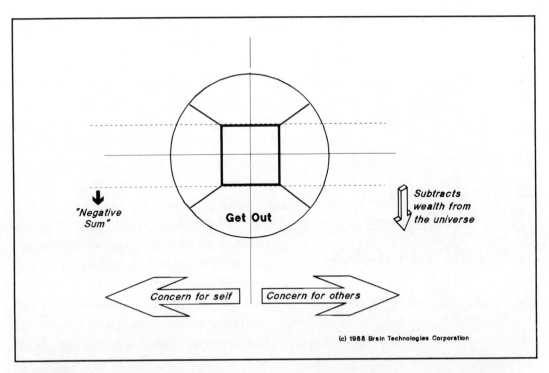

(c) 1988 Brain Technologies Corporation

et-out can be a life strategy—a very damaging one. As seen above, Get-out is a "negative-sum" strategy; it is the only one of the dolphin options that subtracts wealth from the universe or an individual. A person who uses Get-out to excess or exclusively is someone who avoids involvement with others, strongly resists intrusion by others into their private spaces, and reacts against situations that force them into making unwanted choices. The result is predictable: low payoff, low relationship, low energy, and low drama—often just what a severe loner is looking for.

Dolphins play Get-out for other reasons, however. They use it:

- When the outcome doesn't matter that much.
- When more pressing needs exist.
- When emotions need to cool so more basic problems can be addressed.
- When they need to gather information.
- When they need time to assemble their resources.

Life is a lot more like riding a bike than building a fortress. A rider needs alertness, flexibility, intelligence, and skill. The fortress mentality is stupid in this world and we're more likely to be done in by our psychological and spiritual armor. CHARLES MILLIGAN

After enlightenment—the laundry. ZEN SAYING

■ When it is clear that nothing good is going to come from a situation other than a painful learning experience.

Those are tactical reasons. Dolphins also use Get-out strategically. In part, dolphins are dolphins because they put much effort into being *on purpose* in the sense that airplane pilots are *on course*. When dolphins sense in advance that a situation, opportunity, or relationship isn't for them because it runs counter to their best aims, goals, and purposes, they have access to a variation of Get-out that can save them much wear and tear. In fact, Stay-out is one of a dolphin's most productive options. By avoiding situations that harbor little or no promise, dolphins can save valuable time, energy, and resources. Stay-out, then, is an important contributor to doing more with less, though only for the dolphin. There is no opportunity for a net gain for the "universe at large," since there is no opportunity to leverage with others. To create a net gain in wealth for the larger community, dolphins turn to that part of the pool featured in the accompanying diagram, that is their special harbor and domain.

Breakthrough!

Playing Stay-out keeps a dolphin from getting into wasteful situations.

The most sensible outcome for the group is also the most sensible outcome for each individual.

Economist Garrett Hardin has sensitized us to "the tragedy of the commons." From each cattle farmer's perspective, it makes sense to keep adding animals to the herd he grazes on the public pasture. But what makes sense to one farmer also makes sense to the others, and eventually the "commons" becomes overgrazed, the grasses die out, and everyone loses. Should a cry of warning be raised suggesting that the herds be reduced, sharks can be expected to respond by shouting,

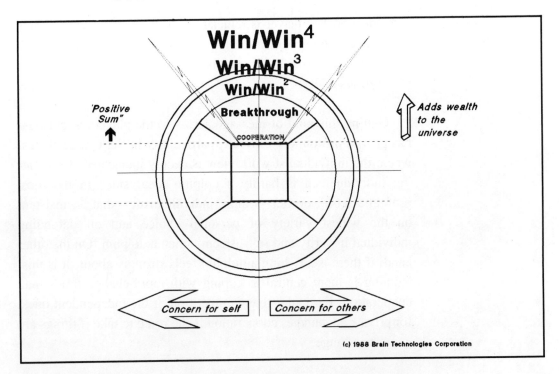

''Anybody's but mine!'' and rushing to add more animals while there is grass remaining. We can also predict the response of the carps: ''Alas, it is destiny.'' Unless there is a dolphin involved, there's a significant chance amid the drama of blame-laying, name-calling, and territorial contention that no one will point out the obvious: that the most sensible outcome for the group is also the most sensible outcome for each individual.

In *No Contest: The Case Against Competition*, Alfie Kohn cites several other examples in which cooperation is more productive:

- The economist Fred Hirsch pointed out that each individual in a crowd is able to see better by standing on tiptoe, particularly when others are doing so. But everyone would do better if no one stood on tiptoe.
- Each individual thinks it in her interest to rush for the exit when fire breaks out, but a cooperative escape protects everyone's interests and saves lives.

- Each hockey player is reluctant to wear a helmet when others are not doing so, since it restricts his vision. But a group decision to wear them benefits everyone by reducing the risk of serious injury.[9]

Getting this kind of message across to the players in business has proved profoundly difficult, particularly in the United States, where the individualist worldview is deeply inculcated. Eliminating individualism is hardly a dolphin idea, since in the most profound sense, no one is more individualistic—that is, insistent on the widest variety of personal choice and on defending individual integrity and self-esteem—than a dolphin. On the other hand, if there is anything a dolphin feels strongly about, it is this: Nothing is more central to coping with rapid-change times than cooperation. Far better than competition or the independent quest for private advantage, cooperation is the route to take if things are going to change.

A sense that this is so has produced a spate of theories on team- and spirit-building, negotiating and organizing loosely clustered around the idea of seeking "win/win" outcomes. It is an idea that, in the abstract, a dolphin can be expected to applaud. After all, it is a start. At the very least, perhaps a Trade-off can be arranged. But if something substantial needs to happen, if it looks like folks are just playing nice to be nice, if survival is a real question, or if a genuinely creative outcome is essential, a dolphin will quickly brush aside win/winners as dilettantes in the art of collective action.

Dolphins may brush aside win/winners as dilettantes in the art of collective action.

Playing win/win—cooperating—is merely the doorway, the beginning point, of playing Breakthrough. Check it out on the segment of Figure 1.2 reproduced earlier, the part of "the pool" where sharks and carps don't so much fear to tread but *have* no tread, no traction, no means of acceleration capable of pushing them through their limits. Not, at least, until dolphins enter the picture.

Rather than be celebrated overlong, many win/win players must be understood for what they actually are, a species of thinker caught in the twilight that precedes dolphinhood, a twilight that combines much promise with much pain. We call them pseudo-enlightened carps, and because we count many of them as close, personal friends, we celebrate their gifts and talents at the same time that we agonize at the paralysis that has settled over their self-development.

This is the unconscious testimonial of the pseudo-enlightened carp—our PEC.*

> I am a PEC, and I believe in a universe of absolute abundance. Therefore, I believe in no true evil and no true losers—it's just a matter of time before everyone wins. Because my primary need is healing, *I'm not comfortable with retaliation or escape, so I simply can't demonstrate love with power.* This makes me impotent, and my impotence makes me angry, but since maintaining an image of spirituality is important to me, *I express my anger covertly.* I believe that all we really need to do in life is learn to let go, *to flow, to let ourselves be a channel for a greater force,* and this is how I justify my existence.

On the positive side of the ledger—and they are enormously important pluses—are the PEC's skills and sensitivities in the art of healing the emotions. The PEC worldview is clearly at a more enlightened level than that of the shark. It processes at a higher order of complexity and begins to utilize a range of choices unavailable to the shark mentality. Moving toward better health psychologically takes time, and PECs, partly out of rebellion

* Our choice of this term is a subject of controversy. We selected it after long deliberation to stress the critical obstacle that persons viewing the world in this way place in the path of their self-development. There are two problems in the belief that you are enlightened. The "PEC" worldview creates a new carplike hypnosis that blinds you to the creation of additional choice. And in a terrible new debilitation, the PEC trap also triggers the *shark* disease—addiction. The PEC is addicted not to crisis but to the healing process.

against the addictive agitations of the shark and partly out of a new appreciation for the dynamics of becoming, will take time to help others heal. Thus we have a PEC *safe* place, where wounds can mend, self-discovery can be pursued, and the jagged edges of conflict blunted if not entirely avoided. Whether their special interest is in bringing protection and healing to battered women, victims of the corporate jungle, the ghetto child, the surburban rat race dropout, or casualties of sexual or substance abuse, PECs are as ritualistic in their design and defense of safe places as Native Americans were in establishing their distinctive campfire conclaves at each night's stop. When psychological healing for the badly abused is the critical need, PECs and their safe places can make a profound difference.

Of course ... there *is* a global transformation going on, but it's mental, not spiritual.... [Confuse] "global" with "spiritual," and you think the God squad is on the way."
KEN WILBER, QUOTED IN *NEXUS*

However, the Achilles heel of the PEC is also found in her concept of the safe place. Gone is the plain vanilla carp's hypnotic attachment to a sense of absolute scarcity. In its place, the PEC is now hypnotically attracted to a sense of absolute abundance.

The PEC belief in a benign universe leads to a shirking of personal responsibility.

Operationally, those PEC "safe places" are governed by the presumptions—the false beliefs—that there are no limits to be faced or feared, no boundaries to be enforced in the pursuit of human potential, and *no end to be expected to the healing process.* Unwilling, perhaps in many cases unable, to recognize the realness of human limitations, the sometimes unyielding and unforgiving nature of "the universal condition," and, in the most critical way, the need to get well, PECs fail to understand that their flawed belief in an all-knowing, all-loving universe that will *always* provide leads in finality straight back to the old carp cop-out: a shirking of personal responsibility. And when people won't be personally responsible, whether because they don't think they can win or because they think a benign universe will take care of them, the results are the same: eventual disappointment, pain, loss, and the concomitant triggering of denial or rage.

P ractically speaking, PECs oscillate between two extremes. One is the belief that anything is possible. So believing, they will often seize on the remotest evidence, the most gross overgeneralization, that can be cited to suggest that the world of reality in fact matches the utopian world of their dreams and visions. The hundredth-monkey episode is merely a case in point. A dubious piece of research into the behavior of a group of potato-washing Japanese monkeys grew almost overnight into a worldwide PEC claim that merely doing something in large enough numbers could result in the new practice propagating itself instantaneously to other users or localities. Supposedly, when the hundredth monkey in this group learned to wash his potato in the surf, all the monkeys in the vicinity of the Japanese island began washing their potatoes. On closer scrutiny, the research itself didn't stand up; the facts just weren't there. But PECs of many nationalities and involvements immediately seized on the hundredth-monkey story as evidence that you can transform behavior merely by manipulating the *number* of participants. In a similar sense, apparent isolated breakthroughs in parapsychology—remote viewing, clairvoyance, or psychokinesis—are immediately labeled by PECs as qualities of which all persons are capable. Evidence that some minds at least appear to be capable of willing a spoon to bend is quickly amplified to suggest that minds are capable of lifting a human body or even a truck. The PEC's trancelike belief in the absence of limits makes her vulnerable to this assumption: that anything that is possible is therefore probable *and* universal.

When the pendulum swings, an enraged PEC is created, enraged that the world isn't changing instantaneously, that there are limits, and that the PEC belief system is so powerless against sharks.

*I*n a world of rapid change, boundaryless PECs are eventually driven to define themselves and their safe places almost solely by what they are against, and so they and the targets of their ire find them constantly lashing out. It isn't so much the anger of the victimized carp, however. It is more the outrage of a mind and spirit capable of sensing the higher potentials of the human species but in doing so of being confronted with serious hobbles. Central to the PEC's Sisyphean predicament is his belief that he must "be healed" to be powerful, and yet deep down he seeks to avoid personal power at all costs. Thus real, liberating healing is thwarted, and the PEC remains without power to move humanity toward actualizing his all-consuming utopian vision.

The position of the PEC is riven with paradoxes. Though they view themselves as perennial and consummate "rescuers" (to cite the Drama Triangle again) determined to lash out against the *most hideous* of injustices, PECs most often aim their protests at the *least threatening* of targets. (Protesting apartheid, for example, by building shantytowns on the Administration Building lawn.) They tend to grow angry at shark habits and attitudes, but by thrashing around madly and ineffectually in the water, they draw the attention and retaliation of the very creatures they profess to detest (the Kent State tragedy and the 1968 "Chicago police riot," for example). PECs damn "the system" but actually depend on it for their very existence: They *need* the system to keep

> *By thrashing around in the water, PECs tend to draw the attention of the very creatures they wish to avoid: the sharks.*

from having to change. And so, once again, we are back to carplike dynamics: the need to be the victim. Without the trappings and feelings of victimization—either for themselves or their codependents—PECs are sorely pressed to defend their denial of personal responsibility.

The organization may encounter PECs in one of two forms: the *metaphysical* PEC or the *social* PEC. The former is more likely to be an employee of the firm; the latter, an outsider lashing at the organization for its failings, real or imaginary.

Metaphysical PECs heavily populate the "cohort" that occupies middle management in the 1980s. Now in their late thirties and forties, these people are in every sense the children of *The Big Chill,* the sensitizing 1960s. The truest thing we can say is that an unsympathetic world of sharks has beaten the *%*$#%&*& out of them, so much so that they are in severe retreat from the basic assumptions of the Western world and Judeo-Christian culture. In their flight from a realpolitik world, they prefer to believe in the feminine, the ethereal, the untrammeled flow of the Universal— and eschew any acknowledgment of evil at all. Defined as are most PECs by what they oppose, the metaphysical PEC is

> Evil is considered by a lot of liberals to be a religious concept—that knocks me out. So what you're left with is this sort of social-sciency sterilization. They think evil can be *corrected.*
> HARRIET TYSON-BERNSTEIN, QUOTED IN *NEWSWEEK*

- **Antimatter.** Secretly enraged that we humans are material beings living in a material world, the metaphysical PEC often seeks to escape through drugs, seances, channeling, studies of the metaphysical, "dropping out," meditation, spiritual therapies, and other avenues and activities that would appear to promote "dematerializing."
- **Antimasculine.** As one well-known metaphysical PEC—a man—has counseled, "The human male should be disqualified from high office. Government and testosterone are an unholy and lethal combination."
- **Antistructure.** Structure, of course, implies limits, an idea PECs do not accept.

The other kind of PEC, the social PEC, is more likely to assault the organization from without, believing that the ills of the world issue primarily from the shark-dominated "industrial-technical complex." Social PECs seek to surround themselves with what is natural, pure, pristine; they launch themselves in pursuit of the "holistic"; they view with suspicion anything smacking of the multilayered. Therefore, in their negativism, social PECs are

- **Antitechnology.** Technology can disrupt "the flow," which they see as a universal answer to problems of the human condition.
- **Anticomplexity.** Complexity offers too many places to hide, and PECs in general view the catacombs of human abstract thinking as conveying a tactical advantage to sharks.
- **Anti-authority.** To accept the view that authority is a requisite for organizing a society is to be forced to accept the reality of evil.

> There was a conspiracy years ago to put the small farmer out of business. The people who put it together thought it was a real intelligent idea that we get rid of all the little guys and let the big guys handle it. COUNTRY AND WESTERN SINGER WILLIE NELSON

In summary, whether metaphysical or social, the PEC is consumed by a blinding infatuation with a new discovery: the ever-questing and perfecting life force of the universe. So captivating and inviting is this new treasure source of hope and healing that PECs cloak it in the gilded trappings of spirituality. Failing to see that their newfound power is self-generated, PECs develop strong allegiances to their fresh "spiritual" wellspring of potency and contentment and work to become aligned to it and attuned with it. Not psychologically comfortable with generating power internally, PECs resist embracing self-direction, and therefore— like the carp—their outlook is, in the end, still sacrificial. Characteristically, all PECs

- Believe only in abundance; there is no room in their worldview for scarcity, evil, or ultimate judgment or failure.
- Avoid personal responsibility for correcting the mischief and malice of society. Enough, they assume, that they point it out. Thereafter, everything is expected to right itself magically and mystically.

- Believe being in "the flow" is very much a universal answer, failing to understand as the dolphin does that there are times when it is impossible and ill-advised to be in "the flow."
- Understand that there is a need for purpose but seek to be resonant with it without necessarily having sought it or thought it through.
- Have an overwhelming faith in a positive outcome, believing "the universe" will always take care of matters.

P sychologically and spiritually, PECs need kindness, rest, companionship, and healing. They need all the encouragement possible to get them to travel on, appropriate personal power, and develop a choice-seeking, dolphin-oriented worldview so their many talents can be used to solve the organization's and the world's many problems. However, inauspiciously, most indications are that for most PECs, their healing will never end, their cookies will never get done. The solutions they propose and the avenues they pursue in their often highly emotional, highly energized attempts to right the wrongs they can so clearly see simply take

To the PEC, the dolphin looks for all the world like the shark from which she is in retreat.

too long or simply have little lasting effect. For the PEC herself, her worldview can be an insidious trap, preventing the movement to dolphinhood. And because of her sense of personal power and her dexterous use of it, the dolphin looks to the PEC for all the world like a shark from which he is in retreat.*

This, then, is the world from which much of today's so-called win/win philosophy issues. Such "dolphins-in-waiting" understand intuitively that there are valuable payoffs to be enjoyed and

---

* We are often asked if there is such a belief set as a pseudo-enlightened *shark*. We think it possible but rare. The addictive quality of the shark worldview makes it difficult for the shark-oriented individual to adopt healing methodologies. Much more common are sharks in carps' clothing. By faking their interest and skills in healing, sharks routinely take the role of "guru" and just as routinely "fleece the flock."

better relationships to be had by getting people to the point of cooperative, collaborative behavior. But, alas, for too many of today's win/win consultants and their unfortunate clients, those payoffs are unlikely ever to be achieved because of the players' tendency to embrace as outcome that which to a dolphin is merely prologue. Playing win/win simply raises the *possibility* of a Breakthrough outcome but doesn't produce it, particularly if your win/win-playing coterie remains surrounded by sharks. And place your bet with confidence! Where win/winners are gathered together, there are or soon will be one or more sharks close by, hungrily eyeing the prospects.

Three crucial, dolphinlike elements are missing from most of the win/win formulas now being avidly introduced to the business and organizational community:

- A genuine understanding of how to use the brain to do more with less, exceeding everyone's expectations.
- An appreciation for what it takes to use resources, especially *human* resources, elegantly.
- The ability to exercise power, including leaving with integrity and retaliating when it is appropriate.

Political scientist Robert Axelrod helped us to understand better than anyone else thus far what is important about retaliating.

To do so, he chose to use a favorite research tool of psychologists, a game called Prisoner's Dilemma. How it works doesn't matter here; it is a bit complicated. In brief, each of two players has a chance to cooperate or defect. Viewed from the individual's perspective, the best strategy is to defect. But as the game unfolds, it quickly becomes obvious that from the pair's perspective, *each* player does best when he is cooperating.

*A*xelrod wondered about how to get players in any situation—but particularly national governments—to realize the merits of cooperation quickly. The most difficult situation for getting players to cooperate, he concluded, would be when they couldn't communicate—when their moves themselves must be the communication.

To explore such circumstances, he invited skilled game theorists throughout the world to submit computerized strategies for playing Prisoner's Dilemma; each submission was paired against all the others. In the first round, the triumphant entry was Tit for Tat, a strategy that began by cooperating and thereafter, just as the name indicates, "did as the Romans do"—reciprocating the opponent's last move; that is, cooperating if the opponent had cooperated. Retaliating if the opponent had retaliated.

> *Carps always "die" first because they don't discriminate among players.*

After informing his participants of Tit for Tat's success, Axelrod ran a second tournament. Although these entries were more devious, the result was the same: Tit for Tat won again. Axelrod believes that Tit for Tat approaches of *strategically limited retaliation* "succeed by eliciting cooperation from others, not by defeating them." He adds:

> Cooperation based on reciprocity can get started in a predominantly noncooperative world, can thrive in a variegated environment, and can defend itself once fully established.[10]

Most startling of all, perhaps, is Axelrod's "5% Solution." Place five skilled, cooperating, motivated Tit for Tat-playing dolphins in a pool with ninety-five sharks, and it is, other influences being equal, all over for the sharks. It may take a while. Of course, the people who *always* play nice—the carps—will "die" first. Carps, unfortunately, don't make any discrimination about who they are playing with and have a dismal tendency to end up as bait fish or shark dinner. But eventually, says Axelrod, the sharks must convert or become cannibals and eat each other, which they often do and thus don't last all that much longer.

Can this *really* be true? Can Axelrod possibly be right? Is it at

Over a period of time I learned to trust certain catchers so much that I actually let them umpire for me on the bad days. The bad days usually followed the good nights.... On those days there wasn't much I could do but take two aspirins and call as little as possible. If someone I trusted was catching ... I'd tell them, "Look, it's a bad day. You'd better take it for me. If it's a strike, hold your glove in place for an extra second. If it's a ball, throw it right back. And please, don't yell." No one I worked with ever took advantage of the situation, and no hitter ever figured out what I was doing. And only once, when Ed Herrman was calling the pitches, did a pitcher ever complain about a call. I smiled; I laughed; but I didn't say a word. I was tempted, though, I was really tempted. RON LUCIANO, *THE UMPIRE STRIKES BACK* all reasonable to think that five dolphins can triumph over ninety-five sharks?

Axelrod's experiment was conducted in the artificial world of simulated games and was a bit simplistic. But even while acknowledging these limitations, we invite you to comb his data, premises, and principles repeatedly as have we and others have done[11] and see if *you* can determine a basis for denying his conclusions.

When you are caught in a situation from which you cannot escape and the others involved aren't cooperating or communicating, you have only three choices:

1. You can be a carp.
2. You can be a shark.
3. You can play Tit for Tat.

And if you are playing Tit for Tat, you are playing Breakthrough in the dolphin-populated part of the pool.

Here's how dolphins play Tit for Tat:

They understand that if "the boss" doesn't support cooperation, it takes longer for Tit for Tat to win.

It may be necessary to resort to guerrilla warfare and may even be necessary to take out the boss. A key is making connections quickly with other dolphins and increasing interaction among the cooperative players.

They enlarge the influence of the future over the present.

The more that players know they will see each other and must deal with each other, the greater likelihood that cooperation will develop. Knowing this, dolphins act to make interactions more durable. Geopolitically, they put emphasis on the rituals of diplomacy—the toasts, the exchanging of gifts, the ceremonies, and the parades. In a business context, they meet contractual expectations promptly, act quickly to resolve disputes, take notice of opportunities to offer "the human touch," and observe the rituals and folk aspects of business.

They avoid unnecessary conflict by cooperating as long as the other players do.

Such a policy of "basic reciprocity" is critical, since any attempt to take advantage of the other party's cooperation even occasionally can trigger the Echo Effect. Echo is a potentially serious side effect of Tit for Tat in which two parties get "locked in" on mutual competition. Dolphins guard against triggering or getting locked into Echo with two strategies:

- When finding it necessary to retaliate, doing so at only "90 percent" of the strength of the other player's move or action.
- Finding ways to demonstrate that, although they are strong and capable of playing Echo indefinitely, they are willing to break out of a mutually competitive pattern and pursue a more generous strategy.

They respond promptly to a "mean" move by retaliating appropriately.

The importance of maintaining a "hairline trigger of provocability" surprised Robert Axelrod. He admitted coming to his computer tourney believing the best policy was to be slow to anger. However, the results convinced him that waiting to respond to the other player's provocation invites being misunderstood—of sending the wrong signal. Whether the problem is your upstairs neighbor playing the drums at midnight or an employee abusing his sick leave, your silence can be read as acquiescence, approval, or cowardice. Dolphins retaliate promptly to avoid being misunderstood or underestimated.

A policy of unconditional cooperation tends to bring exploitation by an adversary whereas a policy of consistent coerciveness tends to lead to a fight. However, a strategy that begins with firmness—including the threat or use of coercion—in the early stages of a dispute and then switches to conciliation appears generally to be effective in securing cooperation from an opponent. Apparently, the demonstration of one's willingness to use coercion, and the poor outcomes of an initially competitive relationship, usually cause an adversary to welcome, and respond positively to, a later chance for cooperation. MARTIN PATCHEN, *JOURNAL OF CONFLICT RESOLUTION*

While quick to retaliate, dolphins are also quick to forgive.

The moment the other party shows signs of being willing to cooperate again, dolphins take them up on it.

Dolphins take pains to avoid being too clever.

Being too clever can confuse others. Having a clear, consistent strategy telegraphs immediately how your response should be interpreted. Responses that are inconsistent and highly complex may prevent the other side from getting a clear picture of how you are thinking. If this is the case, they may not know how to adjust easily to your patterns of actions.

They do creative things to the payoff.

If one side perceives that mutual competition will produce greater payoffs than mutual cooperation, you can't expect that cooperation will evolve. Instead, the sharks will triumph. So dolphins work to make the long-term incentive for mutual cooperation greater than the short-term incentive for defection. They also play from a position of power so they can always "get out" with integrity. This may mean developing multiple sources of income, for example, so they can always tell the truth and leave with impunity if an organization tries to control their behavior with economic sanctions.

*T*it for Tat is how you "go for Breakthrough" when playing with sharks. Its aim is to help mutual cooperation evolve. Once in place, mutual cooperation sets the stage for the truly exciting, productive aspects of playing Breakthrough, aspects that have high survival value for *all* players, both short and

[Once] a manufacturer begins to go under, even his best customers begin refusing payment for merchandise, claiming defects in quality, failure to meet specifications, tardy delivery, or what-have-you. The great enforcer of morality in commerce is the continuing relationship, the belief that one will have to do business again with this customer, or this supplier, and when a failing company loses this automatic enforcer, not even a strong-arm factor is likely to find a substitute.
MARTIN MAYER, *THE BANKERS*

long term. When playing Breakthrough with friendly, supportive colleagues, friends, relatives or organizations, dolphins go for a win/win,[2] win/win,[3] win/win,[4] or even greater mutual wins with these injunctions:

- Develop trust and rapport.
- Tell the truth so you can clarify everyone's needs explicitly.
- Specify, clarify, and define the desired outcome.
- Commit to it and see yourself achieving it.
- Stay "centered" *in the present* during conflict—this helps others to avoid being hooked by guilt and the regrets of the past and the anxieties and fears of the future.
- Focus on what's happening *now*—this is where and when solutions emerge.
- Remain flexible and able to respond.
- Remove all blame and focus on what works.
- If strong negative emotions surface, acknowledge the feelings and ask, "What needs to happen now? What needs to change? What can I do to use this energy constructively?"
- If resistance arises, explore it and use it rather than creating a battle of wills.
- Develop the belief that you have the power to affect your life directly and that you will ultimately be supported.
- Suspend judgment.
- Be willing to be illogical.
- Focus on going beyond "winning" as opposed to merely "not losing."
- Give everyone permission to win.
- Talk about what you are doing that is not working.
- Search for alternative meanings that will satisfy the situation and everyone's needs more productively.
- Ask, "What if . . . ?"
- Use metaphors, analogies, and stories that match the situation you are facing.
- Use humor. If this situation were funny, what would you be laughing at?

- Be willing to identify and go beyond habit.
- Seek the unexpected.
- Make time to receive unconscious messages.
- Search for the second, third, or fourth "correct" solution.
- Accept the stress needed to motivate you to a higher order of processing.

*E*ven though the Breakthrough strategy requires more time and energy "up front," this approach is easily the most efficient strategy available for creating and implementing novel, innovative, powerful long-range solutions, saving you time in the long run.

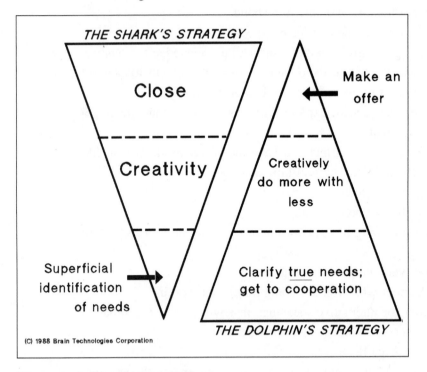

THE SHARK'S STRATEGY

Close

Make an offer

Creativity

Creatively do more with less

Superficial identification of needs

Clarify true needs; get to cooperation

THE DOLPHIN'S STRATEGY

(C) 1988 Brain Technologies Corporation

Figure 1.3.   Leveraging

Breakthrough also offers a new dolphinlike perspective in other areas. An important one is featured in Figure 1.3, a chart design first used to our knowledge by consultant Marshall Thurber to show the salient differences in the way sharks and dolphins approach human interactions. At a glance you can see that sharks tend to focus the bulk of their efforts and time on that venerated ritual of sales—the close. Very little time is devoted to an area that is sacred to dolphins, the trust-and-rapport-building rituals, exchanges, and mutual explorations of *true* needs that lead to cooperation. From that point, dolphins then up the ante, the heat, and the expectations, expecting that the bonds of mutual cooperation will hold. In the end, dolphins look for the outcome to sell itself as the best of all possible worlds: a "net gain" in wealth for all parties involved. Thus the two most important features illustrated in Figure 1.3 are these: the dolphin's strategy stands the shark's strategy on its head and puts by far the greater emphasis on establishing a workable relationship. And the use of creativity by the two approaches is vastly different. For the shark, creativity is aimed at setting up a close that "traps" the prospect into responding in the way you want them to. The dolphin's creativity is based on the idea of elegantly exceeding everyone's expectations and needs by leveraging the available resources by taking the time to go for breakthrough outcomes. (The area of each segment of the two triangles is intended to relate to the proximate time spent in pursuing each task.)

*U*ntil recently, the "strategy of the dolphin" was seldom needed. In a final analysis, compromise—the spirit of trade-off—was usually capable of producing the desired results when what you were doing didn't work.

Then time quickened. The computer emerged to augment the human mind. Our abilities to leverage what we know soared overnight. On myriad related fronts—ranging from the acceleration of world births and gains in prolonging life to the sudden, serious depletion of vital resources such as oil, timber, potable water, clean air, and the atmosphere's ozone layer to a shrinking of the learning curve—old equations crumbled and new uncertainties loomed. More and more, the hard-wired litanies we unquestioningly play through and play out in our individual and collective brains sound like the ditties and siren sounds of lemmings headed unthinkingly for a plunge off the precipice into the sea.

Carps sing, "I can't win," and repeat this message in all of its change- and possibility-negating variations, even to the point of denying the true consequences of failure:

- "Ignorance is bliss."
- "I was helpless before, and I will always be helpless."
- "My suffering has a purpose."
- "Losing comes with life."
- "In all important gains there is an element of sacrifice."
- "Turn the fourth and fifth cheek; go the twentieth and thirtieth mile."

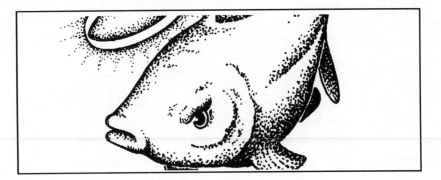

Pseudo-enlightened carps believe, "All fish should love and care for each other. To make it so, all I have to do is to believe it is so."

They promote this philosophy in various ways:

- "It's not who wins or loses—it's how you play the game."
- "It's not the payoff that counts but the journey."
- "All I have to do is continually 'let go' and everything will be all right."

Sharks croon, "I have to win." And their propaganda includes these variations:

- "After all, it's a shark-eats-shark world out there."
- "I really didn't mean to cut off your hand at the wrist, but I had no choice when you reached for your chips."
- "I really meant to cut off your hand at the wrist, and before you reached for your chips you should have remembered my warning."
- "I really meant to cut off your hand at the wrist when you reached for your chips, even though I had assured you that was never my intention."[12]
- "Competition is inevitable."
- "Competition motivates us to do our best."
- "Competition is the only way to have fun."
- "Competition builds character."[13]

The dolphin says, "I want us both to win—and win elegantly and resoundingly, no matter what the odds or the difficulties or the time it takes."

Leaving the lemmings if necessary to plunge into the sea, the dolphin replaces the siren songs of competition, disaster, confusion, and sacrifice hard-wired into the human brain with the soaring melodies of change and creation. The important stanzas to the dolphin's song are these:

- "We must learn to *leverage the wave.*"
- "We must learn to *create and act on compelling visions.*"
- "We must learn the process of *releasing and letting go.*"
- "We must learn to *break set.*"
- "We must *develop—all of us—strong self-esteem.*"
- "We must learn to *work cooperatively.*"
- "We must focus on *doing more with less.*"
- "We must learn to *be open to surprise and to the future.*"
- "We must *be responsible.*"
- "We must *discover and act on personal purpose.*"

So run the lyrics undergirding the strategy of the dolphin.

DOLPHIN WORK

Exercise No. 1

Below is a list of circumstances that have happened to people. Reflect on each entry and make brief notes on a separate sheet about the changes you believe each of these events would bring to your life and how you would respond:

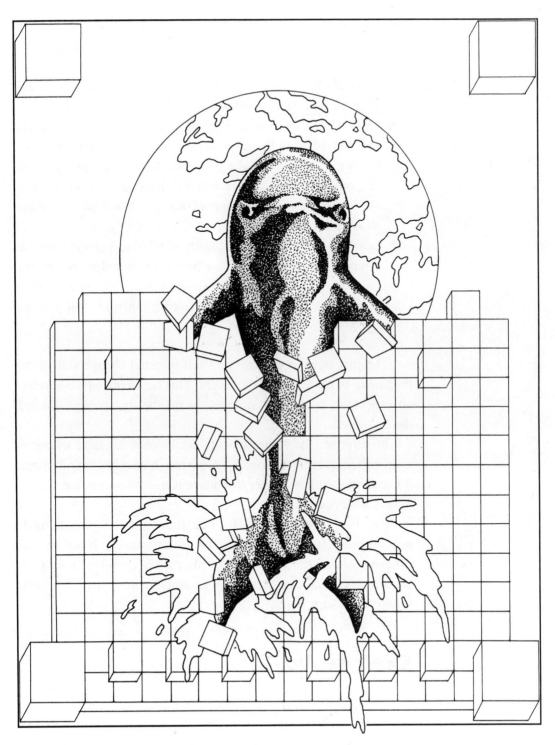

- *Story A:* One of your children, your closest friend, or someone you greatly admire, claims to have had a vision in which he spoke directly with God.
- *Story B:* Your organization or company suddenly eliminates your job and puts you on the street.
- *Story C:* Rushed to a hospital emergency room, you are pronounced dead. However, persistent doctors revive you. Now you are faced with deciding whether to tell others that you had an ''out of body'' experience in which the mind seemed to rise above the frantic life-saving efforts and observed everything taking place in full detail.
- *Story D:* You are accused unjustly of robbing a grocery store at a time when you were with a friend. Pressured by police and prosecutors, the friend testifies against you, and you are sent to prison. After two years, new evidence emerges, and you are freed.

The first step for empowering self-directed change skills is to prepare to be surprised by the future. This requires that we develop an expectant, beckoning attitude toward the unexpected, toward the unknown.

In surprise, the future reaches back, changes, and triumphs over the past. It offers the past a new start, a new beginning. Since for the infinite game player the future is always surprising us, the past is always changing.

Recalling your thoughts about the four situations just outlined, ask yourself: Is there a pattern to my responses? If so, is this pattern positive or negative? Does my current thinking about such circumstances indicate that I have an attitude open, partially open, or closed to surprise?

Exercise No. 2

By thinking through the various ways you could respond to the following outlined situations, you will increase your ability to recognize the strategies typically used by the carp, the shark, and the dolphin.

Read each of the situations carefully and then create a response that exemplifies the Get-out, Give-in, Takeover, Trade-off, and Breakthrough strategies. If you need to review our descriptions of each of these strategies, refer to the appropriate locations in this chapter.

- *Situation A:* A person for whom you care deeply has just prepared a dish for you that you strongly dislike (perhaps chicken liver or meatloaf). When you express reluctance to eat it, she says, "If you loved me, you would like chicken liver [or meatloaf or whatever]!" How do you respond?
- *Situation B:* Your new art teacher has told you that you need more "spontaneity" in your work. You like the teacher and want to please him, but you know that if you *plan* to be spontaneous, your work will actually lose its spontaneity. How do you respond?

Exercise No. 3

On a separate sheet of paper, identify the ten most important *long-term* relationships that are directly involved with the most important objectives/outcomes you currently wish to achieve.

Now, return to the beginning of the list and in turn identify the *primary* strategy (Get-out, Give-in, Takeover, Trade-off, or Breakthrough) you use in this relationship. Place a "/" after the designation of each relationship, and write in this strategy for all ten entries (for example "My daughter/Takeover").

Since you have identified these relationships as both critical and long-term, and since all zero-sum strategies (Give-in, Takeover, and Trade-off) degenerate into lose/lose over time:

- Are there any changes you need to make in the strategies you utilize in these critical relationships?
- In each of these relationships, are you both mutually aware of your true needs? If not, what would the real needs be?
- Given both of your real needs, how can you work even more creatively together to do more with less?

2
LEVERAGING THE WAVE: THE DOLPHIN'S SPECIAL SECRETS

S eals get enthusiastic about beach balls and dolphins about symbols, and for roughly the same reasons. Both possess substantial buoyancy and maneuverability. You can toss them to and fro, testing them for loft and stability. You can shunt them aside if they lose their appeal and efficacy, then ponder the consequences of no longer having them around.

As the twentieth century ends, two of the most important beach balls/symbols for dolphins are these:

> The $=$ sign in Albert Einstein's formula, $E = mc^2$.

And

> the word "nanosecond."

Here's why:

To the dolphin, Einstein's equals sign is an indication that, all things considered, what goes around comes around. If we attempt to gain on energy, what we get is matter. And hedging with matter

I reckon I got to light out for the Territory ahead of the rest, because Aunt Sally she's going to adopt me and sivilize me and I can't stand it. I been there before. MARK TWAIN, *ADVENTURES OF HUCKLEBERRY FINN*

"Is there any other point to which you wish to draw my attention?"

"To the curious incident of the dog in the nighttime."

"The dog did nothing in the nighttime."

69

"That was the curious incident," remarked Sherlock Holmes.   ARTHUR CONAN DOYLE

Future shock is the dizzying orientation brought on by the premature arrival of the future.   ALVIN TOFFLER

puts us back in the energy business. It is a zero-sum, seesaw affair, as Einstein's equals sign indicates. No leverage there—to speak of. Instead, the leverage lies in the expansion of knowledge and information—in how much we have of it, how rapidly we can process and package it, and what we do with it. That's not to say that there are *no* limits to information and its speed of processing. As Sherry Turkle notes in *The Second Self: Computers and the Human Spirit,* "Everyone knows that the game is going to end 'sometime,' but 'sometime' is potentially infinite."[1] Mention an expanding universe to a dolphin and he immediately thinks of information—and of nanoseconds.

A nanosecond is symbolic of a new time perspective, one where dolphins can expect to be the managers and leaders of choice. One nanosecond is one billionth of a second. How fast is that? Extremely fast. In the time it takes to snap your fingers, 500 million nanoseconds have passed. Social critic Jeremy Rifkin notes,

In the industrial context, *organization always lags behind strategy.* Because of the assumption that you have to know what it is you want to do before you can know to do it, all organizations based on the industrial model are created for businesses that either no longer exist or are in the process of going out of existence! That is a terrible state of affairs.
STANLEY M. DAVIS, *FUTURE PERFECT*

> [Though] it is possible to conceive theoretically of a nanosecond, and even to manipulate time at that speed of duration, *it is not possible to experience it.* This marks a radical turning point in the way human beings relate to time. Never before has time been organized at a speed beyond the realm of consciousness.[2]

In dolphin terms, the new time perspectives introduced by computers and other forms of information processing, storage, and delivery mean essentially this: *There are more waves "out there" to ride or to create than ever before.* Great, looming, incredibly energized waves of *change!* And whereas those waves once took shape almost glacially, over thousands and thousands of years, today they are taking shape and crashing against us with ever-accelerating rapidity. Some observers—Jeremy Rifkin is one—

want to apply the brakes to "the new nanosecond culture." But dolphins are more adventurous, more hopeful, more aspiring to push through, and take responsibility for the consequences that come with pushing through, their limits.

*D*olphins understand that the single most important organizing principle of the late twentieth and early twenty-first centuries is "the wave." The wave of change. And that managers and leaders who don't learn to ride—and enjoy learning to ride—the wave run the risk of being marooned in an ever-receding pool overpopulated by frantic, confused, dispirited (and sometimes mean-spirited) sharks and carps. Or else being pummeled into ineptitude and ineffectiveness by the unpredictable and unforgiving gyrations of a riving ocean of change.

You can expect this chapter, then, to be a thoroughly nautical experience. Our goal is this: to equip you with a dolphin's understanding and finesse in navigating today's—and tomorrow's—great crescendo waves of change, ignorance of which is destined to doom many a hopeful enterprise and dash dreams that otherwise might have thrived.

Lesson 1: The waves are accelerating.

*T*he appeal of the dolphin as a symbol for new kinds of management and leadership approaches grew out of Brain Technologies' research into a concept we have called Neuropreneuring®—the idea of taking charge of your own changes, of changing (if necessary) before the times, of developing new personal tools for self-direction.

In large measure, dolphins qualify as dolphins because they understand and respond skillfully to what we call the Neuropreneuring Cycle. Beginning with Figure 2.1, we will focus on the

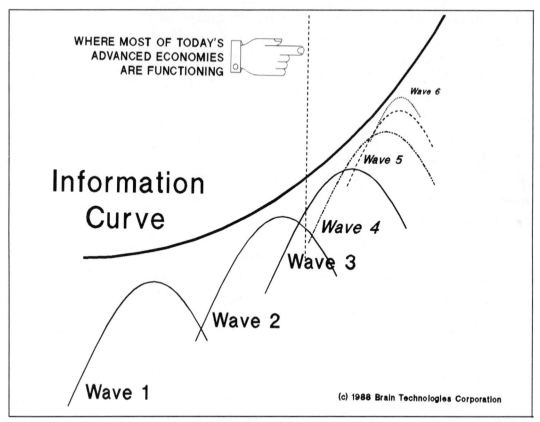

Figure 2.1. Waves of Change

The lag was so long in Wave 1 that people had almost forever to change.

A professor named Alex Bavelas often plays golf with other professors. Once, he took the foursome down to the golf course, and they were going to draw straws for partners. He said, "Let's do this *after* the game." STEWART BRAND

central dynamics of the great waves of change, the spawning grounds, the playgrounds, and the testing grounds for Neuropreneuring's dolphins, using the Neuropreneuring Cycle. Leaving the "whys" for another time and place, the crucial "what" of importance to the dolphin visible in this drawing is this: *Today, waves take shape and take command with astonishing speed compared to earlier eras.*

As futurist Alvin Toffler was the first to remind us, Wave 1—the domain of the farmer—lasted about six thousand years. Between the "arrival" of this wave and the demise of the preceding hunter-gatherer, or nomadic, culture, tens of generations lived and expired with scarcely any change at all in life-styles, work habits, and social bonds, so slowly did the change take place. Indeed, there was such *lag* between waning of the germinal, amorphous "seedbed" era of the hunter-gatherer and the arrival in substantial fashion of Wave 2 that humans had almost *forever* to change.

With Wave 2, the industrial era, the pace picked up. In three hundred years, this wave of change peaked and at this moment is rapidly disintegrating in advanced economies.

T oday's vaunted information age, Wave 3, ushered in by the computer only a few decades ago, is even now being supplanted at the leading edges of idea and technique development; though most of the players in our advanced economies are just beginning to make adaptations and transformations organizationally in response to Wave 3 (see Figure 2.2), prognosticators give it a half-life of only about fifteen to twenty years.

Already on the scene in its beginning stages, its power so potentially awesome that we can only guess at many of its ramifications, is Wave 4, which we are calling the Wave of Productivity because of the enormous gains it augurs in energy, reconstitution of basic matter and life forms, and the further gains it promises in information. At this point, the key technological components appear to be biotechnology, robotics, artificial intelligence, and the advent of superconductivity and other exceptionally productive gains in energy. Would you believe robots so *unimaginably* small that they could penetrate the wall of a single human cell (a million human cells will fit on the head of a pin) and make needed repairs to the cell's DNA? How about a computer so tiny that it could fit between the infinitesimal gaps, or synapses, that separate nerve cells in the human brain? Or a *bacteria-based* computer so awesome that it could duplicate the computational power of *one thousand* Crays—still the queen of today's supercomputers—within the space of a *cubic centimeter*, smaller than a sugar cube?[3] Such are the possibilities at this minute being

Computer simulations [of organizations] have a propensity for luring researchers into Bonini's paradox—the more realistic and detailed one's model, the more the model resembles the modeled organization, including resemblance in the directions of incomprehensibility and indescribability. W. H. STARBUCK

The only person who is educated is the one who has learned how to learn ... and change. CARL ROGERS, *FREEDOM TO LEARN*

Learning is an approach, both to knowledge and to life, that emphasizes human initiative. It encompasses the acquisition and practice of new methodologies, new skills, new attitudes, and new values necessary to live in a world of change. Learning is a process of preparing to deal with new situations. ALVIN TOFFLER, *FUTURE SHOCK*

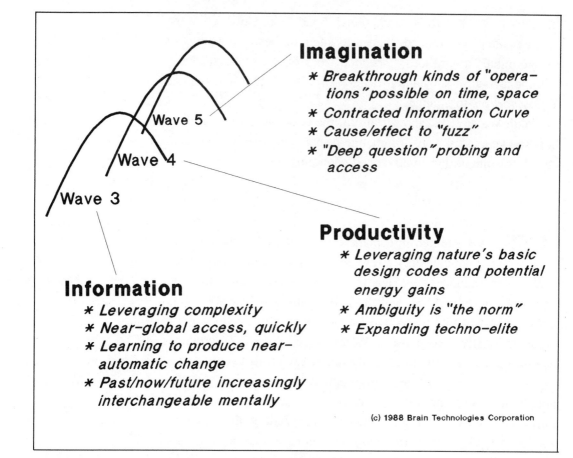

Figure 2.2.   Waves on the Leading Edge

A computer built on bacteria as powerful as a thousand Crays?

seriously pursued by the pioneers—charter members of a new techno-elite—of Wave 4.

Wave 5 we are calling the Wave of Imagination because it can be projected that this new cycle of technologies will equip us to offer a host of new explanations and theories on the most basic questions of the universe. Barring awesome catastrophe, Wave 5 should be almost certainly just around the corner, with Waves 6 and 7 waiting in the wings, provided enough dolphins beget dolphins.

Though they do not and cannot know with specificity the nature of these future waves, dolphins do understand and are preparing to act on the following realities:

Because of the acceleration of the Information Curve, it can be expected that new waves of change in the near future, and for an indeterminate time thereafter, will arrive virtually "on the toes" of the previous wave. Thus, the seeming aeons of time available to our distant forebears for reacting to and getting in synchrony with new developments and challenges are no longer available. The option of keeping one foot in the old and the other foot in the new has evaporated. With the rocketing rate of new information creation, near-exponential gains in rates of information storage and exchange, and the sheer diversity of choices available, the likelihood of stable—that is "flow"—periods of normality grows less and less. As Figure 2.3 suggests, when flux has itself become flow, then every new wave, whatever else we may name it, has become a "brain wave," requiring new brain functions and qualities to accommodate the global changes it brings.

With waves of change bursting forth on the scene every few years, we may soon face a spectacle of unprecedented global diversity in which perhaps as many as four, five, six, or even more "systems of ideas and beliefs"—worldviews—created by these waves of change are vying for dominance simultaneously. Each succeeding shift along the Information Curve has signaled greater and greater stress for individuals and institutions subject most directly to the changing times. The shift from Wave 1 (agriculture) to Wave 2 (the industrial era) triggered a bloody civil war in the United States. Whatever the waves involved, families can be torn apart in so-called generational conflict. Political realities are often stood on their head, and economies may wax or wane along unprecedented lines incapable of prediction or even solid analysis. Dealing with a multitude of shifts within the global and even national communities will be a dolphinlike task for certain.

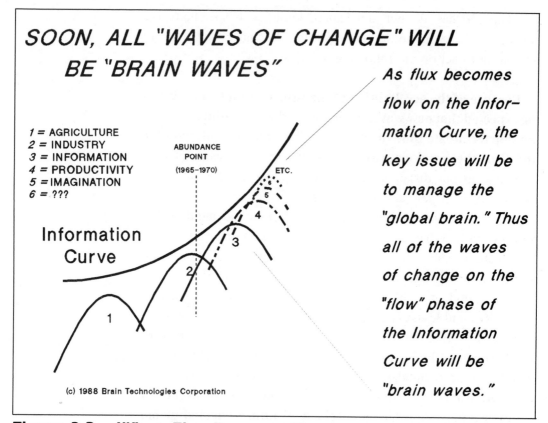

SOON, ALL "WAVES OF CHANGE" WILL BE "BRAIN WAVES"

1 = AGRICULTURE
2 = INDUSTRY
3 = INFORMATION
4 = PRODUCTIVITY
5 = IMAGINATION
6 = ???

ABUNDANCE
POINT

(1965–1970)

ETC.

Information
Curve

As flux becomes flow on the Information Curve, the key issue will be to manage the "global brain." Thus all of the waves of change on the "flow" phase of the Information Curve will be "brain waves."

(c) 1988 Brain Technologies Corporation

Figure 2.3.   When Flux Becomes Flow. . .

Be spontaneous!
A PARADOX

Experience is not what happens to a man. It is what a man does with what happens to him.
ALDOUS HUXLEY

The consequences of attempting to ride the downside of a wave—that is, simply reacting to what's happening in the environment—can be expected to become more and more precarious. Not only are waves of change arriving more and more often, they are also arriving in a compacted state—that is, within the wave itself, developments are on a fast track. The computer system you bought nine months ago may already be obsolete. The ''confidential'' tip you received last week on an important business development in your industry was a headline in this morning's *Wall Street Journal*. The brainstorm you had yesterday for a new product or service has actually been under development in California, Sweden, or West Germany for several months. The market you were counting on to propel your company to its next phase of growth has been preempted—or eliminated.

What powers the Information Curve?

The ability of men and women to tell each other what they have learned or discovered and to leverage off the knowing.

Buckminster Fuller told this story. Two shipwrecked sailors are washed to shore on a terribly isolated sand spit of an island, far from the normal sea lanes. They separate and begin to forage the place for something to eat. One discovers a tangle of vines with red berries. He hurriedly crams a handful into his mouth—and dies.

When the other sailor finds the lifeless body, he realizes the berries are poisonous.

Later, remarkably, two attractive young women also are washed ashore on the same island. Scarcely believing his luck, the surviving sailor rushes to greet them. And what is the first thing he tells them?

"Don't eat the red berries!"*

That's the essence of the Information Curve—the transmission of the outcomes of learning and discovery and the willingness to share information openly, truthfully, and creatively so we all can leverage off of it.

And with the electronics that make possible the communication of information on red berries and other topics turning over so fast that virtually all information technologies are obsolete in two to three years, the Information Curve is headed into shore at full speed. In addition to avoiding red berries, dolphins will be brushing up on the navigation of change, which is another way of describing what this book is about.

Lesson No. 2: Timing is everything.

In terms of the wave, life is essentially divided into three sections; *any* kind of life: the life of a project, the life of a single

---

*A participant in one of our Australian seminars puckishly suggested this answer: "Just one of you eat the red berries!"

Long before the bottom line indicates that the organization is in trouble, everything inside has gone to hell in a hand-basket.

JAMES RENIER

individual, the life of a business, the life of a product, the life of a society.

No experience on the wave is ever exactly the same over time, but the dynamics of the wave remain amazingly constant. Dolphins go to unusual lengths to assess, moment by moment, month by month, where they are *on* the wave, how they are interrelating *to* the wave, and what they can expect over the expanse of the future *from* the wave.

In a word, dolphins are survivors. And they are survivors because, in large measure, they know how to *leverage the wave with a minimum of nonproductive stress or with strategically targeted productive stress (or eustress)*. Because they understand the nature, nuances, and notions of the wave, they enjoy the three traits pinpointed by psychologists Suzanne Kobosa and Salvatore Maddi as the core characteristics of survivors: a clear focus on what it is they want to achieve in their work and career; an ability to experience surprises as challenges and setbacks as valuable learning experiences, refusing to be immobilized by change; and a firm sense that most of the time they are in control of their actions and the meanings they assign to events, and not in the control of the events themselves.

Survivors have a clear focus, handle surprises well, and believe they are in control.

The finer points of reading and riding the wave will be addressed in the chapters ahead. By way of introduction, however, we invite your attention to Figure 2.4.

Figure 2.4 portrays the wave in three temporal, or time-defined, segments. Within the unfolding of each of these time segments on the wave, a dolphin's behavior may resemble only remotely "typical" business or organizational behavior and may, in fact, be just the opposite.

Discovery Time: Early in the wave—when time (the *X* axis)

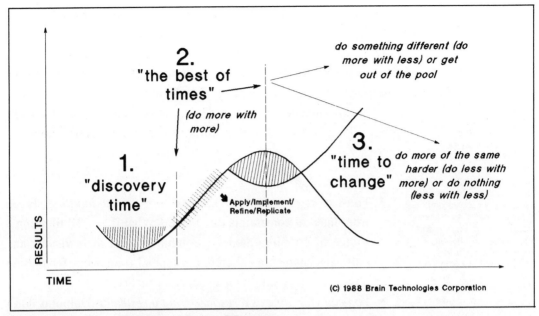

Figure 2.4. Timing Your Moves

is young and results (the *Y* axis) are meager or nonexistent—dolphins are involved in a crucial reversal: They act first, *then* develop their strategy. That is to say, dolphins tend to launch new flurries of activity immediately, though usually manageably small ones, and address the need to "attack the logic" of what happens later.

"This allows you to see your business and organization in the future, interpolate your way backward into the present reality, and then manage your implementation more powerfully," says consultant Stanley M. Davis in *Future Perfect*. "The only way an organization's leaders can get there (the objectives of [a] strategy) from here (the current organization) is *to lead from a place in time that assumes you are already there, and that is determined even though it hasn't happened yet.*"[4] Davis dips into the rules of grammar to buttress his core theme: that an "action before strategy" approach requires that we treat the future as if it has already happened. If you say, "By summer, I will have expanded into eight new markets," you are using what grammarians call the future-perfect tense of the verb. The thought that you have expressed is phrased as if it exists simultaneously in the past *and* the future. Such a way of picturing events allows you, as Davis notes in *Future Perfect*, to treat the present as if it were the past of the future. By so doing, you can then pull your strategy into the future rather than be pulled *by* your strategy.

By thinking in the future-perfect tense during the discovery phase of the wave, you as a dolphin can enjoy such benefits as these:

- *You can clear a path for the best use of your intuition.* Freed from internal constraints that make "What if. . . ?" thinking a source of crippling anxiety, dolphins act on their visions and only later involve a coherent conceptual framework for pulling physical reality into their conceptual reality.
- *You can view time as a resource, not a restraint.* Dolphins don't say, "Time is money." Rather, they say, "Money is time." What's the difference? The difference is in where you place your emphasis or your priorities. In the carp/shark world of Newtonian controls, money is viewed as the primary resource, and you get a sense of how well you are making use of that resource by using time as a measure. In the dolphin's world, time is the resource you leverage, and money is the measure of how much value you create.
- *You can avoid "the Utopia syndrome."* Sir Thomas More named his famed distant island "Utopia" in 1516; it means "nowhere." Nowhere *is* where many carps and even sharks end up because of believing self-talk like this:

The "regular" carp: "I'll never arrive, so why leave?"
The pseudo-enlightened carp: "It's the journey that's important, not the destination, so it doesn't matter whether you arrive or not."
The shark: "It's the destination that's important, so get there as fast as you can, no matter who gets hurt in the process."

The Mexican sierra has seventeen plus nine spines in the dorsal fin. These can easily be counted. But if the sierra strikes hard on the line so that our hands are burned, if the fish sounds and nearly escapes and finally comes in over the rail, his colors pulsing and his tail beating the air, a whole new relational externality has come into being—an entity which is more than the sum of the fish plus the fisherman. The only way to count the spines of the sierra unaffected by this second relational reality is to sit in a laboratory, open an evil-smelling jar, remove a stiff colorless fish from the formalin solution, count the spines, and write the truth. . . . There you have recorded a reality which cannot be assailed—probably the least important reality concerning either the fish or yourself.

It is good to know what you are doing. The man with his pickled fish has set one truth and recorded in his experience many lies. The fish is not that color, that texture, that dead, nor does he smell that way. JOHN STEINBECK

The dolphin says, "Balderdash! The fact that you are on the journey means you have already arrived. *This is it.* You are here! If everything important to you lies 'out there,' then you don't have it and can never expect to get it. The power of visionary leadership comes from knowing that you already are what you want. The task you are now involved in is to develop your strategy for dealing with your arrival and to help others understand and act on your new reality."

"The Best of Times." Not long ago, one of our business acquaintances volunteered, "I think there is some kind of 'genetic code' that determines whether you are successful or not. No matter what I do, it's successful. And then some people can't do anything right, no matter how hard they try."

Most of us know people like these—both types, in fact. But your authors would offer another kind of interpretation for this individual's current successes, an interpretation based on the wave. This fellow, a successful contractor, has simply caught the wave many times and navigated it well. He has great instincts for changing. At

> *In the flow, if it ain't broke, you don't fix it.*

this particular moment, he's in that part of the wave we call "the best of times." He's on the power track, riding the swell of the wave almost effortlessly. In an organizational sense, he's enjoying what Dr. Mihaly Csikszentmihalyi of the University of Chicago—in *Beyond Boredom and Anxiety*—called "flow." Flow, said Csikszentmihalyi, results when challenge and ability are more or less evenly matched—that is, the difficulty of a challenge and a person's (or organization's) ability to meet it are in balance. This is the power sought by surfers in the great breakers of Hawaii and Australia. And this is the power sought by dolphins as they develop strategy for their intuitive actions.

When a dolphin feels the wave surge powerfully beneath her, she adopts the motto of the nonperfectionist: "If it ain't broke, don't fix it." As we see in Figure 2.4, "the best of times" are times where you *apply* what you know, *implement* what you have

We cannot, and perhaps should not, interfere with the unfolding of evolution in the realms of nature. But when it comes to evolution in the realms of history, the case is different. Here *we* are the actors, and it is *our* future that is at stake. ERVIN LASZLO in place, *refine* any rough edges you identify, and *replicate* the process that has brought you to this delicious point where you seem equal to the occasion and the challenge.

This isn't to say everything is idyllic or even comfortable—that wasn't Csikszentmihalyi's point. Rather, because your sense of mastery is a match for the challenges being thrust at you by the environment, you can enjoy the pleasures of problem-solution using your capabilities for controlling the uncertainties and the novelties. As Michael Hutchison writes in *Megabrain,* "[Flow] is not boring, or easily mastered, nor is it so extraordinarily difficult as to cause overwhelming anxiety."[5] For a dolphin, "flow" is what is experienced in the power track of the wave.

For a carp or a shark, this part of the wave is just another day at the office filled with drama, games, and the crippling fallout that comes from not having a suitable answer to Henry David Thoreau's question "What are we busy about?"

Time to Change: As the curve tops out, it reaches what the Nobel Prize-winning scientist Ilya Prigogine; George Land, the author of *Grow or Die;* James Gleick in *Chaos;* and others have called "the bifurcation point." Because of its absolutely critical importance in the life of any and every organized, ongoing activity, you would think that the bifurcation point—the top of the wave—

As the wave plunges, carps may work in their own worst interest.

would be a frantically crowded, busy place, with everyone—dolphins, sharks, and carps alike—testing the waters, eagerly searching for clues and portents to what might come next.

Actually, though, the crest of the wave is typically about as crowded as a swimming beach in the midst of a wintry blow—that is to say, not very crowded at all. There is much to learn from the reasons why—*don't-eat-the-red-berries* kinds of reasons at that.

At the bifurcation point, the wave inexorably sloughs away from its apogee, losing power, momentum, and opportunity. It is headed into a trough, increasingly abandoned by the creative forces of the environment, heretofore the invisible sculptor of the wave's outer shape and dynamics.

For the carp, the point at which the wave begins to descend fails to register because of sheer fatalism, the refusal to acknowledge that something different can, should, or might be done. Unwilling to challenge the status quo or create radical alternatives, the carp can hardly be expected to be a veritable early-warning DEW Line for change, and of course she isn't. If, as the steepness of the wave increases and the plunge toward disaster and disintegration grows, the carp doesn't opt out altogether, she can be counted on to continue working hard in her own worst interest.

*S*harks aren't congregants in large numbers at the bifurcation point because they invariably greet the first signs of slackening in the wave's momentum with a mad retreat into more familiar waters, waters where they have enjoyed success. They are absent because they don't want to be identified with failure (so they deny it and don't learn from it) and because they have rushed off to reassure—and gain reassurance from—various stakeholders and codependents: their peers, their investors, their political cronies, their brokers, their allies, and their sycophants. Few waves come apart overnight, and there is nearly always advantage and benefit to be enjoyed in transitional times if you are well enough protected and rapaciously

Sharks aren't at the bifurcation point because they're out beating the drums.

Anybody can *be* unhappy, but to *make* oneself unhappy needs to be learned, and to this end some experience with a few personal blows of fate simply won't do. PAUL WATZLAWICK

quick-witted enough to grab and defend what is yours, whatever the moralities or ethics of your actions. If there are changes to be made, sharks would prefer that they come only after they have secured what is theirs, and they would prefer that those changes happen on someone else's watch. So at the bifurcation point you find few sharks; they're out beating the drums and spreading such messages as "It's just a minor correction," "All we need to do is get back to the basics," and "It's only a matter of hanging tough."

And dolphins? In most cases, don't expect them to be visible at the bifurcation point, either: They likely bailed out of the wave and began a new discovery process some time before it became plainly evident that something different would need to be done. Dolphins both intuit and reason the need to change rather than wait until the environment bludgeons them again and again with sharper and sharper reminders. Sensing that fundamental shifts are in the wind or the wave, dolphins begin their disengagement and their pro-active explorations of new possibilities well before the crest of the wave. The result is that by the time of the bifurcation point, dolphins have worked through much of the start-up lag of new beginnings and are firmly in command of their strategy and their program for the new era.

Dolphins began their disengagement some time ago.

S umming up, the carp permits itself to be swept along by the wave, even if the wave is in a death plunge. The shark as always is fiercely and furiously in the hunt searching for self-advantage and easy kills, even at the grave risk of entrapment.

Dolphins leverage the wave. When the old patterns and performance gains begin to flag, when people's needs aren't getting met and the faintest hint of changing times and circumstances is transmitted by the future, dolphins begin to raise questions and to play "What if . . . ?" Knowing that the political realities, budgetary considerations, research, pilot runs, and efforts of persuasion needed to put a new vehicle in place successfully for catching the new wave will take months or perhaps even years, dolphins usually disengage from the old wave well before the actual bifurcation point. In that way, when the old wave folds over and begins its downward movement, the dolphin effort is ideally nearing the end of a new discovery phase. While the severity of the learning experience increases geometrically for those riding the old wave down, dolphins hope to be doing something different, something that works.

To say it again, *timing is everything*.

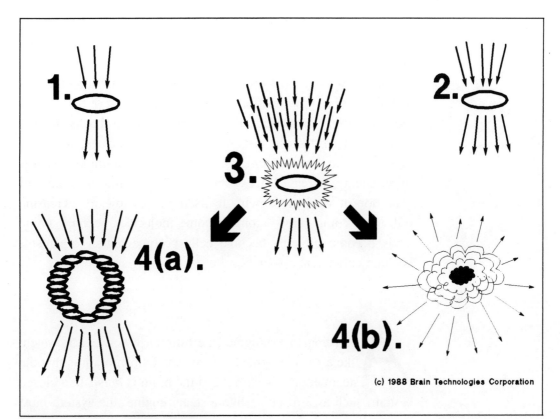

(c) 1988 Brain Technologies Corporation

Figure 2.5. Exit Stress

Lesson 3: Realize that you are the flow.

P lease! Don't get turned off, hung up, or powered down at this point because we keep talking about "flow." Practical thinkers that they are, dolphins tend to opt only for real-time, real-world, real-measure, real-results ideas, methods, and approaches and usually opt out if the conversation and the conversationalists begin to talk too reverentially (as opposed to experimentally) about the part of the universal picture that they don't understand and for which they have no salient explanations.

Be assured: *Flow* is a pure, Nobel Prize-winning, earth-shaking science of a kind so instrumental and fundamental that its discoverer deserves to be

Ilya Prigogine offers us an understanding of a world that is running up.

remembered—and likely will be—as a twentieth-century Isaac Newton. Certainly, Ilya Prigogine will rank with Albert Einstein as one of the greats of postindustrial science.

In few words, what this gifted Russian-born Belgian theoretical chemist has provided for us is an understanding of how, in the face of entropy or inescapable heat loss, a world that is running down can nevertheless sustain all kinds of processes, including human life, that are *running up*. That is, how in a universe that is experiencing increased decay and disorder we find a process of evolution at work in which life itself moves toward increasing order and complexity—atoms become molecules become amino acids become proteins become cells become higher organisms become cultures and societies.

*A*ccording to Prigogine, the difference between a system like a steam engine and, say, the human brain is that the steam engine is *closed* and the brain is *open*. In a closed system, such as a machine like a steam engine, the system must eventually run down. Usually, the closer a closed system gets to stopping cold, the less energy it provides for doing useful work. Eventually it just quits, wears out, or falls apart.

Not so for open systems, which, as Prigogine explains, operate along very different lines than closed systems.

In Figure 2.5 we have converted Prigogine's brilliant ideas into a few simplified thumbnail, dolphinlike sketches. Follow along if you will, appreciating that at the end you will assuredly find yourself.

Sketch 1 clues us to a fundamental difference between closed systems and open ones. Open systems don't absorb or "horde" entropy or "wear and tear" like closed systems, which are totally self-contained, providing little or no flow of matter or energy

> *Open or living systems are always interacting with their environment.*

between themselves and their surrounding environments. Open, or living, systems are always exchanging matter and energy with the outside environment. Humans, for example, take in food, light, oxygen, and information and give off "entropy" in the nature of carbon dioxide, heat, waste, ideas, art, and other excretions.

If the energy load increases as depicted in **sketch 2,** open systems can often deal with it because, in contrast to closed systems, they are self-organizing. They simply increase the amount of entropy they give back to their environment while at the same time probably doing a little quick-shuffle rearranging or repair internally to keep their act together.

At times, however, minor rearranging or repair isn't enough of a response to keep things stable. The environment in which they live, do business, borrow money, pay taxes, invent new products and services, and hire and fire becomes too energized, volatile, and unpredictable to be handled the way they are currently structured. As **sketch 3** illustrates, the system is being bombarded by energy faster than it can be dissipated as entropy. Something's got to give.

Suddenly, once again, we are at the bifurcation point. And a critical point it is, one leaving only two real choices.

As portrayed in **sketch 4(a),** we can be willing to withstand momentary collapse and then escape, relax, change, re-create—however you choose to picture it—to a new pattern in order to reassemble at a higher order of internal organization capable of handling the new complexities elegantly. Or as depicted in **sketch 4(b),** we can resist any changes, ignore and delay our capabilities for evolving structurally, and run the risk of coming apart irretrievably with, like Humpty Dumpty, little hope of being put back together again. A variation of this is to adopt a "wait-and-see" strategy, thinking that we can handle things until we get the drift of the prevailing winds. But too often, during times of rapid change, this approach is a trap: When the crunch truly hits, it is then too late for "the system"—our brains,

When you take Lebbeus Woods' graduate class in architecture, you never know what whirlwind of the mind he's going to be riding. He's at the blackboard scribbling. When he turns to face the class, you read:

- Science rewards the creative imagination;

- Science understands that discoveries come by vision fed by intuition and apparent accidents;

- Set up conditions within which you are compelled to confront some accidents;

- Great art and great science are criminal acts;

- Stop thinking of yourselves only as competent professionals; today's society is changing too fast for mere competence;

- Think of yourselves as intellectual subversives;

- Live dangerously.
  KATHLEEN STEIN IN *OMNI*

Something has to give in an open system where energy exceeds entropy.

When the crunch hits, the tendency is to "go back to the basics."

our company, our economy—to escape to a higher order, and in increasing desperation we go back to the basics, trying what we've always done with more intensity and more investment, only to fail.

The essential lessons, then, of **sketches 4(a)** and **4(b)** are that when the system is being bombarded with more energy than it can handle, there are three primary choices:

- We can do nothing.
- We can do more of the same harder.
- We *can* do something different.

When understood in this way, our views of the wave and the flow undergo an important modification. Beforehand, we viewed the flow as a "state of affairs" in which our abilities and our challenges were equally matched. To be in the flow was to be in that part of the wave where we found the environment to be reasonably supportive of our efforts, a quid pro quo that was inviting and productive.

With Prigogine's insights, however, we find ourselves confronted with a startling new perspective. Each time they change, open systems become more complex. The more complex they become, the more entropy they must dissipate. The more entropy they must dissipate, the more energy they must absorb. The more energy they can absorb, the more open they are to reorganization—to collapse, chaos, change, and creation. Eventually such open systems are scarcely distinguishable from the energy and matter flowing through them. Michael Hutchison offers this analogy:

Think of a windsock, filled by the whipping breezes that funnel through it—its structure is unpredictable, unstable, created, shaped, and maintained by the energy (the wind) which passes through the system; but if the energy/wind ceases, the windsock droops, ceasing to exist as a three-dimensional, open system.[6]

In Prigogine's terms, it isn't so much a matter of being "in the flow" as much as it is that as dolphins *we are flow*. When we reach a stage of human development where our brains are automatically establishing their own conditions for self-change, we literally are the energy and matter that pass through us. When our environment—the world where we live and do business—foists such a surfeit of energy, challenge and change at us that this input can no longer navigate passage through us, then we are at a point of "exit shock"—a point where we must do all we can, courageously and creatively, to trigger and establish the "perturbations" that will bring the reordering we need to survive.

Dolphins understand this.

Dolphins understand that they are *flow*.

Being flow, dolphins understand that the wave is nothing less and nothing more than a measure in time of where they are on the road to collapse, chaos, change, and either re-creation or disintegration as open systems, subject to the "fruit basket turnover" rules of process and living discovered and defined by Ilya Prigogine.

In times of rapid change, dolphins understand that as flow, the closer they come to the "edge" of the wave without initiating steps to change themselves as flow, the greater danger they face from the energy surging through and around them in an increasingly high-energy, unstable, far-from-equilibrium, even volatile environment.

Dolphins understand that there comes a paradoxical time in the development of any open system, including the human brain, when the system becomes autocatalytic—from the words "auto" (self) and "catalyst" (a substance or quality that changes other things while not being changed itself). Suddenly, the brain, the person, or the organization is no

"Exit stress" is self-willed, self-created, self-directed stress.

longer waiting for developments ''outside'' to cause it to see the need for change or to want to change or to make it possible to change. Instead, the brain, the person or the organization is itself creating the situation, circumstances, fluctuations, and elements that will force it to change. Call it self-stress, if you will. We like to call it ''exit stress.'' It's the self-willed, self-created, self-*directed* stress that propels the system into a new pattern, a new state that is more ordered, more coherent, more interconnected, more complex, and more highly evolved than before.

That's why dolphins, as opposed to sharks and carps, invest so heavily in learning how to trigger and how to leverage self-stress—self-collapse, self-chaos, self-change, and self-creation—all subjects that we examine more closely in the chapters ahead.

DOLPHIN WORK

Exercise No. 1

On a separate sheet of paper, take a moment to identify the six most important focuses in your life right now (for example, your spouse, children, other members of your family, close friends, your career, health concerns, educational activities, personal growth investments, your church or religion, etc.). Place the most important entry first, followed by the other five in the order of importance to you.

Now estimate how much of the total time during which you are awake is spent on each of the six priority focuses, and place the number corresponding to this focus on the time line. For example, if you listed your children as No. 1 and you spend about 10% of your time with them, write 10% by this entry. If you listed your career as No. 2 and you estimate that you are spending about 30% of your time there, write 30% by this entry. Act similarly for all six of your focuses. When you are finished, you will have identified graphically how much of your time you spend on each of the six.

Exercise No. 2

Now we would like you to think about what kind of results you are getting from each of the focuses identified in Exercise No. 1 and also how satisfied you are with each. To complete this exercise, continue to use the list you just compiled or, if necessary, create a new list on a separate sheet of paper. In either event, find space for two additional columns on your paper. Label the first column "Results" and the second "Satisfaction."

If, for example, you chose your spouse or someone else with whom you have a close relationship as your No. 1 concern in the previous exercise and you are getting strong results from the time invested in this relationship, then place a triple asterisk ("***") in the "Results" column after that entry. If you are getting only average results, place a double asterisk ("**") in this column; if you are getting poor results, place a single asterisk ("*") in that column. Now make a judgment as to how satisfied you are with this entry or priority. If you are highly satisfied, once again place a triple asterisk ("***") in the "Satisfaction" column after this entry. And so on.

Continue with the remaining four entries until all six are represented in both columns. Then you will have a graphic representation of the balance between results and personal satisfaction for the six most important areas of your life. In the chapters ahead, this information will help you identify whether you are "on purpose."

Exercise No. 3

Finally, on a separate sheet of paper, draw a simple "bell curve" like that seen in Figure 2.2.

In this exercise, you can check to see where your six priorities are in terms of the Change Wave.

Remember that a Discovery Phase occurs at the beginning of the wave. The Flow Area is located on the ascending part of the wave and defines a time when what you are doing is working well—when you merely need to refine and duplicate a known process. The Recovery Phase is on the back side of the wave and is when you are attempting to recuperate from a change in the results you are getting from doing things the way you always have.

Once again, determine where you are on the Change Wave with each of your priorities and place the appropriate number for each priority at that point. For example, if you are in the flow with your No. 1 priority, place a "1" at that point on the curve. Then continue with the other five priorities. This will provide you with a picture useful in orchestrating the most important areas of your life.

Thinking back over the insights provided by this exercise, what does the total picture tell you about where you are now? Were there any surprises?

To "actualize" a vision of where you want to be, you must first understand clearly where you are now so that you know what to correct and change. If the future were giving you signals about what and if you need to change, what would the changes be, what would the new profiles look like, where would you need to correct, and how? What would these changes tell you about the direction of your life? What things would not change, and what does that tell you?

3
UP PERISCOPE: THE CRITICAL DOLPHIN SKILL OF BREAKING SET

"Breaking set" sounds like something tennis pros Ivan Lendl or Martina Navratilova might be good at. For certain, dolphins (the human variety as well as the seagoing variety) are very good at escaping the self-imposed barriers to new perspectives that tend to keep the mind anchored to only one idea, a single rule, or a solitary dimension. Without such skills, we often find our outcomes and our opportunities set in concrete.

Set in concrete because we've never taken time to challenge our ideas, habits, or assumptions. Set in concrete because, to now, everything has worked. The most difficult sets to break are those supportive of our egos or those supportive of our social values—the values our friends and colleagues also view highly. Breaking set is invariably required to keep organizations healthy and on purpose, especially in times of rapid change. Every day, and on some days every hour, you in some way need to break set—take a different perspective, challenge the status quo, ask a different kind of question, see the world another

Argue for your limitations and sure enough, they're yours.   RICHARD BACH, *ILLUSIONS*

To play as a dolphin plays, you must take responsibility for how you respond to what happens to you.

93

way, and help yourself and your colleagues ask, "How would we really like it—how do we really *need* to have it?"

To play as a dolphin plays, however, we must take responsibility. For what happens to us? No. No one can possibly control—and thus be responsible for—everything that happens. Dolphins make no such erroneous assumption. To play as a dolphin plays, we take responsibility only for how we *respond* to what happens. In most situations we have a wide choice in how we respond—if, that is, we choose to be responsible about our choice-making powers.

Sharks often take what has traditionally been a masculine stance for responding to events: the use of force. Carps, both the plain vanilla and the pseudo-enlightened variety, favor a feminine solution: the use of effort. Dolphins at their best opt for the androgynous, seeking the best of all combinations in a response of elegance, grace, and finesse. Dolphins understand that what counts is what works. To find what works, you must be willing to be responsible, acting to discover your choices. It may not be in your best interest at all to stay in the pool with the sharks. Instead, you may want to get out of the pool or avoid it altogether.

> [There] are two different types of change: one that occurs within a given system which itself remains unchanged, and one whose occurrence changes the system itself.
> PAUL WATZLAWICK AND COLLEAGUES, *CHANGE: PRINCIPLES OF PROBLEM FORMATION AND PROBLEM RESOLUTION*

In rapid-change times, preservation is not an option.

The critical points to remember are:

1. In rapid-change times, preservation is not an option, and choice is at a premium. As others have noted, if you have only one choice, you are a robot; if you have two choices, you are in a dilemma, and if one way doesn't work, the tendency is to do the opposite (which usually doesn't work either); but if you have three choices, you are finally beginning to develop a functional variety of behaviors for responding to change.

2. It's not what happens to you but how you respond to what happens to you that determines the quality of your experience.

3. How you respond is determined by the meaning you assign to an event. Carps and sharks focus on their limits, dolphins on their possibilities.

To be skilled at breaking set, the foremost quality of the dolphin, you may need to step away from some of those cherished "unwritten rules" of management and begin to grow comfortable and confident operating under an altogether new set of assumptions and realities—a set that replaces, as theorist George Land has phrased it, "a world view of exclusion and exclusivity, of this *or* that, and this *versus* that [with] one of this *and* that."[1] To think like a dolphin, it makes sense to hone our skills at breaking set, just in case when tomorrow we look back on today, we realize that it was one of those days on which the universe changed.

Every psychological extreme secretly contains its own opposite or stands in some sort of intimate and essential relation to it.... There is no hallowed custom that cannot on occasion turn into its opposite and the more extreme a position is, the more easily may we expect ... a conversion of something into its opposite. C. G. JUNG

Life is a sword that wounds, but cannot wound itself; like an eye that sees, but cannot see itself. ZEN MASTER

For a dolphin, there is a deliberate, daily effort made to avoid "If only . . ." disappointments and disasters by using a constant "What if . . . ?" frame of mind. Unfortunately, the attitude is not widespread. On Black Monday—the day in October 1987 when the stock market plummeted an unprecedented 508 points—the horror of this reality was indelibly stamped in the minds of thousands of investors. "I knew we were due for a correction," one shaken owner of stocks volunteered, "but I didn't expect it to come all in one day." We never do. Even investors who on that fateful day quickly realized what was happening were often unable to get through to their brokers. One woman tried to dial her discount broker more than a hundred times before giving up. The chairman of that firm later told reporters, "If we'd known the magnitude of this downturn even a day or two in advance, we could have had several hundred extra people here to help." If only. Of course, after the fact, one "if only" and fifty cents in hard currency will buy us a cup of coffee. If, that is, after the shock, we have fifty cents left, and if anyone is left in the coffee business, and *if* there are any beans left for making coffee.

There is less and less time these days for learning and reacting.

In educational circles, the idea of learning by reacting to

We first raise the dust and then claim we cannot see. BERKELEY

If I don't know I don't know, I think I know.

If I don't know I know, I think I don't know. R. D. LAING

events is called *maintenance/shock learning.*[2] Typically, we humans have used a pattern of continuous maintenance learning disrupted by short bursts of innovation triggered by some shocking, unexpected turn of events. Some observers, including your authors, argue that during times of rapid change, such a *Que sera, sera* attitude is a prescription for disaster—for individuals, for organizations, for societies. Here's another opinion:

> The conventional pattern of *maintenance/shock learning* is inadequate to cope with global complexity and is likely, if unchecked, to lead to one or more of the following consequences: (a) The loss of control over events and crises will lead to extremely costly shocks, one of which could possibly be fatal. (b) The long lag times of maintenance learning virtually guarantee the sacrificing of options needed to avert a whole series of recurring crises. (c) The reliance on expertise and short time periods intrinsic to learning by shock will marginalize and alienate more and more people. (d) The incapacity quickly to reconcile value conflicts under crisis conditions will lead to the loss of human dignity and of individual fulfillment.[3]

[The Age of Alibi is a philosophy] which for decades has induced us to believe that human fault must rest always on somebody else's shoulders; that responsibility for behavior damaging to society must invariably be attributed to society itself; that human beings are born not only perfectible but identical, so that any unpleasant divergences must be the product of unpleasant environments.

While we pursue the unattainable we make impossible the realizable. ROBERT ARDREY

These authors advocate *innovative learning,* which seeks to anticipate the need to change and to enlist everyone who would benefit in making change, or learning, happen. That's a dolphin idea, one that the primary approaches to breaking set are designed to assist. Here are mental tools for "a change of change," important and yet little-used principles for shifting gears (doing something different) as opposed to merely injecting more fuel (doing more of the same harder):

Take time to talk about how you have been talking about the problem.

The notion of talking about how you talk may produce momentary mental paralysis. But it makes a lot of sense once you understand that nearly all our personal and organizational limits are imposed not by menacing, unapproachable outside influences but are self-imposed by ourselves *using language* or other forms of memory storage.

Consider this sentence: "America is steadily losing blue-collar jobs, and we've got to act now if we hope to save our manufacturing base." Do you agree? If you do, you probably are in favor of stronger "protectionist" laws limiting trade between the United States and other countries. Why? Why, to protect America's manufacturing base from more erosion. Yet this is just what Britain tried to do—to the virtual ruin of much of its late twentieth-century economy. In *Frontiers of Management,* Peter Drucker points out that it has been the countries that, in the past twenty-five years, have *reduced* most rapidly the number of blue-collar workers per unit of manufacturing production that have remained the healthiest.

Once the trap concerning blue-collar workers has been pointed out, it is easily seen. But when you are caught up and shielded from other perspectives by the language that you yourself have chosen for describing your problem and outlining the solution you believe must be applied, seeing matters in any other way can be perniciously difficult.

In their book *Change: Principles of Problem Formation and Problem Resolution,* psychologist Paul Watzlawick and his colleagues offer numerous examples of people and their institutions trapped by their own so-called solutions that they have self-imposed ("self-described") for themselves:

■ *A four-year-old girl so upset at the prospect of being left by her mother at kindergarten that the mother believed it was necessary to remain with her at school day after day.* (Then one day her father took her, and the child showed no stress at all, remaining by herself all day that day and every day thereafter.)

It often happens that we only become aware of the important facts if we suppress the question "Why?"; and then in the course of our investigations these facts lead us to an answer.

Let us suppose ... that the game is such that whoever begins can always win by a particular simple trick. But this has not been realized; so it is a game. Now someone draws our attention to it; and it stops being a game.

What turn can I give this, to make it clear to myself?—For I want to say: "and it stops being a game"—not: "and we now see that it wasn't a game."

That means ... the other man did not draw our attention to anything; he taught us a different game in place of our own. But how can the new game have made the old one obsolete? We now see something different and can no longer naively go on playing.

For an answer which cannot be expressed the question, too, cannot be expressed.   LUDWIG WITTGEN-STEIN

- *A middle-aged man so progressively paralyzed by agoraphobia (a fear of open spaces) that he found it unbearable to go even to the supermarket.* Finally, he decided to get in his car and commit suicide by driving to a nearby mountain. He expected that within a few blocks his overtaxed heart would kill him. (Actually, he drove all the way to the mountain with no ill effects, and five years later he remained fully cured of his phobia.)

- *During the Chinese cultural revolution, the Red Guards ordered the destruction of all public signs (of streets, public offices, public facilities), thinking it would signal a radical break with the past.* Then they carefully renamed everything. (Later, partisans of the past reasserted themselves, deposing the Red Guards, in part because in changing all the names they had reinforced the Confucian belief that proper naming will produce proper reality. That is, rather than institute radical change, the Red Guards had actually reemphasized a key age-old feature of Chinese culture.)

Whether you completely understand the psychological dynamics in each of these examples isn't important—not at all. *Whys* do not matter all that much to dolphins, just *whats*. (Psychologists have a grim joke about the adult bed wetter who after years of therapy says, "I still wet the bed, but I now understand what my problem is.") Watzlawick writes:

> It is precisely [the] unquestioned illusion that one *has* to make a choice between *a* and not-*a*, that there is no other way out of the dilemma, which perpetuates the dilemma and blinds us to the solution which is available at all times, but which contradicts common sense.[4]

How do dolphins "talk" themselves out of dilemmas? They use techniques such as these:

When they see that what they are doing isn't working, dolphins stop doing what it is they are doing and focus on what

works. By not doing what you've been doing, you create the opportunity to do something else.

Dolphins create new words to talk about their problem. A Zen master, Tai-Hui, showed his monks a stick and said, ''If you call this a stick, you affirm; if you call it not a stick, you negate. Beyond affirmation and negation, what would you call it?'' Well, shucks, master, call it an apple or a thingamajig or the Monday morning after. Call it anything if it works. That's the point. Call a financially leaky department a sponge and see if that prompts any new possibilities. Label a difficult employee a prisoner in his own cell and explore the insights in that image. Practitioners of neurolinguistic programming, a psychotherapy approach based on uncommonsensical communications, are often gifted at renaming things. They talk about frogs and princes and chunking information, and it frequently makes a difference. NLPers—and dolphins—never forget that language is movable, and that, above it, it is language that shapes ideas.

The way out is through the door. Why is it that no one will use this exit? CONFUCIUS

Dolphins talk a lot to each other about the process.

Whatever you are doing, talk about how you've been doing it. That is, put aside for a time the talk about solutions and talk instead about how it is that you have been trying to reach a solution. If meetings on the problem are getting you nowhere, talk about what your meetings are like. If you've been unsuccessful in being creative, talk about how you've been going about being creative. If you aren't communicating well, talk about how you typically communicate with each other. Dolphins talk a lot to each other *about* the process and as their reward often discover the solution *in* the process, where it was all the time.

Videotape your problem-solving meetings and review them, or appoint an observer who can later talk to the team about how the team talks to itself. Either way, you get a chance to ''metacommunicate'' about a situation—that is, communicate about communicating, which usually is necessary at some point for you to get from an old into a new framework on an issue or need. Suddenly you find yourself shifting gears—and saving fuel.

There is nothing either good or bad, but thinking makes it so.   WILLIAM SHAKESPEARE

Whatever you do for the next five minutes, don't think of the color blue.
NEUROLINGUISTIC PROGRAMMING PARADOX

Chunk up. "Chunking" was mentioned earlier as a term invented by the inventors of NLP. It refers to dealing with ideas one step, or class, at a time. By "chunking up," we mean looking at a problem in a larger context. If your problem is recruiting quality employees, take a little time to ask, "Is this really part of a larger problem? If so, does this shed any new light on things?" If supporters of protectionism legislation in Congress would "chunk up" on the blue-collar-worker issue, they would quickly see that there is a much more serious problem here, with needed solutions that may not fit in the context of blue-collar unemployment alone.

Do what you fear.

Psychologists—good ones, who are good at using this approach—call this "prescribing the symptom." Dolphins that they are, they understand that we often get cut off from a more suitable future by the hidden tenacity of our old solutions. *False* solutions. False because they aren't working, and perhaps never have.

Our "solutions" actually become the problem when they don't work.

When we are habitually involved in pursuing solutions that don't work, our "solutions" have become our problem. Somehow we've got to find ways, as psychotherapist Matthew McKay and his colleagues described it, "to seek what is habitually avoided, to disclose what is habitually hidden, to choose what is habitually rejected."[5]

In psychotherapy, dolphins who are skilled at guiding their patients to a genuine cure, tell insomniacs to stay up all night. They order fainters to fall down. They instruct perfectionists to make mistakes. In providing clients with instructions to do what they fear—and getting their agreement to do so—these therapists create a new situation where the old "solutions" don't make any sense. If you plan to stay up all night, then it suddenly seems silly to worry about not being able to fall asleep.

*I*t isn't always easy to do what you fear. Or do what you can't. Or get where you can't go. But then, it isn't always that difficult, either. Viktor Frankl, the father of logotherapy, helped invent the "do what you fear" approach to problem-solving. He told the story of the schoolboy who was late. Upbraiding him, the schoolmaster demanded to know why. "It was so icy, every time I took a step forward, I slid two steps backward," the boy replied. "How then did you get here?" the indignant master demanded. The boy answered, "I turned around and walked home."

Dolphins know they can often make significant changes for the better by making themselves vulnerable. By doing what they fear. One obstacle that can push us away, push us back, is what has been called the Bannister Effect. Until miler Roger Bannister appeared, no human had ever navigated 5,280 feet *on foot* in four minutes or less. Once Bannister crashed through this invisible, largely psychological barrier, others quickly followed. Virtually anything new that also carries with it a degree of risk has a similar psychological barrier attached. Creators of the Outward Bound program understand this. In insisting that individuals confront their fears of leaping from heights, making their way up steep inclines, or participating in other feats made safe through precautionary harnesses or other protective measures but yet daring enough to challenge mental barriers, today's change agents are encouraging more and more people to challenge their limits.

This is the meaning of [philosopher Immanuel] Kant's great doctrine that teleology [the study of design or purpose in nature] is brought into nature only by the intellect, which thus marvels at a miracle that it has created itself in the first place. It is (if I may explain so sublime a matter by a trivial simile) the same as if the intellect were astonished at finding that all multiples of nine again yield nine when their single figures are added together, or else to a number whose single figures again add up to nine; and yet it has itself prepared this miracle in the decimal system.

ARTHUR SCHOPENHAUER

*A*nother barrier to breaking through, to breaking set, may be the Wallenda Effect. Karl Wallenda was one of the great tightrope walkers of all time. Then during his final performance, he lost his balance and plunged to his death. Later, analyzing the tragedy, members of his family recalled that Wallenda had more than once expressed concern the night before about falling. They surmised that whereas he usually concentrated

Do what you fear— and do it with a variation.

If the reader feels that these studies are somewhat abstract and devoid of applications, he should reflect on the fact that the theories of games and cybernetics are simply the foundations of the theory of How to Get Your Own Way. Few subjects can be richer in applications than that! *w. ROSS ASHBY, AN IN-TRODUCTION TO CYBERNETICS*

on making it across the wire, this time he had concentrated on not falling. You can get an unshakable sense of the difference by envisioning how easy it is to walk across a bridge of two-by-four planks if they are laying on the ground. In this case, all you need do is put your attention to getting across. But if those planks are suspended twenty-five feet in the air, then you are only human if suddenly your concern *is not falling*. Yet in making that your concern, you increase substantially the likelihood that you will, indeed, lose your balance.

"Doing what you fear" can be an extremely difficult pact to make with yourself. In *The Book of Lists*, a fear of public speaking topped the category of greatest fears, surpassing even a fear of nuclear holocausts. The barriers that exist in our heads can be formidable, which is all the more reason to challenge them. You should, however, proceed with caution, understanding that breaking set is more than some people can handle. In substantial measure, dolphins are successful because they have mastered a key principle of pushing through paradox: the *principle of variation*.

Here are some examples:

- *Advertise what you usually hide.* ("To be honest with you, I'm not sure I'll get through this speech, I'm so nervous.")
- *Do alone what you usually do with others.* (Spend a week in the wilderness—alone with your future.)
- *Don't say something you usually say.* (This time, don't say, "The buck stops here.")
- *Hide what you usually reveal.* (Keep the bank balance a secret . . . for once.)
- *Do it with someone different.* (A friend, a consultant, one of your children?)
- *Rearrange the sequence.* ("The last shall be first . . .")
- *Do it at a different time or a different place.* (Your place this time.)

- *Say the opposite of what you usually say.* ("Looking ahead to the nineteenth century . . .")
- *Do it slower or faster, harder or easier.* (And let God work her wonders in mysterious ways.)
- *Do it in pieces.* (The sum of the parts sometimes is preferable to the whole.)
- *Exaggerate or minimize the usual actions.* (Don't bother to make sure everything is shipshape next time. Or, on the contrary, make sure for once that it is.)
- *Remove one step in the usual sequence.* (This time make a decision without doing an exhaustive marketing study.)
- *Add an unpleasant but beneficial task.* (Clean out your closet.)
- *Do it twice in a row, or more often.* (Let the person you trust least chair the meetings for a month.)[6]

> Civilizations die of suicide, not by murder.
> ARNOLD TOYNBEE

> Through my own experience, I learned that striving for a positive mental attitude will get you nowhere unless you have the ammunition to back it up. You develop a positive mental attitude by being prepared, by understanding the realities of what it takes to succeed, and by being good at the necessary techniques. It's a cycle: The more prepared a person is, the more positive his attitude, and, therefore, the better his chances of succeeding.
> ROBERT J. RINGER

The late Milton Erickson was a genius at getting people to do what they feared but with a variation. For example, there was the young man he cured of nail biting by getting the patient's agreement to confine all his biting to the nail of one finger. And the compulsive diet breaker, who could lose weight easily enough but then immediately put it back on. Erickson's solution: get her to agree to *gain* twenty pounds before she began her next dieting experience.

Doing what you fear is an excellent way to break set, especially if you do it with a variation.

Play a skilled game of "paradoxical tennis."

Even sharks have difficulty controlling a situation in the presence of a quick wit capable of using word games to create change in an unwilling, unwitting brain. One of our favorite stories is about the medieval city that posted guards at the moat to ask strangers this question: "What business have you inside the gates?" If the strangers told the truth and were not wanted, they

Techniques for playing paradoxical tennis the dolphin way.

were turned away. If they lied and were discovered doing something else, they were hanged. One day a dolphin arrived at the gate and was asked to state his business. "I've come to be hanged," he replied. If you are being treated like something you aren't, it may be time to exaggerate what it is that they are acting like you are. We once witnessed a young physician of Chinese extraction do an exceedingly brief but devastatingly effective imitation of a coolie when being ordered around by a senior doctor. The harassment ceased immediately.

To cite another example, from World War II, the Nazis posted a pompous poster that read, "National Socialism or Bolshevik chaos?" An underground group promptly printed a small sticker and went around Germany affixing it to hundreds of these posters. The sticker read, *Erdapfel oder Kartofel?* (Spuds or potatoes?)

Sometimes this is also called the "yes *and* no" strategy. When the Nazis ordered all Jews to wear the yellow star of David, King Christian X of Denmark showed his great skills at paradoxical tennis. He slammed the ball back into the Nazis' end of the court without accepting their terms, which is the intent of paradoxical tennis. Danes recognized no differences between Jewish and non-Jewish Danes, the king announced; therefore he would be the first to wear the Star of David. Other Danes overwhelmingly endorsed the king's idea, and the Nazis were forced to cancel their order.

Here are some techniques for playing paradoxical tennis the dolphin way:

Do explicitly the very thing that the other party thinks you want to avoid. Learn to say, "No, thank you" creatively. That is, refuse—firmly but with tact—to take responsibility for having to deal with a problem the way the other party has set it up. That's what King Christian did to the Nazis. Much to his satisfaction, one of your authors has finally witnessed a TV crime show where the intended victim used an effective paradoxical answer when a thug

If a person offends you, and you are in doubt as to whether it was intentional or not, do not resort to extreme measures; simply watch your chance and hit him with a brick.   MARK TWAIN stuck a gun in her ribs in a crowded shopping mall parking lot and ordered her to accompany him. "Hell, no," she replied. "If you are going to shoot me, do it here in front of all these people." (By no means are we suggesting this as an "answer in stock" for all situations of this nature, but if you are about to be transported to a remote area and slain, it does seem to have its merits.)

Answer questions with a pointed question. You may find it useful to reply, "That's an interesting question. Why do you ask?" Or, "That makes sense. Can I ask why that's important to you?"

State the obvious. Ask, "Nancy, why are you putting all this pressure on me?"

Probe. If you are told that your price is too high, ask, "Which means. . . ?" On learning that someone is unhappy with a situation, follow up with, "You say you are unhappy, Paul: What does unhappy mean?" If told something is too expensive, ask, "Compared to what?" If told everyone is doing it, reply, *"Everyone?"* Ask for specifics: who, what, when, where? It is good, if you are a dolphin, to probe anytime you are confronted with "play it safe" words, carp words—words that leave you in the dark and allow the other party to escape commitment. Words or phrases like "maybe" or "possibly" or "it appears" or "looks good" or "every opportunity" or "try."

Anyone who can spell a word only one way is an idiot. w. c. FIELDS

Go "off the record." Going off the record is generally a condition that politicians or others in sensitive positions attempt to place on journalists. Supposedly, information revealed "off the record" isn't to appear in print. Used in business or everyday conversation, the phrase may be useful in getting people to open up, lighten up, or "own up."

Use unconscious resistance. When people insist that they cannot perform or change or make progress in any fashion, you usually have an opportunity to help them make progress by using their own resistance. "That's right," you will want to reply. "I can see now that it's impossible for you to come up with even a single creative solution to this problem." Suddenly you have placed them in a double bind. Their feelings of resistance are as strong as ever, and yet now if they resist you (by showing you that they can, too, come up with a creative solution), they must give you what you want and themselves what they really need.

Be a carp. When dealing with someone who is attempting to apply pressure, make unreasonable demands, or put you in an unfavorable or unfair situation, play dumb. Profess not to know. Suggest that if things are really that bad, what's left to do? Maybe the jig's up. If things are really *that* bad, why are the two of you even bothering to talk about it?

Reframe—or create choice by changing the meaning of an event.

There will never be a better way to illustrate what has been called "the gentle art of reframing" than the story of Tom Sawyer:

"Hello, old chap, you got to work, hey?"

"Why, it's you, Ben! I warn't noticing."

"Say—I'm going a-swimming, I am. Don't you wish you could? But of course you'd druther *work*—wouldn't you? Course you would!"

Tom contemplated the boy a bit and said:

"What do you call work?"

"Why, ain't *that* work?"

Tom resumed his whitewashing and answered carelessly:

"Well, maybe it is, and maybe it ain't. All I know, is, it suits Tom Sawyer."

"Oh come, now, you don't mean to let on that you *like* it."

"Does a boy get a chance to whitewash a fence every day?"

That put the thing in a new light. Ben stopped nibbling his apple. Tom swept his brush daintily back and forth—stepped back to note the effect—added a touch here and there—criticized the effect again—Ben watching every move and getting more and more interested, more and more absorbed.

Presently he said: "Say, Tom, let *me* whitewash a little."

When we reframe, then we "change the conceptual and/or emotional setting or viewpoint in relation to which a situation is experienced and . . . place it in another frame which fits the 'facts' of the same concrete situation equally well or even better, and thereby changes its entire meaning."[7]

Dolphins frequently reframe the meaning of events and issues using techniques such as these:

Asking "What if . . . ?" What if we ask, "what if . . . ?"? For one thing, we are reminded of Antoine de Saint-Exupéry's observation that truth is not what we discover but what we create. (Or Robert Ardrey's observation that "A territory, for example, cannot exist in nature, it exists in the mind of the animal.") When we ask "What if . . . ?" we raise the possibility of looking at a situation—a problem—from a variety of viewpoints. Asking "what if . . . ?" may be sufficient to remind us that it was likely we who created a "reality" to being with, only we've forgotten having done so. Now, reminded that we were indeed the creator of a "reality," we can set about to change it.

Usually, reality is what we make of it.

One of our spouses provided an excellent example of this. Faced with an opportunity to move to a larger suite in our office complex, the male of the species fixated immediately on the expense and inconvenience of having to change the suite number—from 3 to 2—to match the old suite number on business cards, stationery, and printed products. "What if," interjected the dolphin thinker in our midst, "we just exchanged suite numbers? Call the old one '2' and the new one '3'? That way, we keep our current address and no reprinting is necessary."

Makes the point beautifully, doesn't it? In nearly every instance, "reality" is what *we* make of it.

Seeing through someone else's eyes. Much of modern philosophy, from Immanuel Kant forward, has had as one of its central focuses the intent of helping us understand that we can

"Showing the fly the way out of the fly bottle."

avoid the supposed anguish of one "reality" simply by abandoning or replacing it.

This is the idea behind Ludwig Wittgenstein's interest in "showing the fly the way out of the fly bottle." Since "realities" or "territories" or "games" are often inventions of the brain, it is almost always helpful to ask how or imagine how other brains view the subject or topic of *our* interest.

Royal Dutch Shell used such an approach prior to the Arab oil embargo of 1973 and enjoyed significant benefits because the huge firm acted on what it learned. If they were the Arab oil potentates confronting the same world oil situation as Shell and the other major players, what would *they* do? Suddenly it was very clear: They would sit on their oil, leaving it in the ground and letting the price rise. And that, as we need no reminder, is just what the Arabs did.

Identifying the opportunities in our obstacles. That's what the Colorado-headquartered brewer Coors did with beer that did not meet its quality-control standards. By Coors' usual standards, that is "bad beer." But is bad beer necessarily *always* "bad" beer? Not in the eyes of cattle feeders. "Bad" beer can suddenly become very "good" beer if it is viewed as a source of nutrients for livestock. Coors now sells its "bad" beer to cattle feeders. Suddenly "bad" beer is "good" beer, and nothing has changed but the thinking about the beer. But for this kind of transition to occur, categories must shift. Or to quote the implacable Austrian thinker again, we must get the fly out of the fly bottle.

Using the Confusion Technique. Our debt once again is to the late Milton Erickson, the gifted dolphin in psychotherapy. He once described this encounter:

One windy day . . . a man came rushing around the corner of a building and bumped hard against me as I stood bracing myself against the wind. Before he could recover his poise to speak to me, I glanced elaborately at my watch and courteously, as if he had enquired the time of day, I stated, "It's exactly ten minutes of two,'' though it was actually closer to 4:00 P.M., and walked on. About half a block away, I turned and saw him still looking at me, undoubtedly still puzzled and bewildered by my remark.[8]

One remarkable ''truism'' stands out in our studies of breaking set: *It is ''not getting it'' that takes the time and creates the pain.* We typically put enormous energy into resisting a new, useful solution—into avoiding the obvious. No wonder, when we finally *see it*, we shout ''Eureka!,'' have peak experiences, and feel our world reorder.

There is an interesting rule that seems to apply to life in general. It's called the 80/20 rule, or Pareto's Law (after Vilfredo Pareto, the Italian economist and sociologist who created it). It says: ''Twenty percent of what you do produces 80 percent of the results, and conversely, 80 percent of what you do produces only 20 percent of the results.''

In every work of genius we recognize our own rejected thoughts; they come back to us with a certain alienated majesty. RALPH WALDO EMERSON

In sales, this means that 20 percent of your customers generally produce 80 percent of your revenues. In management this means that it's important to separate the ''critical few'' from the ''trivial many.'' In dolphinhood it means developing our skills to determine quickly the 20 percent that matters and focus our change skills here, letting the 80 percent that doesn't matter much to sort its way out at our convenience.

This is a breakthrough insight. To perform as a dolphin, we need deal only with the critical 20 percent. And how do we do *that?* Pay attention to what isn't working and do something different, using the dolphin techniques outlined in this chapter.

DOLPHIN WORK

Exercise No. 1

If what you are doing isn't working, you need to do something different. But what? To arrive at a successful answer, it helps to explore two areas: (1) "What have I learned?" and (2) "What do I need to learn?" Reflect on the thoughts and ideas that come to you after reading each of the following questions:

1. If this situation were funny, what would I be laughing about?
2. How would I view/solve this problem if I were twenty years older? Or twenty years younger?
3. What would I do (think, say) differently if this problem were an opportunity?
4. How did the old solution work in the past? Why is the solution now the problem?
5. What would happen if this situation meant exactly the opposite of what I think it does?
6. How would this situation look from another's point of view?
7. What is the larger issue for which this is only a part?
8. What does the person creating this problem *really* want?
9. Is this problem the system? If so, how do I bypass it?
10. What emotions am I feeling or blocking that are causing me to react—react out of habit or old brain programming rather than behaving with freshness and creativity?

Exercise No. 2*

On a separate sheet of paper, write exactly what it is—what few critical outcomes—you feel you need to achieve to be successful.

Next, think for a moment about what is preventing you from achieving them, and list these obstacles.

Now ask yourself, "If I were 100 percent responsible for what I want and do, what would I do differently?"

---

* We are indebted to Michael Higgins for this exercise.

4
BEING "ON PURPOSE": AVOIDING "THE FATE THAT ACHES"

One of the most miserable creatures in all of life is a fish out of water. For a *real* fish suddenly ejected from *real* water, it's a very grave situation indeed. For the human creature, death isn't imminent when we find ourselves tossed up on the beach. Our fate is more that of a chronic discomfort, often so vague in character and puzzling in nature that after a time we simply accept it as one of life's "givens," a condition like eczema, arthritis in the knee joints, or chronic ingrown toenails that nature has cruelly saddled us with.

Carps and sharks are the most susceptible to this "fate that aches." Dolphins are quick to challenge any signs of drift or disengagement.

Dolphins insist on a synchrony among *what they are doing, thinking, and feeling; why they are here;* and *who they are.* Dolphins search for inner contentment and congruity. Dolphins do not accept, for very long and for very often, the status of a "fish" out of water.

John Sculley is the CEO of Apple Computer, Inc. Before taking this job in one of America's most publicized executive job changes ever, Sculley was Pepsi-Cola's youngest president ever at age thirty-eight and a likely heir apparent for giant Pepsico's top

It was astonishing. A new vice president was sent in, gave my boss six days to get out, and fired me before we had exchanged ten words. I counted them.   QUOTED BY PAUL HIRSCH IN *PACK YOUR OWN PARACHUTE*

111

Migrating from the waters of the shark to the waters of the dolphin.

post. At the time, Sculley was also arguably a shark. Then, suddenly, he discarded assured fortunes and further fame for a very chancy endeavor. Moving from one coast to the other, he stepped into a dicey and difficult leadership role in the dizzying, highly decentralized free-for-all atmosphere of Apple Computers. In doing so, Sculley discovered that for years he had been a fish out of water. In doing so, he migrated from the waters of the shark to the waters of the dolphin.

In his autobiography, *Odyssey,* he writes:

I loved tinkering with electrical things as a child. I hardly ever played with toys. When I was five, I remember getting a dry-cell battery, a buzzer, and hook-up wire for Christmas. I started blowing fuses in our apartment at that age, too. . . . I became a ham radio operator at the age of eleven. At fourteen, in 1954, my fascination with electronics led me to invent a color television cathode-ray tube. . . . My father helped me find a patent attorney. . . . As a teenager, I'd wake up at 4:00 A.M. to sit and chat with [my grandfather] about the future. A tale about a flying saucer he spotted in Bermuda so fully captivated me that the next day I stalked out on patrol, a pair of binoculars in hand, searching the sky for aliens. Failing to find any, I eventually invented a flying saucer myself on a new circular-wing design based on Bernoulli's principle. . . . My single-minded concentration on success at Pepsi somehow caused me to discard my early interest in inventions and technology.[1]

We learn ... that there's a utility in death because ... the world goes on changing and we can't keep up with it. If I have any disciples, you can say this of every one of them, they think for themselves.
WARREN S. MCCULLOCK

When Sculley resigned at Pepsi to go to Apple, Pepsi officials were unbelieving. How could he give up an assured future—one that virtually guaranteed him the top post in a powerful company admired worldwide—for such an iffy situation in the (at that time) still unproved world of personal computers?

The answer may not even yet be fully understood by many of Sculley's former colleagues and mentors. But really, it is a simple thing. Suddenly, after years of growing more and more beached, Sculley was back in the swim. Suddenly, after years of moving more and more off course, John Sculley was back *on purpose*.

He knew it—beyond any doubt—because he felt it.

A fundamental difference between dolphins and their fellow sojourners in "the pool" is that dolphins understand the importance of knowing what their purpose in life *is* and whether at any given time they are *on* purpose, and carps and sharks often do not.

We can define "purpose" in several ways. For one, when we know our purpose, we have an anchor—a device of the mind to provide some stability, to keep the surprises of a creative universe from tossing us to and fro, from inflicting constant seasickness on us. Or we can think of our purpose as being a master nautical chart marking shoals and rocks, sandbars and derelicts, something to guide us and keep us on course. Perhaps the most profound thing we can say about being "on purpose" is that when that is our status, our condition, and our comfort, we find that our lives have *meaning*, and when we are "off purpose," we are confused about meanings and motives.

When we are "on purpose," we find that our lives have meaning.

Dolphins aren't always on purpose; life is too complicated for that. But—and this is a critical point—when they are off purpose they realize it almost immediately. A search for what has been lost or muddled is launched forthrightly, with intensity and dedication.

"Off-purpose" individuals and organizations find themselves in the same kind of situation that former University of Texas football coach Darrell Royal described when discussing the dangers of throwing a pass. "Three things can happen—two of them bad," said Royal. When you are "off purpose," the only good thing that can happen is that you luck out. You do the right thing even though you don't know why you did it or how. The outcome simply clicks, and you

> *"Off purpose," we can stumble from one mistake in life choices to another.*

find yourself feeling more together, more focused. Typically, however, it does not work that way. Typically, being "off purpose," we stumble blindly from one mistake in life choices to another, suffering from "the fate that aches." For example, we may take jobs—again and again—because of inwardly inadequate and unsatisfying reasons: It pays a better salary, it offers a chance to move up, there's a lot of prestige involved, or "it's just the thing to do." But once there, because we are off purpose, we once again find ourselves miserable, victims of "the fate that aches," once more having set ourselves up for failure.

In such circumstances, we have four choices:

- We can get out.
- We can change the organization or the environment.
- We can change ourselves.
- We can suffer.

Dolphins can be expected to act on the first three choices. Typically, carps, pseudo-enlightened carps, and sharks either elect to suffer or else blunder into suffering, silently or not so silently, passively or not so passively, sometimes making themselves the target of recriminations, sometimes not, sometimes taking out their revenge by sabotaging or attacking others, sometimes not. However the role is handled, the end product for any organization is diversion from its targeted goals: Hour by hour, day by day, the organization is inexorably pulled off course.

> *The key is knowing what your purpose is and honoring your deepest values.*

We have art in order not to die of the truth.
NIETZSCHE

The key to avoiding "the fate that aches" is knowing what your personal purpose is and using this knowledge to make choices that are aligned with your deepest values. When you enjoy this kind of synchrony, you are assured of the ability to function with a sense of integrity.

*O*nce we are "on purpose," what remains in our quest to act with integrity is getting in touch and in sync with our deepest values, the values of our very inner world where the issues of purpose and other weighty matters are hammered out—the world of beliefs, of standards against which and by which the whole of the external world of our lives is judged.

Dolphins understand that teams, groups, families, and individuals can share a similar purpose when they are "on porpoise" and yet be applying exceedingly different standards or values. Thus one of the critical skills of the dolphin is appreciating and being able to respond supportively to the values of others as they seek to "actualize" their purpose in life or in the organization. When dolphins put on the spectacles of values and beliefs and examine "the pool," this is what they see:

*L*ate in the twentieth century, a new field called the cognitive sciences confirmed something dolphins had already intuited: The brain is a house of mirrors—and a gifted one, at that.

This organ that we think, emote, and "engineer" with has an extraordinary ability to construct an "inner" world of its own with deep selectivity. Working with hidden logic and a filtering system that puts the best "clean room" technology of the computer industry to shame, the brain selects with an iron-willed autocracy what it chooses to know and how it chooses to know it.

In this house of mirrors, ill-fitting information from the outside can be handled in one of several ways. If the brain's defenses are prepared, "alien" information may not register at all. If it does, this information may be distorted in carnival fun-house fashion until it manages to pass muster. Or if it arrives in such quantity and with such vigor that it can't be ignored or distorted, information that threatens the brain's carefully tailored assumptions about "the *real* world out there" may trigger neural alarms, leading to denial, anger, bargaining, and grief strategies. If such circumstances

Each time we changed our environment, our environment changed our behavior, and our new behavior demanded a new environment.
LAURENCE J. PETER

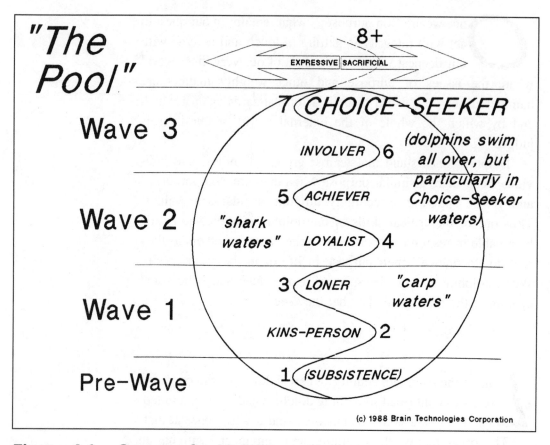

"The Pool"

Wave 3

Wave 2

Wave 1

Pre-Wave

8+

EXPRESSIVE | SACRIFICIAL

7 CHOICE-SEEKER

INVOLVER 6

(dolphins swim all over, but particularly in Choice-Seeker waters)

5 ACHIEVER

"shark waters"

LOYALIST 4

3 LONER

"carp waters"

KINS-PERSON 2

1 (SUBSISTENCE)

(c) 1988 Brain Technologies Corporation

Figure 4.1. Systems for Valuing

The brain's "house of mirrors" is its worldview.

The tools of the mind become burdens when the environment which made them necessary no longer exists. HENRI BERGSON

happen frequently, an individual is clearly "off purpose" and suffering inner, and probably creating outer, confusion.

We call the brain's "house of mirrors" its worldview. For all their potential eccentricities and individualities, worldviews do not exist independent of "outside" existence. Just as the brain shapes the world, the world shapes the brain. Just as the brain shapes information, information shapes the brain. As the brain is shaped, so goes its worldview or its house of mirrors. Recalling Chapter 2, we are aware that the world has thus far experienced three great "waves" of change. Each of these great waves shaped, and was shaped by, the brain. A brain, as you've no doubt heard by now, has two hemispheres that produce very different drumbeats. One hemisphere provides the primary drumbeat of the carp; the other, the primary drumbeat of the shark.

Dolphins understand that two great forces—the distinctive hemispheric processing "personalities" of the brain and the three great waves of change in human history—have combined influences over the past forty thousand years to create six major patterns for being "on purpose." These six "houses of mirrors" are captured in the view of "the pool" portrayed in Figure 4.1. (Worldview 1—*Homo sapiens existens*—is pictured but seldom encountered in the adult world except in the mentally ill or in the senile and will not be treated extensively in our discussions.)

Carps typically swim in waters of "the pool" on the right—the right-hemisphere–dominated side of what's possible, and sharks in waters on the left—the left-hemisphere–dominated side. Because they swim predominantly on the right, carps are vulnerable to the right hemisphere's tendency naively to assume too much and ask too little. The "carp" hemisphere is perfectly happy to substitute figure for ground or ground for figure—to make decisions based on snapshots or cartoons when, in reality, more serious analysis and reflection of a more extensive nature are justified. Across the canyon—the corpus callosum that conjoins the two hemispheres with its two hundred million nerves—the left hemisphere also has its operating limitations. This hemisphere can be said to store hundreds of variations of itself on the shelf, each variation fine-tuned for specific kinds of circumstances and each waiting to be inserted in mental reality like an audiocassette tape. Like a disk jockey with too many requests and too many musical selections to choose

One hemisphere may substitute cartoons for solutions; the other can create a logjam of solutions that may or may not fit.

Wheeler's universe is a self-excited system, brought into being by self-reference and contingent upon a physics that is just right for the eventual emergence of life and human consciousness. Past, present, and future are "wired together" in this universe in such a way that its birth is held up "until the blind accidents of evolution are guaranteed to produce, for some nonzero stretch of time in its history-to-be, the consciousness, and the consciousness of consciousness, and communicating community, that will give *meaning* to that Universe from start to finish. ERICH HARTH IN *WINDOWS OF THE MIND*, DISCUSSING JOHN ARCHIBALD WHEELER'S VIEWS from, the "shark" hemisphere can easily miss the real mood and meaning of events because it is so busy shuffling tapes or running inappropriate ones or, from its more cynical perspective, miss an important nuance.

*T*he brain of a dolphin obviously also contains the carp and the shark hemispheres, but the command system appears to be much different. Rather than assign control predominantly to one or the other of the hemispheres, dolphins have shifted the "action center" forward to the integrative frontal lobes, or so researchers like Walle Nauta of the Massachusetts Institute of Technology and George Edgin Pugh have suggested.[2] In major part, dolphins are dolphins because they can swim anywhere in "the pool," depending on their wishes and their needs.

In dealing with others, dolphins instinctively take note of another person's inner world—that critical, sense-making "house of mirrors" that governs what is real and important for each of us. Dolphins realize that moving toward the realization of purpose may cause individuals to shift from one system of valuing to another. By careful listening and careful observation, dolphins zero in on the realities they must work with and penetrate to establish a productive, humane relationship and to deal with integrity with the major worldviews to date of the species, which are about to be described.

Worldview 2: The Kins-Person (*Homo sapiens gregarius*)

Chief ideal in life: To live *sacrificially*—for the good of their family, tribe, clan, or group.

Needed to support their values: Security, close supervision, the opportunity to work close by and stay close to family and friends.

The questions always foremost in their minds: Will I be cared for? Can I be with others like myself?

Worldview 3: The Loner (*Homo sapiens audax*)

Chief ideal in life: To live *expressively*—getting one's own needs met and to hell with everyone else's.

Needed to support their values: Opportunities to demonstrate power, daring, and prowess; to stay busy and get lots of hands-on experience; to enjoy immediate personal gratification.

The questions always foremost in their minds: Is this a chance for me to gain power, influence, or dominance over others? Is this a chance to bolster my own defenses or to demonstrate power? Will this satisfy my immediate desires?

Worldview 4: The Loyalist (*Homo sapiens stabilis*)

Chief ideal in life: To live *sacrificially* now for rewards that will come later.

Needed to support their values: Opportunity to serve and prove worthy; clearly defined rules and expectations; a stable, predictable, low-risk environment; confirmation of existing beliefs.

The questions always foremost in their minds: Is this an opportunity to prove myself worthy? Is this a chance to serve? Can I find out more about the rules and what is right?

Worldview 5: The Achiever (*Homo sapiens perfectus*)

Chief ideal in life: To live *expressively* with calculation so as not to arouse the ire of others.

Needed to support their values: High potential for return on their investment; a chance to control and influence; an opportunity for personal advancement, recognition, status, and prestige; fast pace and high growth.

The questions always foremost in their minds: Can I get a high return on my investment? Is this a chance for me to acquire possession, status, or control? Is this an opportunity for me to get ahead? Is this a way to enjoy or display the fruits of my success?

Worldview 6: The Involver (*Homo sapiens aquarius*)

Chief ideal in life: To live *sacrificially*—giving up something later to have something now, for oneself and for others.

Needed to support their values: Situations that are participative, democratic, and team-oriented; situations that are casual, personal, naturalistic, friendly, and fun; opportunities for inner growth and for involvement in worthy causes related to human and other "life"-related rights.

The questions always foremost in their minds: Is this an opportunity for me to be accepted and to participate? Is this an opportunity to "expand consciousness"? Is this going to be fun? Will I experience "inner growth"? Is this a chance to be intimate and share feelings with others?

Worldview 7: The Choice-Seeker (*Homo sapiens delphinus*)

Chief ideal in life: To live *expressively* and *experientially*, taking an altruistic, functional view toward all issues, large or small.

Needed to support their values: High levels of freedom and personal choice; opportunities to associate with highly competent individuals in their areas of interest; chances to enhance the probability of survival and quality of all life on the globe.

The questions always foremost in their minds: Is this interesting and stimulating for me? Does this make sense? Is this a chance for privacy and a time to explore and think? Is this an opportunity to associate with highly competent people?

Failing to appreciate what a brain will do to itself and to others when it "gets beached"—when it finds itself "off purpose" or out of sync with its values—carps, pseudo-enlightened carps, and sharks repeatedly find themselves in awkward, painful, damaging, self-inflicted, and self-defeating circumstances.

It happens again and again—in politics, in commerce, in families. A president of the United States, when viewing the world through the filters of an Involver/Achiever worldview, badly misjudges a powerful foreign leader acting with Loyalist/Kins-Person values and pays in the next election with one of the most resounding defeats in American political history. A candidate for the presidency assumes he can live his personal as well as his professional life out of his Achiever worldview and finds himself hounded out of the race—at least temporarily—by reporters acting on their Loyalist/Loner values. Achiever-oriented U.S. auto executives refuse to acknowledge that millions of once Loyalist-oriented car buyers have either shifted to an Achiever worldview themselves or raised Achiever-, Involver-, or Choice-Seeker-oriented children, who now want competitively priced, quality-constructed, technologically advanced products. And year after year, model after model, technological advance after technological advance, the Japanese eat Detroit's cake, profits, and opportunities. An Achiever father fails to understand his teenage children's Loyalist values and drives a deep, lingering wedge between parent and child with his incessant lectures on the importance of being the best and besting everyone else.

Being "off purpose" or out of sync with one's values is

Consider a man felling a tree with an axe. Each stroke of the axe is modified or corrected, according to the shape of cut face of the tree left by the previous stroke. This self-corrective (i.e., mental) process is brought about by a total system, tree—eye — brain — muscles — axe — stroke — tree that has the characteristics of immanent mind.

GREGORY BATESON, *STEPS TO AN ECOLOGY OF MIND*

A father fails to recognize that his children have different worldviews.

debilitating to organizations and individuals. A single "off-purpose" employee can destroy or damage the chances for success of an organization, a circumstance sometimes referred to as the "trimtab factor":

> On airplane wings, and on the keels of racing yachts, trimtabs are small adjustable flaps that assist in balancing and steadying the motion of the craft. The principle of the trimtab also applies to a ship's rudder. In explaining the trimtab factor, [the late] Buckminster Fuller [architect, inventor, philosopher] used the image of a large oceangoing ship traveling at high speed through the water. The mass and momentum of such a vessel are enormous, and great force is required to turn its rudder and change the ship's direction. In the past, some large ships had, at the trailing edge of the main rudder, another tiny rudder—the trimtab. By exerting a small amount of pressure, one person could easily turn the ship. Thus, the trimtab factor demonstrates how the precise application of a small amount of leverage can produce a powerful effect.[3]

One person, one trimtab. A powerful effect—for good *or* ill.

Each act makes us manifest. It is what we do, rather than what we feel, or say we do that reflects who and what we truly are. Each of our acts makes a statement as to our purpose. Whatever immortality there is, is assured by a continual participation in the productive process. Because of us, things have become more. Something has been left of significance because we existed.   LEO BUSCAGLIA

*D*olphins realize that values come in patterns. That shouldn't surprise us overly much, since the deeper we probe into any kind of behavior, whether nature's behavior in creating a landscape or a lung, or society's behavior in creating a marketplace or a traffic jam, the more we find that seemingly chaotic happenings are governed by laws—the laws of chaos.

Weather is one of the chief contributors to chaos theory. In the 1960s meteorologist Edward Lorenz of the Massachusetts Institute of Technology instructed his computer to calculate what would happen to the weather if wind patterns changed just slightly.

Leaving his laboratory to get a cup of coffee, he left his underpowered computer to "crunch" the numbers. Later, reading his printouts, he observed what has been called the Butterfly Effect. A minuscule change in weather conditions in one locality has the potential to be magnified into massive changes elsewhere. For example, a monarch flapping

A Mongolian blizzard originating with a California butterfly?

its wings in California might eventually produce a blizzard in Mongolia. Suddenly, meteorology and other sciences had new reason to search for "the trimtab" factor in previously unexplored aspects of nature.

Benoit Mandelbrot of IBM Corporation also qualified for the elite new ranks of "chaologists"—scientists looking for patterns in chaos—in the 1960s with his discovery of a new geometry: fractals. Curiously, he was studying the behavior of cotton prices over sixty years. Looking at his price curves, he realized that those showing daily price changes had much the same shape as those of monthly price changes. It mattered not whether the causes of price fluctuation were war, depression, or weather: the fractal pattern— the recurring degree of *irregularity*—was the same for all time spans. Mandelbrot had put us on the trail of nature's convoluted love of what often has been called "the Russian doll effect"— scaling. The production of similar shapes on large scales or the very small.

"All pulchritude is relative.... We ought not ... to believe that the banks of the ocean are really deformed, because they have not the form of a regular bulwark; nor that the mountains are out of shape, because they are not exact pyramids or cones; nor that the stars are unskillfully placed, because they are not all situated at uniform distance. These are not natural irregularities, but with respect to our fancies only; nor are they incommodious to the true uses of life and the designs of man's being on earth. RICHARD BENTLEY

*U*sing the dolphin's view of "the pool" captured in Figure 4.1, we emerge with a charting of worldviews, or patterns of values, that appears to show repetitive scaling, fractal-like designs.

Perhaps it is helpful to think of human systems of values as resembling the Western musical scale, the octave. The late Clare W. Graves, the "Benoit Mandelbrot" of the geometry of human values, outlined a six-note scale of sense-making just as the

In maturity, then, one undertakes commitments to something larger than the service of one's convulsive little ego! . . . religious commitments, commitments to loved ones, to the social enterprise, and to the moral order. In a free society we shall never specify too closely what those commitments should be. JOHN GARDNER

musical octave is an eight-note scale (actually a seven-note scale, since the first note—C—reappears as the eighth note). It is substantially his "model of sixes" you see in Figure 4.1. After thirty years of charting values and after creating his "biopsycho-social" model of worldviews, Dr. Graves suggested a scaling pattern that begins to repeat itself, though in altered form, in every sixth leap; in other words, in designs of six. Viewed in this way, the brain's creation of the Choice-Seeker's worldview—System 7—can be said to be "one great leap for humankind," since it represents a bold new movement into the unknown of human values and sense-making at a higher "scale": Scale No. 2 in our corner of the universe. The Choice-Seeker worldview is the most intrepid of new frontiers in a sense that no previous worldview can claim—the sense of heightened self-awareness without strong components of compulsiveness. If Graves's skills as a "chaolo-gist" prove out over much greater spans of time, the leap this time is momentous in its promise. It represents, for the most part, the essence of the worldview being presented in this book: the soaring, silvery leap of the dolphin.

Mathematicians . . . are well aware that it is childish to try to show by drawing curves that every continuous function has a derivative. Though differentiable functions are the simplest and easiest to deal with, they are exceptional. Using geometrical language, curves that have no tangents are the rule, and regular curves, such as the circle, are interesting but quite special. NOBEL PRIZE WINNER IN PHYSICS JEAN PERRIN

*A*t Brain Technologies Corporation, we have noticed another significant pattern within the Gravesian "scale of six": There appears to be a significant scaling factor of fours. For example, as System 6, the Involver, truly took flower in numerous minds in the past twenty-five years, it has borne an uncanny resemblance to System 2, the Kins-Person. Suddenly the brain returned to the great hunger of tribal people to be in touch and in sync with primal forces—with the archetypes of an inner dominion. A modern search was launched for meanings in ancient teachings. In the Western world, one of the most visible spokes-persons for this application of the Involver worldview has been Dr. Jean Houston, a former president of the Association of Humanistic Psychology. In her work *The Search for the Beloved: Journeys in Sacred Psychology*, Houston writes:

Although we are citizens of at least two worlds, we have forgotten the uses and the ecology of the inner world. As we are about to become citizens in a universe richer by far than any we have ever known, we deeply need our archetype, our Beloved [or Spirit, as it is viewed in System 2] in the depth world, to partner us in this larger citizenship. Our Beloved and godded guide knows the patterns, forms, and places where the vast latencies and psycho-spiritual knowings are coded. In this way love grows reality.[4]

This manifestation of System 6 is an eerie revisitation of System 2's tilt toward the animistic "spirit world," a world of magical incantations and healing. That's the key to understanding what System 6 is all about—about healing, about getting well. Brains that "perturbate" and reestablish their "house of mirrors" to reflect System 6 are in substantial pain psychologically. Dr. Houston's cry is a cry for healing—"great goddess of the inner world, *heal me!*" The danger is obvious and ubiquitous: Once ensconced in this "garden of 'psychic' healing," few people want to leave. Our personal and organizational

The danger of System 6 is that we can easily get trapped in the healing process.

problems today can be immensely difficult, and it is less threatening to stay forever in a state of "being healed" than to get well and take responsibility for finding effective real-world, workaday answers. It is a price no organization intent on staying in business can afford.

Dolphins aren't averse to healing and, having access to System 6 themselves, will retreat to its welcome balm when needed. But dolphins also understand acutely the Achilles' heel of System 6: Though they can speak the lingo of Breakthrough thinking, individuals operating primarily from this worldview cannot consistently forge elegant solutions and do more with less. Why not? Involvers have the greatest of difficulty breaking free and soaring individually. They are poised on the last, great outpost of the first scale of human consciousness, and it is a psychic challenge of

This is the true joy in life, the being used for a purpose recognized by yourself as a mighty one; the being thoroughly worn out before you are thrown on the scrap heap; the being a force of Nature instead of a feverish selfish little clod of ailments and grievances complaining that the world will not devote itself to making you happy. GEORGE BERNARD SHAW great magnitude—an almost impossible feat—for an individual anchored in this house of mirrors to let go, to stand on his own, to get the job done as a "complement of one" *if the group gets clogged and cloying in its perennial attachment to the healing process.*

I f the "rule of fours" and the larger symphonic "rule of sixes" hold, how intriguing are the possibilities! Combining our knowledge of how the human brain crystallizes systems of values— worldviews—with our growing knowledge of repetitive scaling patterns, we find ourselves equipped for the first time to attempt rationally what to now only the "high priests" of metaphysics have been emboldened to try: predict in some rudimentary way the future course of human development. Given

Using the "rule of fours" and the "rule of sixes," we see that a double scaling effect kicks in for the first time at System 5.

the chaotic complications made possible by the fractal nature of human behavior and belief structures, it remains folly to think that we can fill in with very much accuracy the blanks of human destiny some distance out. But that's not the point nor the intent. Here *is* the point: By "marrying" the breakthrough discoveries of "developmental structuralists"—in particular, Clare Graves and his colleagues Don Beck and Christopher Cowan, but also such pathfinders as Jean Piaget, Jane Loevinger, Abraham Maslow, Lawrence Kohlberg, and Elliott Jaques—with the startling insights of the chaologists, we suddenly are encouraged to think about where these blanks *might appear.*

Let's try it, using Figure 4.2.

Systems 1 through 7 are the "worldviews" that have repeatedly been identified often with only minor variations by the work of the developmental structuralists named previously, by the widely publicized Values and Lifestyles Study (VALS) of SRI

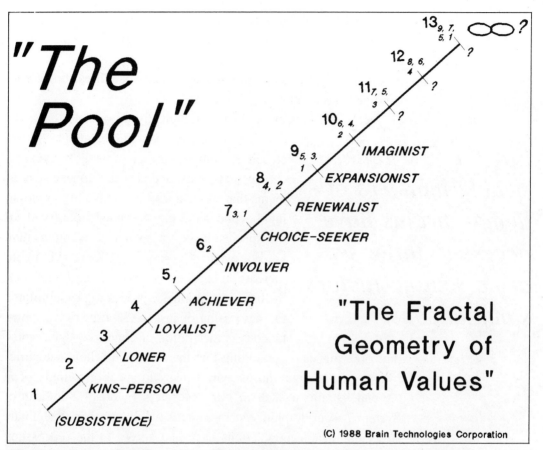

Figure 4.2. Scaling the Development of Human Values

International, and by the studies of more than sixty other social scientists whose work has been closely tracked by researchers at Brain Technologies.

Using our "rules of fours and sixes," we see that a new fractal effect—a scaling-within-a-scaling pattern—"kicks in" at System 5 with the emergence of the Achiever worldview. At that point, with the narrowly survivalist-focused System 1 now overlapping with the new System 5, the brain activates a "biopsychosocial" system of processing that is capable of "playing the game" calculatedly or, to use Dr. Graves's favorite word for it, "multiplisticly."

As noted a few pages back, System 6 strongly reflects much of the values content of System 2 transported to "wineskins" of a

Pathfinders with a purpose are not heroic statue material looking down their holy noses at the grubs who are all the rest of us. Many are people who say: "This neighborhood (or city, school, church, country) is going to the dogs. It's my responsibility to make it better." Most commonly such people find a purpose—or respond when it finds them—at the local level. . . . GAIL SHEEHY, *Pathfinders* higher order of complexity. Their influences combined, these two systems create in contradistinction the oceanic anticipation of major new human potentialities on the one hand and on the other an often fierce resistance to seeing these capabilities through to genuine efficacy and empowerment.

Yet it has happened. In technologically advanced areas particularly, brains today—in substantial and increasing numbers—are processing at levels of choice and in expanded space-time environments that signal a leap in complexity processing beyond anything previously observed in the species. It is not so much an intellectual kind of event; it is something more akin to an increase in capacity; a broadening of access to the brain's multiphasic processing capabilities, the harnessing of just the kind of rich, simultaneous orchestration of cognitive signal sorting, ordering, and combining that has led brain scholars such as Michael Gazzaniga and Marvin Minsky to speak glowingly of a "social" brain in each of our heads. As Figure 4.2 indicates, System 7—our dolphin system—marks the first time in the human story that sizable populations have had access to the processing harmonics of three separate *scaling factors,* or submodalities, simultaneously.

For the first time, sizable numbers of human brains have access to three separate scaling factors simultaneously.

At this point "the fractual geometry of human values" provides a nonpareil opportunity for the inquisitive mind, for the emerging cognitive dynamics of System 7 suggest that just below the horizon of our awareness, in the wings offstage, there exists a *meta*scaling system for shaping human values and worldviews. You have our somewhat intrepid modeling of this development in Figure 4.3.

Those who cannot remember the past are condemned to repeat it.   GEORGE SANTAYANA

Compared to what we ought to be, we are only half awake.   WILLIAM JAMES

Taking a cue both from astrophysicists and the chaologists themselves, we are calling these metascaling forces "great attractors." Acting like giant magnets, they seem to be reaching out to the human brain/mind to exert the most primal kind of tug on its self-defining and self-imaging estimations. For virtually the whole

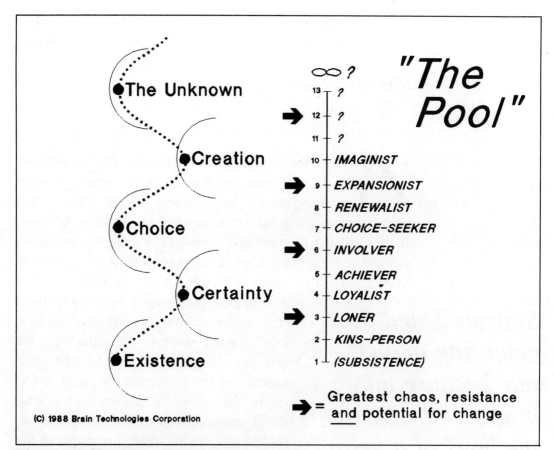

The Unknown

Creation

Choice

Certainty

Existence

∞ ?
13 — ?
12 — ?
11 — ?
10 — IMAGINIST
9 — EXPANSIONIST
8 — RENEWALIST
7 — CHOICE-SEEKER
6 — INVOLVER
5 — ACHIEVER
4 — LOYALIST
3 — LONER
2 — KINS-PERSON
1 — (SUBSISTENCE)

"The Pool"

➡ = Greatest chaos, resistance and potential for change

(C) 1988 Brain Technologies Corporation

Figure 4.3.   The Great Attractors

of its history as an "emergent vessel of morality-forming sentience," the human species has wrestled in one way or another with the tug of the virginal Existence Attractor—the activating icon of survival concerns and issues. Over time, this great attractor was enjoined and eventually surpassed by a second great attractor—the Certainty Attractor. The most immediate result was the synthesis of the Loyalist worldview, the fractal precursor of all great monotheistic world religions and of the Wave of Industry itself. Our much-discussed System 7, the dolphin system, marks the first time that the brain has fallen sway wholeheartedly to the influences of the third great attractor, the Choice Attractor. The enabling leap over the "lip" of the Certainty Attractor's bowl of influence has proved to

I would rather think of life as a good book. The further you get into it, the more it begins to come together and make sense.   RABBI HAROLD KUSHNER, *WHEN EVERYTHING YOU'VE EVER WANTED ISN'T ENOUGH* be an unusually significant one, and we have reason to expect it to provide primal influences in the development of two additional choice-generating new worldviews before the next great attractor redefines the focus of meaning for us.

*A*lready, the emerging Age of Productivity technologies and the incipient reaction of brains sensitive to its potential abuses are pointing us to this further migration—toward (what we are naming) the Creation Attractor. By extrapolating from our scaling model of values, we can suspect that one of the burning aims of brains processing comfortably in Systems 10 and 11—strong Creation Attractor worldviews—may be to migrate permanently from planet Earth into the information-teeming reaches of a meagerly explored universe. And after that? We offer this calculated guess: The fifth great attractor for the human and its environment will be the tug of the unknown on a scale wholly unprecedented in our experience. As with the Choice Attractor, this shaper of life forces will, if the current pattern holds, likely pull the brain toward new complexities of the individualistic kind, perhaps equipping our progeny generations removed to probe dimensions and worlds as shielded from us as the Southern Cross from the residents of Kamchatka.

Systems 3 and 6: confusing and chaotic because they are on the "lip" of the bowl of a great attractor.

Back in *this* world, Figure 4.3 suggests explanations for two readily observable and verifiable "behavioral" patterns in today's population. Of the major worldviews present in most workforces and most communities, none thrusts its users into a more dizzying and tortuous vortex of possibility than Systems 3 and 6—the Loner and the Involver. Chaologists have an explanation for this, and Figure 4.3 pictures it. Systems 3 and 6—and 9 and 12 to come—are confusion-prone "exit systems" from the orbit, or "bowl," or a great attractor. The scientists of chaos tell us that the "lip" of the bowl of influence dominated by a great attractor (represented in Figure 4.3 by the large dots in the center of the half-moon shapes) is the region of highest instability, since it is a region of competing forces. The Loner worldview marks the exit from the tug of the Existence Attractor. Because of the feral energy of this system, our American prisons are jammed with Loner-processing inmates, most of them too high-voltage to be amenable to any overtures of personal change and reform. And as we discussed in detail in Chapter 1, System 6 currently holds much of a generation—the *Big Chill* generation—in its often angry, exercised maw, representing as it does the last outpost of the Certainty Attractor.

This happens in the midst of affluent societies and in the midst of welfare states! For too long we have been dreaming a dream from which we are now waking up; the dream that if we just improve the socioeconomic situation of people, everything will be okay, people will become happy. The truth is that as the struggle for survival has subsided, the question has emerged: Survival for what? Ever more people today have the means to live, but no meaning to live for. VIKTOR FRANKL

In addition to those questions addressed thus far, the model illustrated in Figures 4.2 and 4.3 permits us to speculate to an unaccustomed degree about the emergence and nature of new worldviews—or systems of values—in the near term, such as, for example, the nature of System 8.

System 8 will reflect new values choices plus variations on the familiar contents of Systems 2 and 4.

Figure 4.2 suggests that System 8 will be the second emergent worldview to be shaped by a "triple fractal" effect. There will be new components—and some extraordinary new competencies. But the broth that the brain hath stirred will once again contain some familiar bones and condiments. In addition to the new components called 8, some familiar "harmonics" will be in play—from the Certainty Attractor's Loyalist system and the Existence Attractor's Kins-Person system. Loyalists rally around "the rules" and show almost unshakable allegiance to a sense that "this is the way the world *ought* to be." Loyalists are self-effacing, shunning the spotlight, the glory, and the publicity individually. Loyalists *and* Kins-Persons sacrifice to a higher power, a greater good, and feel noble and rewarded for their fealty. How might these qualities shine forth from a brain that has reorganized itself to handle markedly greater complexity? Ours is only an educated guess, since we have not personally encountered even a single person whose demeanor, insights, or self-explanations suggest to us a well-formed representation of the next quantum breakthrough in human worldview making. But speculatively, we can see our successors in the business of tracking worldviews writing something like this:

Worldview 8: The Renewalist (*Homo sapiens restitutus*)

Chief ideal in life: To live *cognitively* and *psychically* in a manner that makes one aware instantaneously of any harm that may come to the cosmos from human actions and equips one, first, to respond quickly and powerfully to neutralize that harm by any means necessary and, second, to renew the planet through proactive stewardship.

Needed to support their values: A deep anonymity that shields them from the glare of individual exposure; a recognition and acknowledgment of evil; access to a community of "like minds" that coalesces and dissolves quickly, effortlessly, and powerfully as it acts on specific issues of overriding interest from a global or cosmic perspective; use of a full array of up-to-the-minute monitoring and information processing and analysis methods for tracking the general health of Mother Earth and her denizens; means and methods that are effective in (1) withholding power and influence from individuals and groups judged to pose a threat to the cosmos and (2) retaliating elegantly when necessary; and resources to reestablish the livability of the planet.

The questions always foremost in their minds: Is this safe for the cosmos, and does it support its ultimate purpose? Is it my responsibility to play a role in neutralizing an element or activity before its damage to the life fabric grows too heinous? Do I have sufficient "blessing" of my colleagues and the cosmos itself? Have I thought through my strategy and tactics to the point where the desired outcome has the highest degree of probability possible?

If you are beginning to share the suspicion that System 8 has the ominous ring of totalitarianism, you are sharing a concern held by Dr. Graves—and one of our own concerns. What System 8's emergence will mean for the individual liberties those of us in the West celebrate as central to our way of life is a real concern. It is one more reminder that every perturbation of the brain brings the potential for peril as well as progress. It is, however, something we'd best get used to; as we have indicated with our ''infinity'' symbol in Figures 4.2 and 4.3, the brain seems to have a near-infinite capacity for reweaving and reformulating itself to adjust its sense of being ''on purpose'' to assure that the life-support systems and resources it needs to survive and thrive are at hand. We will take a stab at describing the values content of System 9, the exit system for the Choice Attractor as well as the final shaper and ''shapee'' of the Age of Productivity, by calling it the Expansionist (*Homo sapiens extensus*) System. As each system does in turn, System 9 can be expected to rebel somewhat against the previous system, 8, which we anticipate will rapidly exhaust itself with its mission to restore order and hospitality to a planet suffering from the Achiever System's roughshod abuse of its resources, the Involver System's ineptness at acting functionally and systemically, and the Choice-Seeker's reluctance to hang around long enough to challenge dysfunctional systems.

System 10? It can be expected to take shape within the powerful orbit of a new great attractor—the Creation Attractor. And it will have at its command the powerful technologies of a new era—the Age of Imagination. Capable as we suspect they may be of extraordinary manipulations (for us) of time and space, denizens of that epoch will likely be justified in referring to themselves as Imaginists—and that's our naming choice. System 10: the Imaginist (*Homo sapiens imaginatus*) worldview.

And after that?

Dim regions await, filled no doubt with additional yet to be detected great attractors, waiting to ''scale'' the human brain at even greater symphonies of purpose-making.

Even if all these needs are satisfied, we may still often (if not always) expect that a new discontent and restlessness will soon develop unless the individual is doing what he is fitted for. A musician must make music, an artist must paint, a poet must write if he is to be ultimately at peace with himself. What a man can be, he must be. This need we call self-actualization. ABRAHAM MASLOW

If a germ cannot be presumed aware of the living state of the body it dwells in, how can man's somewhat similarly circumscribed view afford him much more comprehension of the total aliveness of his planet today.... The physical essence of Earth life may be termed a spherical biofilm rotating in gravitational, electromagnetic and nuclear fields—a sort of gyrating bubble of evolving potency, a cosmic node of ferment. GUY MURCHIE, *THE SEVEN MYSTERIES OF LIFE*

Obviously, being on purpose and being in sync with one's values as that purpose is pursued represents power, promise, and progress. Thus dolphins know that one of the most empowering actions they can contribute to is to help others get "on porpoise" and to themselves become aligned, if only temporarily, with the purposes of others.

Looking at "the pool" through the values prism, dolphins see a world of simultaneity and spontaneity that requires mental agility and responsiveness. In any organization of any size, all six fully functional worldviews are likely to be present, as we see in Figure 4.4. There is a need to shift from one wave or worldview to the next, perhaps in a matter of minutes or even seconds. There is a need to get the work done using any or all of these systems of

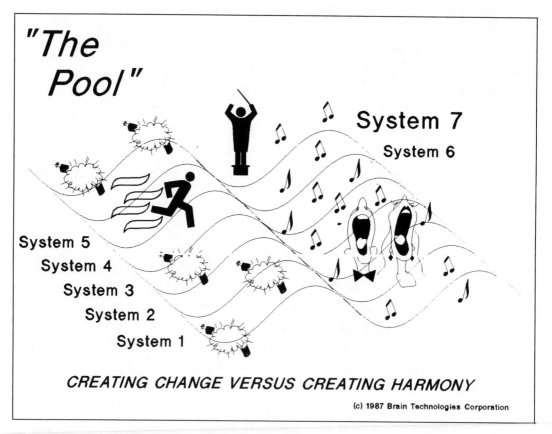

"The Pool"

System 7

System 6

System 5

System 4

System 3

System 2

System 1

CREATING CHANGE VERSUS CREATING HARMONY

(c) 1987 Brain Technologies Corporation

Figure 4.4. Change or Harmony?

worldviews, these multiple houses of mirrors. For the individual, there is the challenge of using the strength of each of the systems in context, as the opportunity arises.

With humanity spread out in such a wide psychological caravan, dolphins usually use their knowledge of purpose-making and values to achieve one of two ends:

To help people change. If it makes sense, dolphins aren't afraid to perturbate the system. Shake it up. Create stress. Inject puzzlement and mystery. Issue challenges and place people on their own resources. Every great reformer—whether a Martin Luther King, Jr., in race relations, an Alfred P. Sloan in management, a Susan B. Anthony in politics, an Albert Einstein in science—traffics in surprise and the unexpected. The same can be said of great teachers, great athletic coaches, great leaders in any sphere. Their actions and their expectations are not always predictable. They have the capacity to use approaches such as these to challenge people's sense of purpose or examine their personal values:

- *Disappear.* In war, the unexpected loss of a platoon leader in the heat of battle may ''perturbate'' the brain of a lowly grunt who steps into the leadership role and is changed forever. Dolphins don't wait for war. They watch for opportunities to disappear strategically—to play Get-out—as a way of encouraging people to ''pop'' into a different worldview or at least take steps in that direction.
- *Perturbate the troops.* When done well and timed well, laying down the law is a move that can help people ''pop.'' As one National Basketball Association coach observed, ''When you apply the quirt to a thoroughbred, he responds. When you apply it to a jackass, he balks.''
- *Lead from the balcony.* The right catalytic insight, placed in the right context, symbols, and perspective at the right time, can help people see the light and move in its direction. Such is the brilliance, for example, of Alcoholics Anonymous, a change-maker par excellence for effecting a single, if vital, move in sense-making. AA moves people, some people—those who are

suddenly afraid of dying and destroying everything valuable to them—from System 3 to System 4. How does AA do it? By promising them an Aston-Martin, Acapulco, and a little private action in the next big deal? No, that's System 5—too advanced a leap on the Scale of Human Sense-Making. By urging them to reestablish their roots with Mother Nature and reenter the spirit world of natural mystery and the cycles of the seasons? No, this isn't the kind of *sacrificial* sense-making that strengthens their resolve to quit drinking. Instead, in her visits to AA, the alcoholic hears, "Surrender to a higher power—that's your only hope." And that, of course, is the essence of System 4, the Loyalist. Surrender now to gain rewards later. This evolutionary, rifle-targeted insight may save the alcoholic Loner. Any greater movement on the Scale of Human Sense-Making would be too great. Dolphins, like AA, target their interventions with great care on the sense-making scale.

- *Toss something new in the salad.* Radishes, maybe. It's not only what you toss but when and how. A sudden threat to declare bankruptcy. A sudden change in the expectations and rewards. The unexpected merger of two warring departments. Abrupt surrender on a key point. An announcement that rocks people back on their feet. Doing the very thing that people never thought you would do. Asking for something people never thought you would ask for. Embracing something people never thought you would embrace. To be thorough about it, you are likely to perturbate the members of an organization any time that you change:
—its leadership
—its membership
—its task
—its organizational climate or structure
—its environment

These are dolphin techniques for shaking up the brain. They can help people "pop" from a sense of direction that is ill serving them to one better suited for their times and needs.

To create harmony or "functional resonance." A disconsonant orchestra is an orchestra whose instruments—and musicians—are working against each other. A maestro worth his pay brings depth and power to the sound by creating functional resonance to the pieces making the music. Dolphins often choose to view the brains making up an organization orchestrally. The goal is "functional resonance," the creation of richness as well as power for achieving a common purpose. Even though people are at different places on the Scale of Human Sense-Making, they can work in common rather than work in discord if they are in skilled hands. Here is how a dolphin seeks to create this harmony:

- *Put people in touch with their values:* Using learning tools like Brain Technologies Corporation's MindMaker6 instrument and other measuring systems for valuing, dolphins will act to help everyone in the organization understand more clearly their central underlying worldview. From that beachhead, dolphins will then guide people they lead or manage in exploring and expanding their insights into how this worldview supports a common purpose and shapes what they want of themselves and others.
- *Put people in touch with purpose:* If both the organization's purpose and the individual's are clear, the individual has the greatest opportunity to choose—that is:
  —to get out
  —to change "me"
  —to change the organization
- *Celebrate diversity.* Every worldview has its blindspots. A true team of people will help each other compensate. And every worldview has its unique contribution to make, acting out of a unique heritage of human endurance, exploration, and sense-making. Dolphins will hire smart and lead smart, acting on their knowledge of where people are coming from, purposewise and valueswise.
- *Be discriminating in issuing assignments, anticipating results, and creating payoffs.* If an individual is placed in a position that throws him off purpose, only harm and disappointing outcomes are to be anticipated. Knowing what is important to the other

person by knowing when she is "on purpose" helps the dolphin as maestro bring resonance—power, synchrony or harmony, depth, endurance—to the mutual outcome.

■ *Understand that being "on purpose" and in sync with your values is only half the formula for getting humans who live or work together to share a common aim effectively.* Being on purpose and having an appreciation for each other's values help people to like and appreciate each other. But by and of itself, common purpose-making and values appreciation are not enough to help them solve problems elegantly or to do more with less. If this were not so, then the thousands of organizations that have spent untold hours in teams and committees giving voice to their missions and principles and goals would have gotten great benefits merely from creating and publishing the results. Purpose has the most power when as many shareholders as possible have been involved in its creation. This allows for a greater alignment of intent among the organization's members. But merely framing a company's "Principles for Doing Business" and putting them up on the walls or typesetting them for insertion in pay envelopes or distributing them in plastic as billfold reminders seldom make much difference at all. Knowing what it takes to be on purpose is a critical piece of the puzzle. But even when you know your purpose—the "why" behind what you are doing—you still must know where you are starting from, how you got there, where you want to go, and how you intend to get *there*. If a team of people hasn't built itself a shared vision for achieving its purpose, it isn't likely to get anywhere very fast or very satisfactorily.

To bring home the importance of achieving purpose through a *shared* vision, we often have members of groups visualize the perfect home for themselves and (if they have one) their families. As they are visualizing, we assist them in "walking through" the visualization by pointing out the various rooms usually found in a house and the wide range of choices available for design, size, colors, shapes, fixtures, amenities, surroundings, and even geographical locations they might consider in the perfect home.

After the visualization part of the exercise is complete, we ask our group members to share and discuss their personal visions. You—and they—will find that people can quickly and clearly visualize their ideal. But when they share these ideals with each other, they will realize that one person's perfect home may have little resemblance to another's. *This is an important point.*

Many organizations will define their purpose (the counterpart to our "identify the ideal house" directive in this exercise) clearly, but without a shared vision people will go about realizing that purpose in a variety of ways, and may even cancel each other's efforts in the long run because of their individualized visions. When we "empower" people without first developing a *shared* vision, we are merely enhancing their ability to cancel each other out.

On the other hand, having a shared vision helps to focus and empower a group effort through alignment and direction.

Having made this point to the group, we give its members this assignment:

Remembering to take into account where you are now (your "rationale"), your values, and your stakeholders, imagine and design a "time-share" vacation home that you will build together. In this case, your purpose is to build the perfect home collectively. And your vision will be in hand once you complete the task you have just been assigned—to come up with a specific, detailed, ideal, future-perfectly stated articulation of a plan for a perfect home. You are to describe the floor plan and draw the home in as much detail as possible. If you think you are finished, check with everyone to see if your plan is compelling and inspires excitement and commitment. If it doesn't, go back and review the purpose, stakeholders, and values of the group to see how you missed creating a vision that works.

Dolphins appreciate that creating a common vision—the directions for getting there—is a task that points the brain in another direction all together. Recognizing what it is like to be on purpose depends for the most part on tapping the brain's ability to "sense" when, *in the past,* the future was most successful in tugging its user forward toward important purposes. Competent vision-building must depend on the brain's ability to lock in on what, *in the future,* is most likely to create success in the present. Here the key is, as we shall see in the next chapter, the extent to which the brain can see itself and its user operating in front of the times rather than moving through them.

5
"VISION BUILDING": STEERING THROUGH THE BRAIN'S "TIME WINDOW"

*I*n the sixteenth century, they were still issuing manuals to European armies and the princes who financed them that pictured cannonballs doing strange things. Strange, at least, by modern reckonings. On being propelled from the mouth of the cannon, the ball reputedly shot away from the earth at the angle of the cannon's tilt. When the energy from the gunpowder waned, the ball was said to plunge straight down, speeding up as it sought "the happiness of being close to the center of the earth." Scientists claimed this was so because Aristotle's laws said it was so. But artists knew better. Leonardo da Vinci, for one, sketched cannonballs curving in their trajectories. The soldiers knew better, too. They could see that their arrows followed a curved path, and they assumed cannonballs were no different. But not until 1551 did scientists themselves have a better idea. Tartaglia, a professor of mathematics at the University of Venice, blew the whistle on Aristotle with a drawing that showed a cannonball that followed a curved path, which only heavenly bodies were supposed to take.

To be shaken out of the ruts of ordinary perception, to be shown for a few timeless hours the outer and the inner world, not as they appear to an animal obsessed with words and notions, but as they are apprehended, directly and unconditionally, by Mind at Large—this is an experience of inestimable value to everyone.
ALDOUS HUXLEY, *THE DOORS OF PERCEPTION*

Soldiers knew that cannonballs curved in flight before scientists would admit it.

141

Three centuries later, science fiction writer Jules Verne still didn't have it right. In *From the Earth to the Moon*, Verne had his "rocketeers" take aim at the moon and fire away. If it ever occurred to Verne that by the time his moonship reached its target the target would have moved tens of thousands of miles away, he never mentioned it.

In 1969, when Neil Armstrong stepped out on the surface of the moon from his Apollo spacecraft, we had obviously learned a thing or two about taking aim. In point of fact, the Apollo craft had traveled the 240,000 "straight line" miles to the moon while being off course approximately 80 percent of the time. And yet it landed within a few feet of its planned target. This will come as no surprise to navigators of jet aircraft, oceangoing vessels, or sport parachutes. Maneuvering for any length of time in water or space requires constant correction. *Most* of the time, as was the case with the Apollo moonshot, you are actually off course. You get there by knowing where you were at your starting point, by knowing where you want to go, and by correcting when you get off course or off speed. What if you don't correct? In all likelihood, one of two possibilities, neither very desirable. You miss your target. Or you repeat the experience of the fellow who fell off the penthouse balcony of a tall skyscraper. Reportedly he was heard to say as he zoomed past the second floor, "I'm okay so far."

> *Most of the time the Apollo moonshot was off course, and so most of the time are we.*

Of all the obstacles to a thoroughly penetrating account of existence, none looms up more dismayingly than "time." Explain time? Not without explaining existence. Explain existence? Not without explaining time. To uncover the deep and hidden connection between time and existence, to close on itself our quartet of questions, is a task for the future. JOHN ARCHIBALD WHEELER

Constant course-correction is a function of vision-building, and this is where both carps and sharks are prone to trouble. A good vision—a concrete, specific, detailed articulation of your purpose—can result only when you can develop a reasonably clear understanding of *what you want*. And there lies the difficulty.

When at the beginning of the change process, you ask the carp or the shark to idealize, to "imagineer," to "blue-sky" what they would have if they could have it in any way they want it, what you typically get back is a list of negatives. Rather than with what they want, they tend to reply in surprising detail with what they want to avoid. Focusing on what you don't want does two things, neither of which is very helpful: (1) It tends to create precisely what you don't want to happen, and (2) it creates an effect similar to driving a car through a rearview mirror in that you know what you are moving away from, but you don't know where you are going. In either case, the long-term consequences are often disastrous. When we only know what we don't want, there also is an accompanying lack of grounding. The would-be vision-builders lack a genuine sense of where they are *now*—of truly what's going wrong, of what needs repair. Finally, the idea of monitoring and adjusting matters as you go, of course-correcting en route, is a process virtually alien to the carp and often poorly understood by the shark. The carp's hypnotic blinders and the shark's addictive compulsions make good vision-building a very problematic affair.

The farther we can "see," the more complexity we can handle.

Time is what we want most, but what alas! we use worst. WILLIAM PENN

Contemporary brain/mind researchers are steadily dispelling our ignorance of the important relationship between vision-building abilities and the ability to handle complex tasks. Evidence grows that the farther into the future a brain can see itself functioning, the more competent that brain is at handling complexity, juggling multiple responsibilities, and integrating tasks. Such ability does not in itself create dolphin thinking or behavior, but it is one of the key measures that contribute to the dolphin mind-set. A person's "time horizon"—the maximum temporal period in which a person can plan and execute specific, ongoing, goal-directed activities—is another of those important aspects a dolphin watches for, since it is a strong indication of a person's openness to information from the future. Looking at "the pool" with an individual's or team's vision-building skills in mind, this is what a dolphin sees:

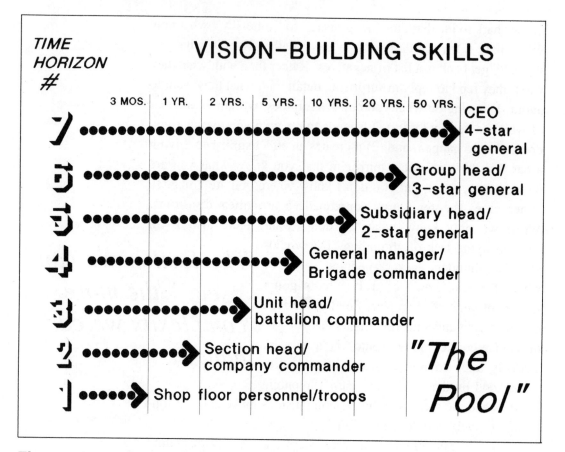

Figure 5.1. Elliott Jaques' "Time Strata"

ritain's Elliott Jaques is Father Time. More than any other researcher living or dead, this professor of sociology has forced us to acknowledge that one of the brain's most important windows is its window on time.

At first during his thirty-plus years of research into time and job competence, Jaques used conventional theories to explain his

Elliott Jaques' seven "time strata": windows on the future.

controversial conclusion: If you determine what a person thinks about time, you can determine the extent of a person's work capacity—what kind of job that person is suited for, the kind of decisions she is capable of making, and how much pay is required for her to be satisfied. Using data from studies in more than fifteen countries, Jaques eventually identified the seven "time strata" for organizing people that you see in Figure 5.1. By "time stratum" Jaques means the distance into the future that persons can see themselves committing to—the forward time span for which they are able to formulate goals and carry them to completion. Working from this basic insight, Jaques has assembled many fruitful, even ingenious findings, often laboriously explained in his numerous writings. From the perspective of vision-building, however, we are attracted most to one of his latest suggestions, one that catapults him squarely into the ranks of brain/mind researchers:

> As perceptions of weight and responsibility increase through movement to increasingly higher levels in executive systems [see Figure 5.1], why does time span increase as well? Moreover, why do a regular series of steps in organization level occur at particular time span levels? The only sensible hypothesis I can construct is that *the maximum time span a person can work with—that person's maximum achieved time span—measures and defines that person's level of cognitive power.* [Italics ours.] I call this measure a person's *time horizon.*[1]

In suggesting that the extent to which a person can cope with a sense of the future may be a dependable measure of how—and how well—that person's brain works, sociologist Jaques has expressed a viewpoint championed to now mostly by researchers tracking connections between brain tissues and time perspectives. These intrepid inquirers have contended all along that we humans have a specific biological component for processing and possessing the future: the prefrontal lobes, that change-sensitive area of the brain forward of the fissure of Rolando. (This is an aesthetically elegant idea, too. Why would the forward-looking part of the brain be at the rear or buried somewhere deep inside?)

One may say broadly that all the animals that have been carefully observed have behaved as to confirm the philosophy in which the observer believed before his observations began. Nay, more, they have all displayed the national characteristics of the observer. Animals studied by Americans rush about frantically with an incredible display of bustle and pep, and at last achieve the desired result by chance. Animals observed by Germans sit still and think, and at last evolve the solution out of their inner consciousness.
BERTRAND RUSSELL, *UNPOPULAR ESSAYS*

S oviet neurosurgeon A. R. Luria remains the best known of the forebrain researchers. Beginning with studies of brain-injured soldiers from World War I and later using data from forty-thousand prefrontal lobotomies—the indisputably dubious "castration" of the brain—Luria arrived at this conclusion: The frontal lobes are involved in a "program which ensures not only that the subject reacts to actual stimuli, but within certain limits foresees the future, foretells the probability that a particular event may happen, will be prepared if it does happen, and as a result, prepares a program of behavior."[2]

In some sense man is a microcosm of the universe; therefore what man is, is a clue to the universe. We are enfolded in the universe.
DAVID BOHM

Commenting on Luria's studies of lobotomy patients, futurist David Loye notes:

> [One] gets the sense of people who in some fundamental way are unable to move ahead, an impression that they have been made captives of the past. They are still able to think and act in certain ways (and this was why well-intentioned surgeons like [Washington, D.C., brain surgeon Walter] Freeman who performed lobotomies were deceived), but their thoughts and actions are confined to sequences that have already been learned. They must fall back upon the automatic thought-action sequences that sustain all of us most of the time, when we are not confronted with a problem requiring that old thought be reshuffled and reordered to produce something new to fit the future.[3]

Combining the insights of Jaques, Luria, and Loye, we begin to get a sense of why carps, pseudo-enlightened carps, and sharks suffer from a diminished sense of what the future can bring:

- **Carps tend to operate** from a very limited "time horizon" dominated by the "carp" hemisphere's tendency to experience time as circular. The deep shadows of the past fall heavily over any carp prospect for the future, limiting the scope and the range of new ideas and the interplay of imagination with possibility. Automatically, the future is retrofit with patterns already in existence, and thus as the future creates the present, the present is freed to re-create the past, and once again the carp's circular view of time is preserved.

- **Sharks fare somewhat better** but not all that much in that the "shark" hemisphere processes time linearly, and anything that operates linearly can be aimed with some precision. You can aim time into the future with the "shark" hemisphere. The limitation, of course, is that though you can aim at the future as a shark, you can't follow time's progress very far. Thus you spend most of your efforts processing the immediate realities. This may render you very effective and influential at the moment, but it leaves you vulnerable in terms of anticipating the location and nature of a moving, changing target. And in rapid-change times, most targets are moving and many are changing, some of them with incredible swiftness.

- **Pseudo-enlightened carps find themselves** in a very odd predicament. In some crucial respects, these individuals are overwhelmed by time. With their brains poised at the brink of a great shift in awareness—one that many PECs will approach but few will actually experience—pseudo-enlightened carps fall victim to an oceanic sense that *everything* is possible *in time now*. Lacking ability to discriminate well among past, present, and future, the pseudo-enlightened carp finds it difficult to develop moorings. Floating free in time isn't the safest of existences. The suicide rate—whether from mountain climbing or drug overdose or ambush in Nicaragua—is substantial for pseudo-enlightened carps, trapped by the "carp" hemisphere's cartoon-creating qualities at their purest and thus doomed to see reality forever taking the shape of the "carp" hemisphere's latest quickie sketch.

The more that researchers of many stripes—from mathematicians to physicists to sociologists to psychologists studying everything from cognition to moral development—probe into mind as a "box of time," the more a consensus is emerging. First, researchers are confirming that humans are time-binding creatures. Each

We live out our lives within the limits we place on time.

individual places limits on what he will allow himself to do with time, and within these limits he lives out his life. Ignorance of this fundamental reality creates much of any organization's, the leader's, and the manager's work-related angst. Instead of matching the "time tissue" of the brain with the nature of work assignments, today's organizational culture and management for the most part continue to treat the brain like a coal furnace. Management just opens the door, shovels in assignments nilly-willy without regard for the recipient's "time horizon," and then wonders why the furnace's combustion levels often don't meet expectations.

D olphins are themselves the best examples so far of what happens when the brain's time envelope is stretched farther and wider. Envision, if you will, an unknown substance—let's call it Factor X—suspended in the air, held by a pliable plastic bag. This bag is confined by all sides and on top and bottom by steel forms that allow it to expand only so far. From time to time the forms are moved back so the bag can increase its volume. When this happens, the air inside expands and the unknown substance grows a bit closer to materializing, to activating its fuller powers, to being recognized for what it is.

The brilliance of Elliott Jaques' work is that he has laboriously traced the emergence of this "substance" in the coping behavior of people. For more than three decades he has prowled the halls of the numerous organizations like an educated Pink Panther, watching for and measuring the emergence of Factor X. Though simplified for quick understanding, here is the gist of what he has learned:

- **When a person's "time horizon" is three months or less, none of Factor X is detectable.** Therefore, this brain/mind likes things very concrete, will work with only one dimension at a time, and will seldom question a task, merely taking matters as they stand. *Brains with this ''time horizon'' are rule-anchored.*

- **When a person's "time horizon" reaches out to one year, a tiny measure of Factor X is discernible.** Therefore, this brain/mind will accept some diversity but handles it by immediately dividing things that are different into piles, so to speak. But the possibility that what works with one pile might work with another isn't considered. If information is fluid and flowing, it creates problems and creates long pauses in this person's activity as he processes it. *Brains with this ''time horizon'' seek judgment and action within the rules.*

- **When a person's "time horizon" reaches out to two years, a touch of Factor X is in the air; but rather than benefit from it, this individual seeks to isolate it and avoid its consequences.** Therefore, this brain/mind starts with the rules and works out from there. A favorite phrase is ''Time will tell''— the thought being that things will work out regardless of one's personal involvement. The importance of things that don't fit simply isn't considered. *Brains with this ''time horizon'' extrapolate from a given rule.*

- **When a person's "time horizon" reaches out to five years, the presence of Factor X is palpable although not yet fully activated.** Therefore, this brain will deal with considerable untidiness but only because she assumes that in the chaos there are rules and underlying themes to be discovered. Once they are found, there is some anxiety over whether the rules will change. Searching for and finding the operative rules for any structure are very important. *Brains with this ''time horizon'' search for, then maintain, an underlying rule structure.*

- **When a person's "time horizon" reaches out to ten years or more, Factor X suddenly, commandingly materializes.** Therefore, this brain listens to the rules and then begins to think beyond them—to establish its own criteria. Rather than seek order, this brain may deliberately induce disorder in its search for new patterns. Alternatives are readily and easily generated, and for the first time, importance is given to what isn't known and what hasn't happened and what hasn't been said as potentially important sources of information. *Because brains with this "time horizon" make the rules, they also feel free to ignore them if they don't fit current circumstances.*

And what is the mysterious emergent Factor X whose absence can so tragically and painfully defeat the best efforts and intentions of carps, pseudo-enlightened carps, and sharks?

Drumroll, please! The answer is:

The willingness to tolerate ambiguity.

Suddenly, at or about the ten-year mark in a human being's ability to feel comfortable with the future, explicit knowing begins to link up with implicit knowing. Suddenly, at this important milestone in the development of forward-seeing, linear thinking and circular thinking conjoin. At this threshold in anticipatory abilities, the "carp" hemisphere and the "shark" hemisphere pool their mutual best interests and their uppermost skills and act together to fashion something radically powerful in human coping abilities. With the "time horizon" widened and expanded to this extent, qualities such as these are now increasingly autocatalytic (self-triggering):

At the ten-year mark, linear and circular thinking begin to link up.

- the viewing of uncertainty as a resource
- thinking outside the rules
- willingness to generate theories
- the use of contradictory information
- openness to all sources
- paying attention to what's left unsaid
- looking for more than one answer[4]

Explanations for what causes time to be so different from one person to another will be left by dolphins to future generations of researchers. Perhaps the most radical route to be explored is the idea that the brain itself conveys the world with a sense of past, present, and future—that time is an invention of mind. Or as physicist Louis de Broglie once expressed it:

> In space-time, everything which for each of us constitutes the past, the present, and the future is given in block, and the entire collection of events, successive for each of us which forms the existence of a material particle is represented by a line, the world line of the particle. . . . Each observer, as his time passes, discovers, so to speak, new slices of the material world, though in reality the ensemble of events constituting space-time exists prior to his knowledge of them.[5]

Already, a Nobel prize has been awarded for laboratory results that suggest information may travel backward as well as forward in time—at least at the subatomic level. For certain, thanks to pioneering work in the biofeedback lab as well as the more esoteric environs of the yogic mind, the meditative voyager, and the daydreamer, we understand more clearly than ever that the brain itself is capable of ticking to different clocks under different circumstances. The consequences of variegated time cannot be ignored, since the kind of time we keep and the size of the "time horizon" we enforce for ourselves are central to the kind of world we are capable of knowing. Ignorance of this state of affairs badly cripples the cognitive performance of carps and sharks, and rather than serve as a liberation, the dawning realization that this is true tends to overwhelm the pseudo-enlightened carp.

There is an underlying, hidden level of culture that is highly patterned—a set of unspoken, implicit rules of behavior and thought that controls everything we do. This hidden cultural grammar defines the way in which people view the world. . . . Most of us are either totally unaware or else only peripherally aware of this.

This was brought home to me recently while discussing Japanese [cultural differences] with a friend, a brilliant man with an usually fine mind. I realized that not only was I not getting through to him, but nothing of a substantive nature that I had said made sense to him. . . . For him to have understood me would have meant reorganizing his thinking . . . giving up his intellectual ballast, and few people are willing to risk such a radical move.   EDWARD T. HALL, *THE DANCE OF LIFE*

The brain is capable of ticking to different clocks under different circumstances.

It is a responsibility of the dolphin, then, to make time a serious component of building and running teams and organizations. Using the discoveries of Elliott Jaques depicted in

Figure 5.1 and other temporal insights into the brain's forecasting nature, dolphins move with deliberation to counteract timebound limitations in teams and organizations that can affect the quality and the positive outcomes of their vision-building. Here are some of the principle assumptions dolphins work with and some of the solutions they apply:

Most of the time, people are reluctant to build a genuine vision for themselves.

Think about what occurs on many occasions when a committee or team assembles.

Under one script, a game of Let's Play Nice gets under way. Behind a facade of what psychologist M. Scott Peck calls "false community," the group ignores its own slate of hidden agendas and concerns and acts for all the world like goody-two-shoes. In this low-energy environment, there are no fireworks or frank exchanges, just as there are no honest assessments and empowering views of what the group might accomplish. The other principal script is The Slugfest. Sharks may lunge for the jugular veins of the conveniently assembled carps or initiate cannibalistic activity amid their own ranks, and any hopes of engaging the frontal lobes' vision-making abilities in the brains present dissolve in acrimony and defensiveness.

Much of the time, people in meetings are attempting to avoid responsibility.

Whichever script is pursued, the behind-the-scenes dynamics are essentially the same: The participants are caught up in a mostly unconscious battle over who is going to take—and who is going to be able to avoid—responsibility. In one script, the participants simply disappear as responsible, thinking entities and refuse to confront any need to change, plan, or risk. In the other, the outcome is "Blame anybody and anything but me!"

Dolphins understand that the issue is whether the old brain or the new brain is calling the shots on the issue of personal responsibility. And the answer is that it is still the old brain components of the carp and shark hemispheres. Not until the frontal lobes of the brain are afforded room in an expanded "time horizon" do they enable the individual to understand that, in most circumstances in life, the person

- can be in control of his or her own destiny.
- should want to be in control.
- will enjoy superior benefits from being in control.
- will create new worlds for himself or herself by being in control.
- measurably improves the success of teams, groups, and organizations he or she is affiliated with when he or she is willing to be in control.

Carps and sharks bring grievous pain on themselves because they give the locus of control away. They put the most crucial outcomes of their lives in the hands of external events and/or others. Time after time, carps place their futures in the hands of sharks and suffer. Sharks place their futures in the hands of dubious schemes and trends and events or overload their capabilities and suffer. When the brain's "time horizon" is too narrow and too shallow to allow room for the frontal lobes to interact freely and realistically with ambiguity and the unknown, the locus of control is external.

In helping teams and organizations build a vision for their future, dolphins seek to help carps and sharks compensate for their own narrow, shallow "time horizons" by providing the ambiguity they can't provide for themselves. It comes through the wider embrace of personal and group responsibility.

There are good reasons to accept responsibility even if you don't deserve it.

Working with their groups, dolphins find ways to emphasize these realities:

- Even though we are *not* 100 percent responsible for everything that happens to us, we might as well act like it and work with

Approaching forty, I had a singular dream in which I almost grasped the meaning and understood the nature of what it is that wastes in wasted time. CYRIL CONNOLLY, *THE UNQUIET GRAVE: A WORLD CYCLE BY PALINURIS* it because we are the ones who are going to have to live with the outcome.

- It is often difficult, and sometimes not possible, to determine what part we *are* responsible for, so we might as well act like we are responsible for everything and start dealing with the consequences.

- If you want things to come out the way you think they should, you probably are the best person to improve chances that they will. By taking responsibility, you gain the leverage that comes from staking a direct claim to the right to control the outcome.

Dolphins invite others to play temporarily in *their* "time horizon" by helping them feel good about the fact that it is okay to take responsibility. In fact, it is a very healthy thing to do. To encourage others to view taking responsibility permissibly and to admit uncertainty for the moment into their awareness, dolphins can find no better question to get the ideas flying than this one:

> **"If you could have it any way you want it, how would you have it?"**

It may take some prodding and more than a few reminders that discussing the problems and the details is to come later, but once you get a group focused on this question, you can literally feel the mental resistance fall away and the energy stream power up as the future comes sweeping in!

Paradoxically, a vision usually will not "take" unless the ambiguity is stripped out of it.

Realistically, dolphins go into any vision-building session knowing that no sooner will they be successful in getting a team or group to explore the unknown than they will need to begin working to eliminate ambiguity from the final outcome.

For an explanation, we need only revisit Figure 5.1 and the idea of Elliott Jaques' "time horizons." Having done so, we are quick to realize that most of the members of any team or organization who bear the day-to-day responsibility for making any vision happen have "time horizons" of two years or less. The challenge is compounded by the fact that it is at the one- to two-year "time horizon" levels that you find most of your section and unit heads, who in your authors' opinions represent the best fit between "time horizons" and responsibilities in most organizations. The minds of these individuals seek the triumph of meaning over uncertainty. *These folks' greatest mental contribution is their ability to search for, apply, and extrapolate from rules.*

The best fit for "time horizons" in an organization is usually found at its lowest levels.

Therefore, once beyond the "any way you can have it" phase of the vision-building experience, dolphins strive for language and understanding of the emerging vision that is:

- clear
- specific
- comprehensive
- detailed
- stated in the "future perfect" tense ("This is how we will have achieved. . . .")
- stated pro-actively (thus taking the focus away from fixing what is wrong and placing it on envisioning what is possible)
- powerful enough and compelling enough to elicit the commitment of everyone involved

The whole difference between construction and creation is exactly this: that a thing constructed can only be loved after it is constructed; but a thing created is loved before it exists.
G. K. CHESTERTON

[A] mind that could know the object-world without any error would know nothing at all.
EMILE AUGUSTE CHARTIER

A colleague of ours, Kenneth L. Adams, may not be the first to make this discovery but he is one of the best at putting it to use: Perhaps the finest, clearest, most specific, most comprehensive, most detailed, most forward-looking, most pro-actively written, most powerful and compelling vision statement ever put to words is that provided by a combination of the Declaration of Independence and the Constitution of the United States of America. Their framers explicitly stated:

their rationale for taking action . . .

[In unforgettable fashion, the declarers listed no fewer than twenty-seven crystal-clear injustices suffered at the hands of the "present King of Great Britain," including these:]

"He has obstructed the Administration of Justice . . ."

"He has made Judges dependent on his Will alone . . ."

"He has erected a Multitude of new Offices, and sent hither Swarms of Officers to harass our People, and eat out their Substance."

"He has kept among us, in Times of Peace, Standing Armies, without the consent of our Legislatures."

"He has plundered our Seas, ravaged our Coasts, burnt our towns, and destroyed the Lives of our People."

their purpose . . .

"We, the people of the United States, in order to form a more perfect Union, establish Justice, insure domestic tranquility, provide for the common defense, promote the general welfare, and secure the blessings of liberty, to ourselves and our posterity, do ordain and establish this Constitution for the United States of America."

their values . . .

"We hold these Truths to be self-evident, that all Men are created equal, that they are endowed by their Creator with certain unalienable Rights, that among these are Life, Liberty, and the Pursuit of Happiness. . ."

who their stakeholders were . . .

[The framers of the Constitution listed the federal and state governments. Then realizing they had left out individuals, they added the Bill of Rights four years later.]

This is the highest wisdom that I own,

The best that mankind ever knew:

Freedom and life are earned by those alone

Who conquer them each day anew.

Surrounded by such danger, each one thrives.

Childhood, manhood, and age lead active lives.

At such a throng, I would fain stare.

With free men on free ground their freedom share.   GOETHE

their vision . . .

[The Constitution is literally a walk in the future. It is written as if the government it describes already exists. The framers sat down and said, as every group committed to create a viable vision must say, ''If we were there now, this is what it would look like.'']

their serious pledge of commitment . . .

[The Declaration closes:] ''And for the support of this declaration, with a firm Reliance on the Protection of divine Providence, we mutually pledge to each other our lives, our Fortunes, and our sacred Honor.''

Pretty potent stuff. It makes for an excellent outline for developing a vision for any forward-looking group.

It should not be assumed that persons holding senior positions are always operating from longer ''time horizons.''

Jaques suggests that, for example, general managers and brigade commanders hold positions that will benefit from a five-year ''time horizon'' and that corporation heads and four-star generals will benefit from twenty- to fifty-year ''time horizons.'' Some holders of these positions unquestionably operate from such ''time horizons.'' But as Mardy Grothe and Peter Wylie noted in *Problem Bosses: Who They Are and How to Deal with Them*, there are numerous reasons why people may rise in the bureaucratic pecking order other than ability or, we would add, the nature of their ''time horizon.'' Some of the reasons listed by Grothe and Wylie include:

- They have outstanding technical skills.
- They work harder than their peers.
- They're loyal employees who have ''good attitudes.''
- They're good followers.
- They know how to play politics with company higher-ups.
- They have advanced degrees.

- They form their own companies.
- They're related in some way (son, daughter, spouse, in-law, friend, lover) to the big boss.

In guiding vision-building activities, dolphins don't necessarily expect the "big cheeses" of the team, group, or organization to show the greatest comfort with ambiguity, preparing for the unexpected, or structuring the unknown. Frankly, our experiences and observations at Brain Technologies Corporation have led to the conclusion that "time horizons" encounter the greatest violation in what we call the Killing Waters, the shark-eat-shark world that lies between high competencies of section and unit leaders and the high competencies at the very top of the executive ranks. In between lies a badly muddled and frequently bloodied zone of often questionable competence in middle and upper middle management created because, for the most part, people have been promoted beyond the capabilities and proficiencies of their "time horizon." We believe that the two locales within most large organizations where brains are most likely to be on purpose are those abutting the Killing Waters—near the bottom and at the very top—and that this is where progress is made. We'd suggest that this is a significant reason why so much of middle management is being replaced by the information-providing capability of computer systems. The nearsighted information focus of middle management is no longer necessary. If we are to retain people in these positions, their efforts must be directed toward futuring, customer interface, and the development of self-managing teams.

> *The Killing Waters can be a bloodied zone of questionable competence.*

> Progress makes life easier for our muscles but not for our brains.   JERZY A. WOJCIECHOWSK

Positive things can be made to happen by temporarily coaching and coaxing people into the next "time horizon."

In his studies, Elliott Jaques and his colleagues have concluded that "an alternate reality" is built into each "time horizon" and is lurking there, awaiting actualization. Here is how Jaques describes the phenomenon:

> This implicit duality [the ''alternate reality''] is implicit in the sense of being active behaviourally, intuitively [in a given ''time horizon''], but as yet not accessible for use as a conscious, explicit context. The qualitative shift, then, from one level to the next higher level is one in which the implicit duality becomes explicit at the next higher level and thus joins the processes at that level—while at the same time a new implicit duality emerges which gives the behavioural intuitive foundations of meaning at this higher level.[6]

In leading teams or groups in vision-building, a dolphin remains alert to the brain-within-the-brain that always is lurking behind the current veil of reality. There is always the possibility that an individual will shift from one ''time horizon'' to the next during a vision-building exercise. If so, it may be a moment of ecstasy for the group. Suddenly, through the eyes of one of their members, they may get a glimpse of a wider future than they had reason to anticipate. If it happens, dolphins act quickly to nurture the experience and build on it. A more likely development is the sudden relaxation of the limits created by the team's current ''time horizon,'' permitting access to the ideas and meanings implicit at that level but not likely to be articulated except during special moments. Dolphins seek to make the moment special by carefully monitoring and orchestrating moods and by bringing into play the breakthrough skills of ''breaking set'' outlined in Chapter 3. In addition, it can be fun and it can be productive to ''take a walk in the future'' by deliberately stepping into the next ''time horizon.'' It is not necessary for participants to know that this is happening. All that is necessary is for the dolphin in charge to, first, recognize what the group ''time horizon'' is and, second, to coach and coax them

You can take people on a walk into the future by coaxing them into the next ''time horizon.''

into examining their circumstances and needs as best they can from the perspectives of the next one. Here are some suggestions for achieving both outcomes:

To help you identify which "time horizon" the group or team is functioning within, ask:

How many people are reporting to most of the individuals in this group?

Time horizon of three months
Probably at most one or two, if any.
Time horizon of up to one year
Up to a dozen or so.
Time horizon of up to two years
As many as two hundred to three hundred.
Time horizon of up to five years
As many as a thousand or more.
Time horizon of up to ten years
Perhaps tens of thousands.

To what extent are these people *really* organizing their lives and aspirations for themselves and for the group, team, or organization?

Time horizon of three months
Are probably just setting a few, very simple goals, incapable even of being called "a vision."
Time horizon of up to one year
Are having some success at envisioning how to improve their work and overcome their work-related problems.
Time horizon of up to two years
Are showing concern both (1) about getting the work done in the next three to six months and (2) about how this will influence events a year or so later.

Time horizon of up to five years

Are examining and thinking about problems they will confront in the next sixty months in pairs: Do they do this or do they do that? (Do they close the factory, for example, or do they retool it?)

Time horizon of up to ten years or more

If they are in the five- to ten-year range, they are probably tracing out second- and third-order consequences of changes they may make. If they are talking about creating the future—putting into place new systems and theories—rather than forecasting it, they are most likely operating from "time horizons" greater than ten years out.[7]

If you want to encourage members of your vision-building group to stretch a little—to see themselves operating from the next most expansive "time horizon"—seek their response to questions such as these:

- What kinds of problems do you think your boss is thinking about? How do you think she will handle them?
- Let's say you all get promoted next month. Will this make any difference in how you see what we've been talking about?
- Okay, we've got our vision in place. What if [outline a problem, development, or event they would not be likely to be asked to find an answer to but that their immediate superior would]?

If they are operating principally from a

Time horizon of three months

Ask them to come up with a list of ideas for improving their work.

Time horizon of up to one year

Ask them to "brainstorm" what the work load might be a year from now and how they might have to change things to deal with it.

Time horizon of up to two years

Ask them to think about what might happen if they decided to do just the opposite of what their vision calls for.

Time horizon of up to five years

Ask them to think about what would happen to them if someone started changing the principal rules they work under. What are these rules? Which ones are most likely to be changed in the next five to ten years?

Time horizon of up to ten years

Ask them what they would do if they were suddenly required to transform all their competitors into ''friends,'' if suddenly they had to get markedly better results with fewer resources, and if suddenly they had to create highly competent contacts in numerous fields and industries abroad.

To encourage your participants to take a more forward-looking view at any point in your vision-building activities, find ways to get them to move their perspectives from

- the old to the new
- one answer to many answers
- the familiar to the unfamiliar
- externally defined meanings and control to internally defined meanings and control
- what they know to what they suspect
- the little picture to the big picture
- the concrete to the abstract
- certainty to uncertainty
- many limits to fewer limits
- the past to the future
- what they don't want to what they do
- the simple to the more complex
- the fragmented to the integrative
- less stress to more stress
- slow information to fast information
- less information to more information
- certainty to doubt

Pushing your participants in vision-building into the next ''time horizon'' is more than merely an exercise that may provoke lively times; develop some new, possibly useful ideas and perspectives; and stoke the fires of *esprit de corps,* any one of which is worthwhile. A more critical reason for doing it is this: Unless you achieve some mind-stretching, you are likely to be involved in just rearranging the furniture of the past and present rather than preparing for the future. As organizational wits have already reminded us, it doesn't do us a lot of good to rearrange the deck chairs on the *Titanic.* Without encouraging tension between ''time horizons'' in our vision-building efforts, we risk deriving a new vision just as rigid and unproductive as the old.

Care must be taken to avoid creating a new vision just as rigid as the old one.

Idle dreamers have given true visionaries a bad name. ROBERT FRITZ

Without a vision, the danger is that most of us will continue to perform at a set level, one we feel unconsciously is correct for us. If we exceed that level of performance, we usually will sabotage ourselves later on to maintain our ''average.'' The importance of having a strong vision is this: If we visualize ourselves performing at a much higher level, our unconscious minds will interpret that as the new level of expected performance and will cause us to correct positively toward the vision without harmful repercussions.

Viewing the future from the frontal lobes, dolphins don't at all mind being ''time bandits'' if it means improving everyone's chances for getting their needs met.

When a dolphin gazes at his own existence or the existence of others, he realizes that at any given time he must peer through several ''lenses'' or layers of meaning. In Figure 5.2 we have graphically depicted those that have been the focus of our explorations in this and the preceding chapter.

In addition to reminding you that every human's sense of perspective and limits to knowing come under multiple influences

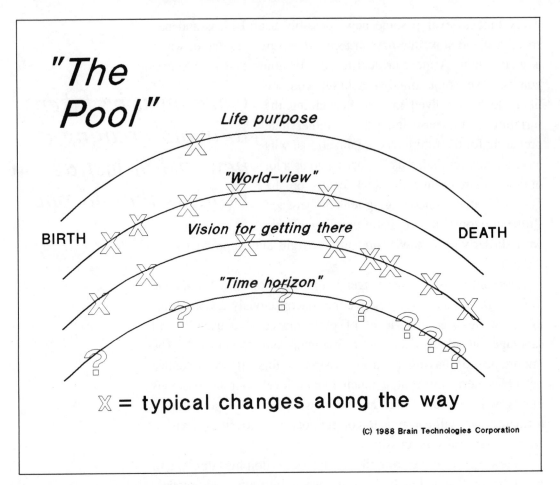

Figure 5.2. Lenses of Meaning

at any given moment, we have chosen to portray ''the pool'' as we have in Figure 5.2 to emphasize that the probabilities of change vary from lens to lens, or from layer to layer.

Over a lifetime, a person's life purpose may change once or twice. It is unlikely to do so repeatedly, although it may appear that this is happening because the individual never manages to identify a life purpose or is continually refining it.

In a rapidly changing world, visions will change more often than any of the other influences on ''the pool,'' particularly if they are products of the minds of dolphins.

And "time horizons"? Elliott Jaques is currently investigating the prospects over a lifetime for expanding the mind's window on the future. For a healthy child provided the physical and intellectual nourishment needed by a healthy mind, it appears likely that three, four, or even five shifts in "time horizon" over a lifetime are perfectly normal. For the extraordinary child provided with unusual opportunities, or perhaps even if provided with unusual hardships, the shifts may number eight, ten, twelve, or more, and others still may be in the offing when the body dies, leaving the brain with no means of life support.

The brain may be able to shift ''time horizons'' beyond the body's life span.

Using Figure 5.2 as Exhibit No. 1, we can amply argue that contemporary brain/mind research has antiquated much of what has been advocated by carps, sharks, and pseudo-enlightened carps for changing the organization and its culture.

Rather than make dolphins arrogant, however, the trip through expanded "time horizons" is a very humbling one. Perhaps the most sobering thought of all is the possibility that we humans currently operate out of a body whose natural life is insufficient in length to afford our brain a chance, in the best of times, to mature fully. Sobering enough is the growing realization that the likelihood that any of our organizations will be in sync for any length of time with the lenses or layers of existence of its employees is very limited.

Improving such matters should be a growth industry, since the trend is for far greater variation, not less, in the way the human brain divides and divines its world.

If a man advances confidently in the direction of his dreams to live the life he has imagined, he will meet with a success unexpected in common hours.   HENRY DAVID THOREAU

The soul . . . never thinks without a picture.
ARISTOTLE

DOLPHIN WORK

Exercise No. 1

In the exercises for Chapter 2, "Leveraging the Wave: The Dolphin's Special Secrets," you began to clarify where "here" is for you currently—that is, where you are "now." This time let's take steps to identify where it is you want to go.

First, focusing on the critical "20 percent" that really matters—that will make 80 percent of the difference for you—provide answers to the following on a separate sheet of paper.

My personal purpose is:

My business purpose is:

My chief values (the guiding beliefs and principles I wish to govern and guide my behavior) are:

My primary stakeholders (people who are going with me, who will be affected by what I do, and who will help me) are:

Next, understanding that a *vision* is the clear, ideal, specific, detailed future-perfectly-stated articulation of your purpose, including the needs of the stakeholders and guided by your values, let's walk into the future and look back on your vision made real. Imagine you are now a newspaper reporter writing a story on the realization of your vision. If you have achieved what you set out to achieve, what would you now be seeing, hearing, and feeling specifically? Where are you now, and how did you get here? And now that this vision is complete, do you sense the possibility of a new vision emerging? Write out your story on your sheet of paper.

6

RELEASE TO A HIGHER ORDER: THE DOLPHIN'S PIÈCE DE RÉSISTANCE

*I*n the late 1980s, an American novelist entered the telephone office in the city of Zhaojue, deep in southern China, about twelve hundred miles southwest of Beijing. He had flown to Chengdu, the capital of Sichuan Province, and boarded the Chengdu to Kunming train. For six hundred sinuous miles, the tracks push south, then a little west, traversing six hundred bridges and 240 miles of tunnels. The writer traveled only about half the route, however. He disembarked in Xichang, capital for a region whose 3.3 million residents include more than a million Yi, a people whom time has almost ignored.

Leaving Xichang behind for the villages of the Yi in Sichuan's blue-gray hills is like leaving the twentieth century for the twelfth, the writer later reported in *The New York Times*. As he placed his call in the telephone office in Zhaojue, a crowd gathered, eventually numbering more than twenty curious, if deferential, onlookers. The gentle telephonist explained in a whisper, "We have never had a call to Hong Kong before."

If you are a maker of pack-animal harnesses and wooden spoons, you probably can find a market among the Yi, who represent one

We're sourcing wheelbarrow tires in Taiwan. What's going to be the next viable tire source? It could be India. It could be China.
U.S. PURCHASING DIRECTOR

Following the Yi is like leaving the twentieth century for the twelfth.

167

of the last remaining enclaves of medievalism. But even the Yi are changing. Although they still lack TV, there is a collective radio with wires reaching to loudspeakers in many homes. The Yi teachers' college has thirteen thousand volumes in its library, although, as yet, only one of them—a dictionary—is written in the Yi language, the rest being in Mandarin Chinese. As the Yi get more roads and begin to use cars and trucks and as they substitute metal utensils for wooden spoons, the last outpost for medieval merchandise will be gone, and even you—you who have followed a primal, primitive wave to its final outpost—must also confront the need to change.

The trend is clear: Beyond the Yi, there is nothing.

Nothing is more real than nothing.   SAMUEL BECKETT

L eapfrogging change is one option. You do it by following the same wave from environment to environment, from market to market, following it even as far as the Yi.

Some companies are adopting this approach, having grown weary from simply trying to keep up and keep ahead. "They get tired of looking over their shoulders," says David Balkin, a management professor at Louisiana State University. "The demands of innovation take their toll."

At times just getting focused on the basics helps to make a temporary difference.

Yet even this limited response to the need to do something different—moving to another location to catch the same wave as it emerges there—is more the exception in today's business culture than the rule.

Faced with the need to alter old methods, old habits, old products, and old technologies, carps and sharks tend to resist, digging in, going back to the basics, doing more of the same harder. Sometimes, getting focused in this way may make a temporary difference. More typically, however, the jolts get greater and greater and arrive more frequently. Finally, anyone with half an ounce of a sense of reality must confront the fact that what they are doing just isn't working, that the distance between where they are and where they need to be is too vast for them to leap. The vehicle for their hopes and dreams has disintegrated.

When the tires of the old vehicle begin to get bogged down, the engine shows signs of disrepair, and the body begins to fall apart, why do carps and sharks fixate on the rearview mirror and push harder on the accelerator instead of shifting gears or looking for a better means for getting around? Why do they dig in, doing more of the same harder instead of doing something different? Why don't they "release" to greater visions, greater capabilities, greater sensibilities and sensitivities? Why do they refuse to be responsible—that is, to respond appropriately to what's happening? And what do dolphins do differently?

Why don't carps and sharks "release"? And what is it dolphins do differently?

Vital questions. There is something about this business of letting go, of releasing, of transforming our perspectives and understanding of what is real, that is absolutely critical to thriving and surviving in rapid-change times, and yet nothing is more fiercely opposed by carps and sharks. Some advocates of artificial intelligence contend that the brain's pernicious resistance—over the aeons—to replacing old beliefs and behaviors with more appropriate beliefs and behaviors is the best argument for pushing the developing of AI. Computer genius Charles Lecht comments:

> We're doing the same damn stupid things we've done since the beginning of time. And unless there's an intervention, one maybe sown by ourselves, in the course of human history, we are *destined* to annihilation. There's no question about it. Jesus Christ didn't need any connection with Heaven to come to that conclusion. All he had to see was how everybody around him was beating one another up. While we are waiting for either evolution or divine intervention, we need some healthy dosages of artificial intelligence to keep us alive.[1]

One of life's most fulfilling moments occurs in that split second when the familiar is suddenly transformed into the dazzling aura of the profoundly new.... These breakthroughs are too infrequent, more uncommon than common; and we are mired most of the time in the mundane and the trivial. The shocker: What seems mundane and trivial is the very stuff that discovery is made of. The only difference is our perspective, our readiness to put the pieces together in an entirely new way and to see patterns where only shadows appeared just a moment before. EDWARD B. LINDAMAN, *THINKING IN FUTURE TENSE*

Perhaps that view is too strong. And who knows whether Lecht and others can be successful in creating, as they are attempting to create, biological computing devices capable of "becoming mind," a mind they hope can be superior to the human mind in its openness to learning and change? Who knows whether they *should* even be attempting to do so? Whatever the answers to these questions, the need is self-evident and the benefits obvious if we can find ways to replace the tormented, self-deluding, self-defeating, socially and personally damaging resistance to change experienced by carps and sharks.

What would we replace this resistance with?

You'll see as we once again visit "the pool" to inquire first about the differences in how carps, sharks, and dolphins deal with "flow," the "change over time" challenge discussed in Chapter 2. And then how a dolphin empowers the life- and progress-sustaining processes of self-direction and self-correction when confronted with the need to do something different.

*T*hink about how it was the last time—or the first time—you were in a boat, whether a runabout powered by a tiny five-horsepower fishing motor or a powerboat equipped with twin 80-horsepower heavies capable of pulling two skiers simultaneously.

Boats create lag.

> A thought which does not result in an action is nothing much, and an action which does not proceed from a thought is nothing at all. GEORGES BERNANOS

In the water. All life-size, propeller-driven boats do. When the throttle is first advanced, boats literally sink deeper, much deeper than they will later, when inertia has been overcome and speed, or flow, achieved. Early on, boats of any size and any power displace a lot of water. Later, if they achieve momentum, they'll be riding much higher, displacing very little.

Early on, too, a lot of power is expended. If, in fact, you were to use this much power-per-foot-advanced-in-the-water constantly, you'd run out of gasoline soon, before getting very far at all.

In almost every new enterprise, what gets displaced in the

early going is not water but results. You can see that in Figure 6.1. There is a noticeable dip, a sagging, in the dotted line as it moves to the right, toward the future, in time.

That dotted line represents doing something different, something new. And the reason for the sagging, for the lag, is that the future must be both discovered *and* created. The discovery part of the future is instantaneous:

What gets displaced early on in new enterprises is results.

To know it is to *be* it. However, creating that future in its myriad details on the basis of your discovery takes time:

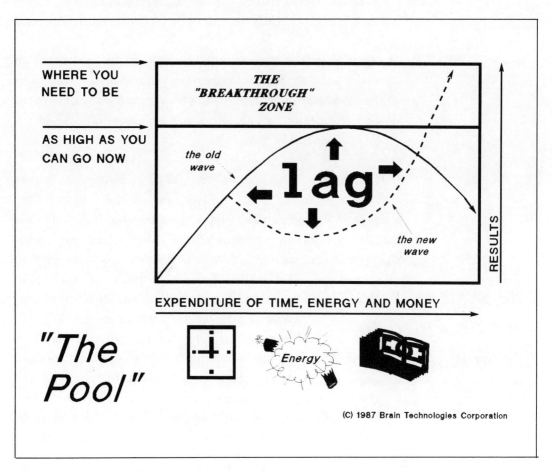

Figure 6.1. Lag and Breaking Through

- **Time to mobilize your vision.** Time to grow conversant, comfortable, knowledgeable, skilled, and effective in directing the new future you have discovered and now are creating.
- **Time to test reality.** Time to sample and study the needs and expectations of the marketplace, correcting as you go, learning as you fail, building on your successes.
- **Time to find allies.** Time to seek out others whose personally discovered, created futures resemble yours, so you can leverage on their interest, their buying power, and their needs, and they on yours.
- **Time to find financing.** Time to persuade money sources that your discovered future, now under creation, can contribute to their goals and justify the risk of their capital, reputations, and futures.
- **Time to gather momentum.** Time to give the "universe" an opportunity to decide whether your newly discovered, now-being-created future represents a path toward greater discovery and complexity for life forces and thus is worthwhile in the general scheme of things.

Ignoring lag, its requirements, and its consequences is perhaps the greatest organizational impediment facing any enterprise. Carps and sharks simply cannot deal well with it in the face of deteriorating circumstances. More than any other "dynamic" that individuals or teams must work through to survive in rapid-change times, lag is a "make or break" phenomenon. The inability to deal with lag is what insightful critics like W. Edwards Deming, the quality expert, are castigating when they assign more than 80 percent of any enterprise's problems to "the system." The system is hardly ever designed to accommodate lag effectively, and the system is equally as powerful an obstacle to successful change as the individual.

The system is hardly ever designed to accommodate lag effectively.

"Lag," then, is where breakthrough kinds of change occur, *if* they occur. To the surprise even of themselves, the "chaologists" are once again providing some of the most valuable, exciting new ideas for understanding change. For dolphins, their notions are timely: Because of the global information revolution, dolphins find it more and more difficult to escape from dysfunctional organizations. (A variant of Gresham's Law seems to rule: Bad information spreads faster than good.) Escaping, getting out of the pool, though it remains a favored dolphin technique, is being foreclosed as "the system" becomes more and more global. Dolphins must then turn to another of their favorite dictums, "When what you are doing isn't working, you must do something different," and the chaologists have some of the most puissant ideas going.

The fact that an opinion has been widely held is no evidence whatever that it is not entirely absurd; indeed, in view of the silliness of the majority of mankind, a widespread belief is more likely to be foolish than sensible. BERTRAND RUSSELL

*H*ere, in the words of artificial intelligence pioneer Douglas Hofstadler, is what these iconoclastic scientists have found: "It turns out that an eerie type of chaos can lurk just behind a facade of order—and yet, deep inside the chaos lurks an even eerier type of order." From the viewpoint of traditional physics and the traditional management sciences, change is getting stranger and stranger.

It helps to walk through a "Dick, Jane, and Spot" condensation of "the chaos game" theory, and we can do so using Figure 6.2. Once again our wave is displayed, only this time, rather than the typical "S"-shaped, sinusoidal repetitions, the wave finds itself being split repeatedly into disc-shaped sections. Over time, each disc-shaped section itself splits at each end into two new disc-shaped sections.

Seeking to understand how organizations do and can change, dolphins are likely to find themselves drawn in particular to two features of this "mapping of change": first, the bowl shapes themselves and second, the region (which we've highlighted in Figure 6.2 as "The Opportunity Zone") surrounding the "bifurcation points," the region where lag occurs—that is, the boundary

Every creative act involves . . . a new innocence of perception, liberated from the cataract of accepted belief. ARTHUR KOESTLER

It's a poor sort of memory that only works backward. LEWIS CARROLL

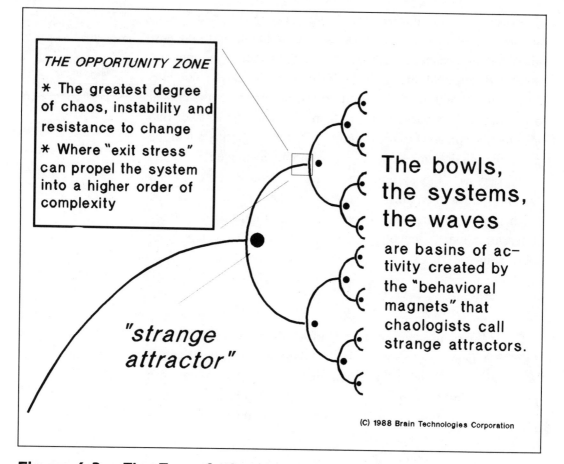

THE OPPORTUNITY ZONE

* The greatest degree of chaos, instability and resistance to change

* Where "exit stress" can propel the system into a higher order of complexity

The bowls, the systems, the waves

are basins of activity created by the "behavioral magnets" that chaologists call strange attractors.

"strange attractor"

(C) 1988 Brain Technologies Corporation

Figure 6.2.   The Tug of "Strange Attractors"

zone between the bowls, the zone where, as James Gleick wrote, "life blossoms."

The midsection of the bowl represents the good times we have repeatedly referred to as "the flow." The bowl itself is formed or dominated by an organizing principle, some operative influence either sufficiently in sync with the environment as to be capable of coexisting with it or more likely one simultaneously also shaping the environment.

If one were to imagine magnifying the shape of one of those bowls, what one can expect, according to the chaologists, is not the nice, sweeping curve seen in Figure 6.2 but a startling pattern of irregular and infinitely complex shapes that, though never quite the same, possess a quality of *self-similarity*. The bowl is "fractal"—a snowflake combination of order and chaos, as is everything else in the universe, including organizations, where nothing ever happens quite the same way twice and yet, during times of relative sanity and stability, enough happens in orderly fashion that people and responses appear capable of being managed.

What is the mechanism that creates the bowl?

As chaos theory developed over the past two decades, mathematicians David Ruelle and Floris Takens gained credit for a concept and a name that continues to create its own turbulence in the physical sciences: *the strange attractor*. The idea has been fueled by British cell biologist and biochemist Rupert Sheldrake, who talks about "morphogenetic forms" giving shape to everything, from inanimate cells to the human species. In nature, in human affairs, in the universe as a whole there appears to be as yet unexplained pattern-makers or templates or attractors that influence mind and matter. Think of them, as Gleick has suggested, as "magnets embedded in a rubber sheet." Or think of them as tethering rings around which pendulums subjected to constantly changing gravitational forces circle.

In Figure 6.2, the bowl shapes are patterns for organizing firms and societies, patterns created by *strange attractors*. Patterns, remember, that when examined closer are seen to be "fractal," or both orderly *and* chaotic. This feature can help explain why information is accelerating. Physicist Robert Shaw was one of the first to understand that because of the fractal patterns they generate, strange attractors are "patterning engines of chaos" and therefore of information.

> *Look closely and you will see a startling pattern of irregular and infinitely complex shapes.*

> God plays dice with the universe. But they're loaded dice. And the main objective of physics now is to find out by what rules were they loaded and how can we use them for our own ends. PHYSICIST JOSEPH FORD

> *"Strange attractors" create patterns for organizing firms and societies.*

It is possible that we do, after all, live in an amnesic world that is governed by eternal laws. But it is also possible that memory is inherent in nature; and if we find that we are indeed living in such a world, we shall have to change our way of thinking entirely. We shall sooner or later have to give up many of our old habits of thought and adopt new ones: habits that are better adapted to living in a world that is living in the presence of the past—and is also living in the presence of the future, and open to continuing creation.

RUPERT SHELDRAKE, *THE PRESENCE OF THE PAST*

For our purposes, the other great insight available from chaos theory issues from the dynamics of "the hump." The hump is our wave, sufficiently energized. Physicist Mitchell Feigenbaum put a brilliant, unconventional mind to work on the environs of the hump, fractionating out all sorts of discoveries.

*T*hose most intriguing to managers and organizational theorists, we'd suggest, concern Feigenbaum's constant. A number. As matters now stand, it appears that Feigenbaum's number (4.6692016090, to be precise) represents a way of determining the exact point on "the hump" at which bifurcation occurs. At this point the strange attractor splits. At this point a new wave of change becomes a reality. Here the consummate manager would aim if she knew precisely how, because here the shift into a new reality for doing business occurs.

At this point it appears that Feigenbaum's constant is a universal: His number applies to *all* humps—to all wave forms in nature. Let James Gleick explain, using a telling analogy just as startling as this:

For want of a nail, the shoe was lost;

For want of a shoe, the horse was lost;

For want of a horse, the rider was lost;

For want of a rider, the battle was lost;

For want of a battle, the kingdom was lost!
DESCRIPTION OF "THE BUTTERFLY EFFECT" FROM FOLKLORE

Imagine that a prehistoric zoologist decides that some things are heavier than other things—they have some abstract quality he calls *weight*—and he wants to investigate this idea scientifically. He has never actually measured weight, but he thinks he has some understanding of the idea. He looks at big snakes and little snakes, big bears and little bears, and he guesses that the weight of these animals might have some relationship to their size. He builds a scale and starts weighing snakes. To his astonishment, every snake weighs the same. To his consternation, every bear weighs the same, too. And to his further amazement, bears weigh the same as snakes. They all weigh 4.6692016090. Clearly *weight* is not what he supposed. The whole concept requires rethinking.[2]

And so does the whole concept of how organizations change.*

Already, the idea of a Malthusian smoothness of steady, linear growth has been under challenge. When the chaologists' discoveries are added to Ilya Prigogene's concepts of dissipative structures and Rupert Sheldrake's morphogenetic, or archetypal, fields, dolphins have a wealth of new vantage points for applying their to now largely intuitive insight that change was a jumpy chameleon.

Eyeing the near future of business, dolphins are more and more likely to manage as "chaologists," understanding that:

- Because of the increasingly global nature of "the system," they are going to be less able to avoid the dysfunctional limitations and irritations of systems—of organizations—than they have traditionally been. Historically, dolphins have not spent a lot of time seeking to make systemic changes because they were unwilling to accept the strictures it placed on their personal freedom. They have either left the system, created their own little insular "bubbles" or "skunk works," or leveraged their influence through their expertise and informal kinds of leadership. Now, like the rest of us, dolphins have fewer shelters. Dysfunctional systems are everywhere.

- When the environment no longer supports a system, the people in the system have several choices. One, they can seek to help the system "pop" into the sphere of influence of a new strange attractor by approaching the threshold defined by Feigenbaum's constant. Chaologists speak of the robustness or the boom-and-bustiness of systems. Too little robustness, and there's no chance of the system perturbating—moving toward a higher order of complexity, creating and catching a new wave, or moving toward the orbit of a new strange attractor. Without sufficient energy, the

> What else, when chaos draws all forces inward to shape a single leaf.
> CONRAD AIKEN

* Whether we'll be able to use Feigenbaum's constant on a large scale in changing human organizations depends substantially on whether managers are able to use the model, first to change themselves and then to develop their skills at targeting what Feigenbaum and other chaologists call the "tuning parameters," which are the energy sources that power the perturbation and bifurcation processes. We can expect that research and application studies into the use of Feigenbaum's constant will be one of the dominant topics in organizational development for the 1990s.

outcome is predestined; the system will eventually collapse. Just enough robustness and you get a steady equilibrium: the flow. Keep adding robustness and soon you create a bifurcation. Suddenly you no longer have just changes within the system, you also have changes *of* the system. As Figure 6.3 suggests, this requires upping the chaos, or the information, gradient massively. Without a "quantum leap" in new energy input, a leap sufficient to perturbate the system, no system is likely to escape to a higher level of complexity. Going for a 10 percent increase in productivity won't muster the energy required. The other choice that may or may not be available is the removal of the system into an environment that continues to honor the "status quo"—that is, in chaos theory terms, the system generated by the original

The 100%+ Shift

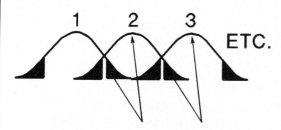

1   2   3   ETC.

Mediocrity in the NEW system
should meet or exceed
excellence in the OLD system.

Shifts in systems usually require an order of magnitude of improvement in performance. A 10% attempt is usually insufficient (it tends to be absorbed by a regression to the mean). However, an attempt to improve productivity by greater than 100% will generally shift the entire system to a higher order.

(C) 1988 Brain Technologies Corporation

Figure 6.3.   Upping the Quality of Mediocrity

strange attractor. If neither of these avenues is pursued, the system probably faces disintegration.

- Change also can be created "fractally." As Edward Lorenz discovered with his Butterfly Effect, the tiniest change can have the most momentous consequences over time in a fractal system. Fractal systems—and those include most human systems—are a mixture of order and chaos. Fractal systems also are open systems, constantly interacting with their environments. Such systems are critically dependent on the feedback of information for survival. To survive, such systems must use this information to *change*. From this great paradox—that to "stay the same," to survive, the system must change—issues numerous "little" paradoxes. Dolphins are unusually sensitive both to the great paradox and the smaller ones because of their ability to gather information from the future and from a wide variety of contemporary sources; because of their openness to ambiguity and surprise and because of their ability to act on information the moment they sense something of value. Now that it is less simple to escape the dysfunctional system, dolphins can be expected to increase their expertise at identifying and taking the small paradoxical steps that can start the system fluctuating. Fractally, these small steps can quickly become the critical influences needed to perturbate a dysfunctional system. For example, the Soviet system is likely to experience profound change as a result of the relatively minor measure of introducing personal computers into it. The paradox is that the Soviets have traditionally prohibited individuals from owning printing devices. Yet the country's leadership must allow the introduction of personal computers and the training of people in their use to remain competitive and technologically competent in the world marketplace. You can't enter the Age of Information and repress information, a reality already changing the very fabric of the Communist system.

What makes chaos theory such a promising new vista for understanding how to manage organizations in times of rapid

[If] life evolves in all of the many universes in a quantum cosmology, and if life continues to exist in *all* of these universes, then *all* of these universes, which include *all* possible histories among them, will approach the Omega Point. At the instant the Omega Point is reached, life will have gained control of *all* matter and forces not only in a single universe, but in all universes whose existence is logically possible; life will have spread into *all* spatial regions in all universes which could logically exist, and will have stored an infinite amount of information, including *all* bits of knowledge which it is logically possible to know. And this is the end.   JOHN D. BARROW AND FRANK J. TIPLER, *THE ANTHROPIC COSMOLOGICAL PRINCIPLE*

change is the new knowledge it brings about what can happen, does happen, or needs to happen in the lag zone. Traditionally, systems have tended to exclude excellence and long-term visioning. If effective visioning is not present and people are only being rewarded and measured on short-term results, then the lag created by doing something different is both unacceptable and intolerable until the pain level begins to force the shift. Companies in this situation do their learning on the back side of the wave, where they are either continuing to disintegrate or have been "downshifted" into the bowl of a less complex strange attractor. (In our part of the United States, where energy, agricultural, and real-estate recessions dominated the second half of the 1980s, "downshifting into the bowl of a less complex strange attractor" has been an altogether too-common event. M.B.A.s have started driving taxis, engineers have started sanitorial services, farmers have started cookie stores, accountants have turned to "white water" rafting, and printers of books and magazines have turned to printing labels. And many of the survivors among our small Colorado high-tech manufacturers are now doing hand-wiring for specialized markets such as cable makers, whereas before they were using leading-edge assembly skills for high-tech customers.)

Most systems are designed to maintain themselves rather than change drastically. Thus, under such circumstances, it usually is mediocrity that gets rewarded as the operative strange attractor continually pulls the organization back toward the center of the chaologists' bowl of familiarity, which in traditional terms has often been referred to as "regression to the mean." Poor performance is punished because it can cause the system to deteriorate, but then, be sure of it, excellence also is punished because very much of it will require the system to change. To say it again, the system is designed to maintain the system, and this makes moving the organization toward the lip of the strange attractor's bowl—where life abounds and where leaps of quantum magnitude into environs of promise are possible—all the more challenging.

ystems designed by carps usually do not plan at all for lag, and if they do, they tend not to confront the reality until the distance between where they are and where they need to be to ascend to the new wave is enormous. PEC (or pseudo-enlightened carp) systems, though they may welcome lag, fail to move people sufficiently toward new modes and levels of performance, and they almost always founder short of their goals. Systems designed by sharks almost invariably go into ever more frenzied turmoil during lag. Eventually, in all cases, there is nearly always new blood in the water.

Yet if what you are doing isn't working and fundamentally you must do something new, lag is all there is. Only by reconstituting your resources and doing something significantly different can you summon the momentum to push through what, in Figure 6.1, we've called the "Breakthrough" Zone. Only by surmounting and surviving lag creatively, responsibly, and responsively can you get from where you are now *to where you need to be.*

Creating and surmounting lag—the process of releasing to a higher order of complexity—is a dolphin specialty. Let's explore how it's done. And why carps and sharks fail in the attempt so often, if indeed they ever make the attempt at all.

Lag is all there is if you want to travel through the "Breakthrough" Zone.

One should not think slightingly of the paradoxical; for the paradox is the source of the thinker's passion, and the thinker without a paradox is like a lover without a feeling: a paltry mediocrity. . . . The supreme paradox of all thought is the attempt to discover something that thought cannot think.

SØREN KIERKEGAARD

arps and sharks get kayoed by lag regularly. First, they may not see lag coming and thus are late in responding to the situations that create lag and the circumstances that accompany it.

Second, when they simply can no longer ignore the need for change, they typically are unable to handle the emotions that lag creates without destructive delay and painful personal and organizational damage.

Figure 6.4 captures what transpires in "the pool" when carps and sharks deny that they themselves are "flow" and continue to ride the wave past the peak and downward toward the shoals of potential disaster and disintegration. In this case, the opportunity for minimizing lag has vanished. Because performance is now falling as results follow the wave down, control is no longer internalized. Control has been handed to external forces—to the environment itself. And one way or another, the environment is a progressively ironhanded teacher.

Hopefully, the lesson will take quickly. After all, you *can*, if you are alert and in a learning mood, get it lightly—with a feather. A dolphin, for one, likes to get his lessons with a minimum of

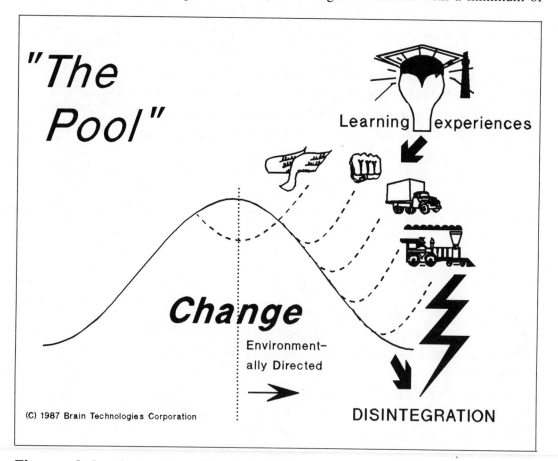

Figure 6.4.   Learning Experiences

discomfort and very little unnecessary expansion of the lag zone and its time-devouring, resources-consuming consequences. In a world of growing complexity, even dolphins don't always see lag coming and react appropriately in time, every time.

If, however, you don't get it with a feather, you surely will have another learning opportunity. Next time the best you may be able to hope for is to get it with a fist.

And if not then, with a truck—a *Mack* truck.

And if not then, with a locomotive.

And if not then, with a lightning bolt.[3]

And *by* then, the whack caves your head in. If you haven't "gotten it" by now, there is little hope of recovery. You have clung to the status quo too long, or too many times reacted to it inappropriately and ineffectively. No longer is the choice one of surmounting lag, of moving to a new configuration, of releasing to a higher order. Those choices are now unavailable.

But even if you "get it" before nearing disintegration, you must still contend with two sobering factors, the first of which is portrayed in Figure 6.5: the factor of "the long road back."

Because you have ridden the original wave so far past its peak, you are now confronted by a truly immense amount of lag. To get from where you are now to where you need to be may simply be unthinkable.

The other concern is what we call the Recovery Trough. That's our name for the chain of emotional stages generated by the brain when change is forced on it externally.

The model you see in Figure 6.6 is adapted from studies of the terminally ill by Elisabeth Kübler-Ross. Such a cycle or something similar to it has been visible in our personal brushes with disaster and those we have observed.

It is a sausage of emotions. At any point you run the risk of getting stuck in this lumpish, action-inhibiting casing of negations and diversions. Over time, most individuals can work through the Recovery Trough: through the shock of failure, the denial, anger, bargaining, sadness, returning finally to a sense of emotional stability. However, every minute, every dollar, every ounce of

When you return to your parked car on an icy day and the lock is frozen, the vertical thinker may try to heat the lock with his lighter in the wind. The lateral thinker may shelter and heat his key with the flame. EDWARD DE BONO, *MECHANISM OF MIND*

You can never have the use of the inside of a cup without the *outside*. The inside and the outside go together. They're one. ALAN WATTS

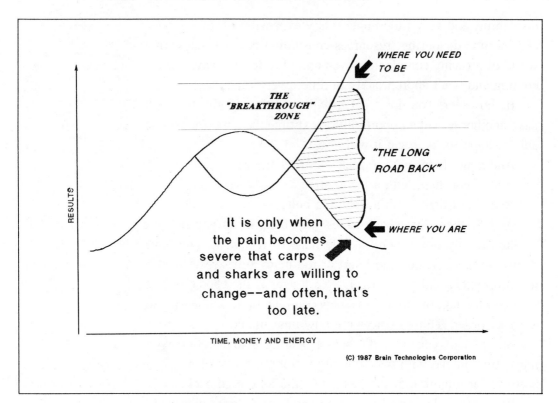

Figure 6.5.   "The Long Road Back"

energy consumed by the Recovery Trough is a minute, a dollar, an irrecoverable dollop of life force forfeited, forcing further delay in our return to performing equilibrium. Is there a better way? Well, we obviously think so: the way of the dolphin. To continue our investigations, let's again return to "the pool," in Figure 6.7.

*E*rnest Hemingway spoke of grace under pressure. It was his definition of courage. We humans think highly of almost any exploit achieved under pressure. For example:

- A political figure eludes a seemingly inescapable trap in a Q&A session by providing an answer showing true mental finesse, and we applaud.
- In sports, our goat reemerges as a hero because, at the last

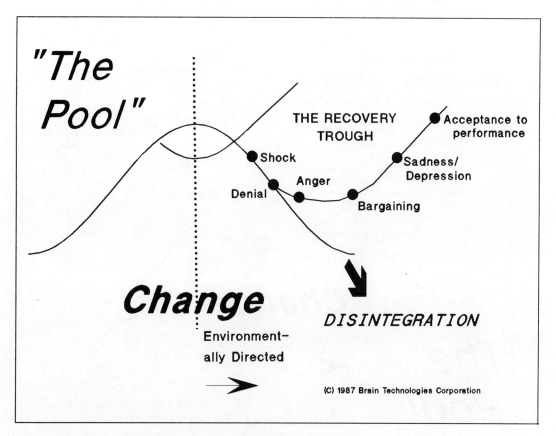

Figure 6.6. The Recovery Trough

moment, he astounds us all by doing the incredible in the face
of almost certain rout.

- Many a Carnegie Medal of Honor has been awarded to an
  ordinary citizen who responded courageously in the face of
  imminent danger.
- None of us who viewed the movie *Coming to America* could do
  anything but marvel at the fluid ability of actor Eddie Murphy to
  take the unexpected and, as we were told he did repeatedly during
  the movie's filming, make it work better than the original script.

Both ordinary and extraordinary persons—in all works of
life—often exhibit ingenuity and finesse and creativity and hero-
ism and wit under pressure.

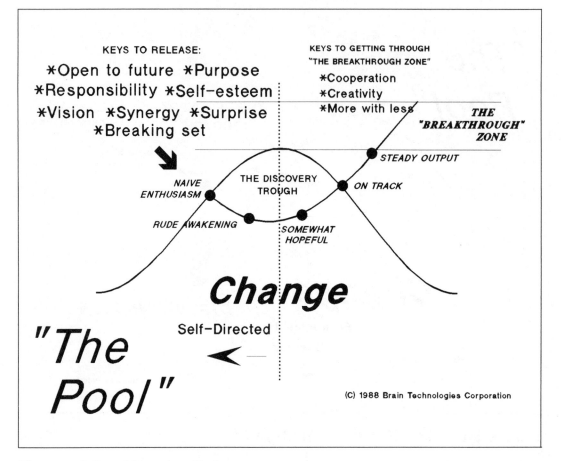

Figure 6.7.   Keys to Release

Is there any difference in the way a dolphin does it when she is self-directing her own changes? Most assuredly.

It can be said even that she does it backward, and if so, it is a reversal of crucial importance.

In rapid-change times, dolphins know it is often wise to begin changing *before* the times rather then run the risk of waiting to change with or after the times. Changing before the times means changing without strong signals, changing on the basis of intuitions and suspicions and perhaps merely dissatisfaction with the current shape of things. Dolphins often don't wait for external pressure to act. They create their own pressure internally, confident that, often enough, the result will be grace—the elegance of

For most of the founders of classical science—even for Einstein—science was an attempt to go beyond the world of appearances, to reach a timeless world of supreme rationality—the world of Spinoza. But perhaps there is a more subtle form of reality that involves both laws and games, time and eternity.
ILYA PRIGOGINE, *FROM BEING TO BECOMING: TIME AND COMPLEXITY IN THE PHYSICAL SCIENCES*

"what works" and works with power, finesse, and simplicity.

Inner pressure. Then grace. Again and again.

It's among the dolphin's most powerful abilities.

Figure 6.7 furnishes us with important clues both to the dolphin's means for producing self-initiated *pressure* and cultivating the chances for *grace*—for abundance, for elegance, for breakthrough.

Dolphins apply their own pressures, then respond with grace to bring change in themselves.

*I*t is not that dolphins don't make mistakes. They do. But because of their openness to learning, they can self-correct quickly. They usually "get it" early on and forgo the need to get it again and again. There is no need to take finals over and over; all the reminder they need is perhaps an occasional pop quiz.

It is not that dolphins never feel discouragement. They do. But they recognize that discouragement for what it is: a fragment of fatigue, a consequence of encountering a blind alley. They use their discouragement as an indicator, signaling the need to take a new direction rather than letting it be a downer, steering them wrong.

It is not that dolphins are immune to fear. Hardly. When the time comes to let go of the trapeze, it is a severely dysfunctional human who at first feels no fear. Feature this: One of your authors is standing at the lip of a 165-foot plunge into a river canyon. How high is that? He later recalls that the tallest hotel in his home city is about nine stories—about ninety feet. The ribbon of river curling beneath his feet is almost twice that far away. Does it matter that he is snugly secured in a climber's harness and attached to superbly engineered "life support"

A checklist for working through your fears of changing.

The alternative to this uncertain world is a certain world. In such a world ... all life would stop. For life as we know it can only exist through the blessing of uncertainty, and security is a myth. Yet security is there. We feel its presence. But ... we must accept the uncertainty of our positions. Without that uncertainty, there is no world.   FRED ALAN WOLF, *TAKING THE QUANTUM LEAP*

lines that will carry him to safety on this twenty-second "ride of his life"? Not at first. Poised there on the brink of decision, he experiences something akin to what everyone—carp, shark, or dolphin—must experience when it comes time to do something substantially, radically different. He feels fear.

He also feels a bit of irony: How many times has he faced audiences to talk about the strategy of the dolphin and run through the steps for confronting and surmounting "performance anxiety"? Numerous times. How many times has he addressed, sometimes rather glibly, what it's like to leave the comfort zone and plunge into the unknown, with all the trepidation it brings? Many times. And on those sundry occasions, what had he told them? Work through your fears. More than on any other occasion in his life, that advice now seems worth repeating.

- *Get clear on the desired outcome* ["Get it over with. Get over *there!* to the other side safely, proud of what I've done and inspired by the feat."]
- *Ask, "What entails the greater risk—moving ahead, or doing nothing?"* ["If I don't jump, how will I feel about myself? How will my colleagues feel about me? What will I have missed in missing this experience?"]
- *Ask, "If I move ahead, what's the worst thing that could happen?"* ["Maybe I'll faint or scream or look like Bossy the Cow falling out of the sky."]
- *Ask, "Am I willing to accept that?"* ["Nobody who has jumped off yet has looked like Evel Knievel."]
- *Ask, "If I succeed, what's the best thing that can happen?"* ["I will have undergone a tremendous personal experience, one that is certain to produce new confidence in my ability to push back self-imposed limits."]
- *Ask, "Am I willing to accept* that?" ["Probably. Yeah, I guess so."]
- *Ask, "Why haven't I taken this risk before?"* ["Because I had a good reason: People in their 'right' minds don't go jumping off cliffs."]

An essential characteristic of intelligent life is that it seeks to protect its own life and well-being.
CHARLES T. TART, *WAKING UP*

- *Ask, "How did my avoiding this risk serve me?"* ["Normally, jumping off a 165-foot cliff kills you. The fact that I haven't made a practice of doing so has no doubt saved my life."]
- *Ask, "Why have more choice now?"* ["Jumping under these conditions will help me better to understand viscerally the concept of risk and support. Now, enough questions—just do it!!"]

And so he jumped. The first twenty feet were free-fall, and for the first time in his life, he perceived directly what it is like to be totally unsupported for that kind of a gap in time and space.

Then the support system caught. He bounced riotously for a moment, stabilized, and began his controlled descent to safety. In the few seconds consumed by the ride across the canyon, his brain changed. Forever.

Figure 6.7 is what the dolphin sees when he looks into "the pool" of self-directed change, when the risk of doing nothing outweighs the risk of doing something different. A dolphin understands that when the old wave surrenders potency, there is an alternative future that must be both discovered and created. In the process, there are salient emotions to be worked through, emotions in oneself and in others—emotions to be handled differently than they are handled by carps and sharks. Here is what dolphins do when they swim in the pool of release, seeking to discover and to create a new future:

Dolphins self-direct.

There's great freedom and exhilaration available in changing before the times.

For the dolphin, being able to choose and to act on one's choice feed self-esteem and help to transform the natural apprehension of confronting the unknown into a life-affirming occurrence.

Much of the "existential" fear triggered by a single human daring to question the entrenched status quo disappears from dolphin reality through the use of approaches and procedures already sketched at length in this book:

- *Identifying and articulating your purpose*—in life, in an organization, on a team, in the context of a given project or framework.
- *Developing a clearly stated "vision"* of how you will have it when you get it—a road map, a snapshot, a movie, a vehicle for establishing in matter what you have conceived as achievable in mind.
- *Being open to the future,* your antennae sensitized to output from both conscious and unconscious processing centers, to formulations of potential outside of ordinary perceptions, to eventualities being shaped by choices that as yet are but indistinct designs at the edges of awareness.
- *Cultivating a love affair with surprise:* Dolphins expect to be surprised. Without it, they understand that play for them is over. Dolphins see themselves as one of James Carse's infinite players. "Surprise," says Carse, "is the triumph of the future over the past."[4]

What dolphins do differently is that they know when to let go. That they are able to is because they understand the process of release.

Dolphins take responsibility for their emotions.

Self-directed change takes you out of your comfort zone. It removes you from "the flow." It places a strain on your relationships with other people, since you are having to leave your niche before others understand the need for it. All the fears of separation anxiety, of the unknown, can be expected.

Courage does not remove anxiety. Since anxiety is existential it cannot be removed. But courage takes anxiety of non-being into itself.... He who does not succeed in taking his anxiety courageously upon himself can succeed in avoiding ... despair only by escaping into neurosis.... Neurosis is the way of avoiding non-being by avoiding being.
PAUL TILLICH, *THE COURAGE TO BE*

Carps and sharks tend to surrender to their fears. And they tend to externalize responsibility for them. "They [or you or circumstances or events] are making me feel bad," they'll say.

Dolphins view feeling differently. Dolphins:

- don't waste a lot of time trying to blame their feelings on someone else.
- don't blame themselves for having feelings.
- don't try to deny feelings, knowing that if feelings are repressed, they can run your life, keeping you in constant reaction.
- don't ignore the fact that they are choosing to feel how they feel—that they are capable of feeling differently if they decide to.

Dolphins analyze their feelings as did one of your authors as he experienced the fear of plunging off a canyon wall.

Second, they recognize their feelings for what they are—fears in this case—and allow them to build, to peak, and to pass.

When feelings aren't dealt with responsibly, what ensues is drama. Conflict. Acrimony.

And when drama is raging, the project, the organization, the team, the family are hemorrhaging. Energy is being lost, plus time and usually resources.

Drama rages in the absence of responsibility. With no one willing to respond appropriately, the scene just goes round and round. Here's what it takes to create drama:

A persecutor: "Johnny, I told you that if you were late one more time, you'd go to bed without your dinner. And boy, I've had it—that's exactly where you're going."

A victim: "You never pick on Susan this way, Dad. It's always me."

A rescuer: [In this case Mom, who sneaks Johnny his dinner on a tray.]

At any point, the developing drama can be interrupted and discontinued by any of the individuals involved taking personal responsibility for acting appropriately. But don't count on it. When we are caught up in drama, it's like having hold of a

Any student of the rise and fall of cultures cannot fail to be impressed by the role played in this historical succession by the image of the future. The rise and fall of images precedes or accompanies the rise and fall of cultures. As long as a society's image is positive and flourishing, the flower of culture is in full bloom. Once the image begins to decay and lose its vitality, however, the culture does not long survive. FRED POLAK, *THE IMAGE OF THE FUTURE* high-voltage wire: It's powerfully difficult to let go. When participants in drama have exhausted the potential in one scene, they tend to switch roles and begin a new one:

Mom: "I really think that was a rotten thing to do to Johnny, Allen." [The new persecutor.]

Dad: "Geez, Jennifer, I was just trying to be a good father." [The new victim.]

Johnny: "Come on, Mom, get off Dad's back—he was just trying to do the best he could." [The new rescuer.]

Dolphins avoid drama by being responsible not only for their actions but also for their feelings—and they allow others to be responsible for theirs. When strong emotions are triggered in others during the change process, dolphins grant the same courtesy that they provide themselves: They permit others to have feelings. They decline to engage in drama: no persecutors, no victims, no rescuers. Just feelings, which usually are temporary. Feelings accepted with the understanding that this is how the other person is choosing to feel right now, whether or not those feelings would seem to be justified by the "facts."

Dolphins are prepared to live with "lag."

Dolphins "psych" themselves for entering the zone of self-directed change by surrendering to challenge, to novelty, to uncertainty. The act of surrender is exhilarating. Possibility floods in like a tidal wave, and dolphins grasp that early in their quest to find a new wave—to perturbate, to discover a new future—they are vulnerable to the emotions of *naive enthusiasm*.[5] Call it the "honeymoon" period. Fueled by the elation of new prospects, dolphins understand that they are vulnerable to forecasting the moon and expecting it. But reality tends to strike soon enough, and that initial enthusiasm gives way to a *rude awakening*—the gateway to a very dangerous time for the prospects of significant change.

The Cosmos is about the smallest hole that a man can hide his head in.
G. K. CHESTERTON

Some carps may get this far on the self-directed change curve. Sharks may also, particularly those flirting with or aspiring to dolphinhood. But at the point of informed pessimism the greatest stress is encountered. Here most people drop out of any attempt to catch the new wave.

Why? It is still too early. The stresses aren't great enough to cause perturbation—the brain's leap to a higher order, to a new configuration, one that permits a more elegant outcome, one that empowers doing more with less. Never is a person's satisfaction at what they are doing at a lower ebb. Results are continuing to drop, and expenses are climbing. Criticism usually is rampant. Now we can see clearly why you need to be crystal-clear about what your purpose is. Without the strength of an unshakable belief in who you are and what your enterprise is about, it is easy, ever so easy, at this point simply to give up.

Don't! Don't destroy the possibilities by letting emotions sear the capillaries of the future shut at the very moment when you and your team may be about to come face to face with the basic generative forces of creation. Every novelist understands this, and every scriptwriter, every folklorist teller of epic tales who has ever lived: The phoenix rises only from the ashes. The new order emerges only because the old was subject to intense energy beyond its capacity and was transformed.

Dolphins know that the emotional road between a *rude awakening* and *somewhat hopeful* is littered with the dead, abandoned carcasses of half-born dreams. By staying the course, staying with their purpose, self-correcting constantly, being responsible, using the brain's powers for breaking set, going for synergy, they stay focused, expecting at any moment to "pop," to perturbate, to identify their niche in the new wave. And often that is the result.

Mirabile dictu! There is light at the end of the tunnel, and for the first time it doesn't look like a train.

> In science . . . the process of prediction is conscious and rational. Even in human beings this is not the only kind of prediction. Men have sound intuitions which have certainly not been analyzed into rational steps, and some of which may never be. It may be, for example, as is sometimes claimed, that most people are a little better at guessing an unseen card, and some people much better than would be a machine, which merely picks its answers by chance. This would not be altogether surprising. . . . Certainly evolution has selected us rapidly because we do possess gifts of foresight much above those of other animals. . . . The rational intelligence is one such gift, and it is at bottom as remarkable and as unexplained. And where rational intelligence turns to the future and makes inferences from past experiences to an unknown tomorrow, its process is . . . a great mystery. . . . JACOB BRONOWSKI

If they have a choice (and usually they do), dolphins always opt for abundance.

The swiftest way to get into "the flow" of the new wave is to go for Breakthrough. Playing Breakthrough as opposed to playing

Get-out, Give-in, Takeover, or Trade-off nearly always creates abundance, not scarcity, when you are dealing with the critical ''20 percent'' that really matters in a must-change situation.

To move past the point that we call *on track* in Figure 6.7—the point where you are starting to get significant results—toward the *steady output* zone of the wave—the zone where mastery and challenge commingle into ''the flow''—dolphins employ a trio of almost superordinate processes or principles:

- *They strive for cooperation over competition* or going it alone. This gives them sometimes astonishing leverage, often with only miserly resources.
- *They push for creative outcomes.* This frees them from the limitations of the past.
- *They aim at doing more with less.* The quest for elegant outcomes establishes itself as an inducement to examine every possible technique, technology, and idea for achieving what is needed with less than was previously required.

It is the road less traveled, but if you begin, in the discovery sense, you already are there.

Traveling this way is the dolphin's *pièce de résistance*.

Why isn't the route more heavily traveled? We may find the nub of the problem in Figure 6.8.[6]

*I*t's one of the medical marvels of the twentieth century, a technique for dissolving tooth decay rather than drilling it out. When researchers at Northwestern University's dental school asked a sampling of dental patients to choose between the techniques, they learned that 60 percent preferred the new approach over the old. Silently, painlessly, and effectively, dentists can remove cavities with a chemical—called Caridex—without using their feared hypodermic needles and their awkward, tooth-scorching, high-speed rotary drills. ''Even so, we suspect very

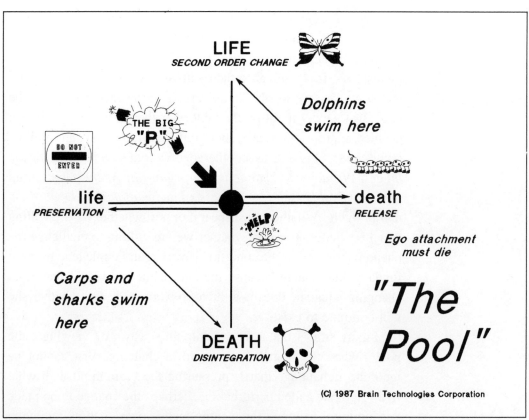

Figure 6.8.   The Essence of Release

few dentists are using it on their patients,''
said psychologist Robert Moretti. Asked why,
Moretti provided a profound insight into why
people don't change easily, even when there
are compelling reasons for doing so. "Dentists
are generally a conservative lot and I think
because drilling has been part of dentistry
since the very beginning and because many
identify with that procedure, *giving it up would require a
difference in the way they see themselves* [italics ours].''

Surrendering to change means seeing ourselves differently.

Hear, hear!

Astonishing though his explanation for the foot-dragging of
much of the dental profession is, Moretti has fingered a universal
truism: Change is often a threat to a person's vital self-estimate.

Even a seemingly minor and thoroughly advantageous thing like replacing dental drills with a better technique for removing cavities appears to be a threat to how numerous dentists see themselves. It is a threat to their self-formulation of who they are and what they are worth. To use Freud's term, it is a threat to the ego. Best we get it out on the table, whether or not it is a subject deemed appropriate to talk about outside of churches and philosophy classrooms and psychotherapeutic conferences. *One of the biggest obstacles to change in the organization, the family, and the individual herself is a fear associated with the Big D word—a fear of dying.* Whether we suspect it or not, whether we are willing to acknowledge it or not, whether we are willing to challenge the phenomenon or not, the condition is very real: People tend to resist fundamental change because the ego of the individual fears that changing what she does is a threat to who she is and whether she will continue to exist.

Figure 6.8 is one way—a dolphin's way—of viewing "the pool" when the brain is faced with a challenge that cannot be ignored, a challenge that is pressuring the brain/mind with what Ilya Prigogine called perturbation. Perhaps the change to be made is adopting a new ego-threatening technology, such as removing cavities with chemical "etching" as opposed to dental drilling. Or something even more momentous, such as choosing to abandon the religion of your childhood or change careers or enter into a divorce or reorganize your company or take an entrepreneurial risk or a courageous, future-altering stance.

In Figure 6.8 resides the essence of a deep wisdom that is central to every great spiritual path and epiphany, every efficacious theory of psychological healing and growth, every significant change of direction in the practice of business and even—as Prigogine has demonstrated—in the reordering processes of change underlying Mother Nature's migration to higher and higher complexity.

A failure to understand the nature of change is crippling to many of the world's billions.

That most of the world's human billions

still haven't "gotten it" is appalling testimony to the crippling powers of the carp brain's hypnosis and the shark brain's addictions.

Consider the situation of a struggling entrepreneur, one for whom all growth thus far has been self-financed. Siphoning off moneys each month from his wife's income as a nurse and supplementing it with his own income as a free-lance accountant, he has developed a new computer program for streamlining cost estimating for small construction companies.

Admirers tell him that his approach is state of the art. Encouraged, he has engaged a commercial artist to design a brochure and has mailed thirty thousand expensive, four-color brochures to small contractors in the lower forty-eight continental states.

That was sixty days ago. For several days, he hurried to the post office to check his mail. Now he clings to very little hope at all: His expensive mailing has produced exactly five inquiries.

His printing bill is due, and because he paid the mailing house in advance and ordered 250 sets of his computer program from a software producer, his funds are exhausted. In terms of Figure 6.8, the conditions for the Big "P"—perturbation—are rapidly developing. The vehicle that has brought him this far—his vision, his worldview, his brain programming, his little business, and his means and methods for getting ahead—is threatened.

Serious times. Where should he turn? How can he possibly feed his family, much less pay his debts and survive?

In short, what is he going to do?

The answer: It depends. It depends on whether he acts as a carp, a shark, or a dolphin. It depends on whether he opts for little "life" or little "death." On whether he seeks to preserve the old order or release to a new one. Using Figure 6.8, let's track the possibilities:

The Carp Scenario: Remember that a carp believes, "I can't win.'' Therefore, if and when the Big ''P'' strikes, the natural instinct of the carp is to give in, get out, and if necessary sacrifice himself.

In terms of Figure 6.8, carps invariably head for little ''life,'' where the risks appear to be minimal, where there seems to be hope that the few cards still remaining can be clutched tightly to the vest. If our fledgling entrepreneur responds as a carp, he'll likely abandon hope and, filled with the neurochemicals of defeat, seek the shelter of sympathy and the familiar.

What he may not realize is that it will not be a comforting harbor for very long. Debts are mounting. Creditors are knocking. Financial ruin looms. Thus what may have first appeared to be a perservative action quickly begins to degenerate toward disintegration, toward big ''DEATH,'' in terms of this particular episode and opportunity. Before long, the carp finds himself moving rapidly toward a major collapse of intents and purposes—a collapse with little expectation of recovery.

At this point, carps typically opt for an ''out'' from among the following:

- *Blame.* Shifting the responsibility to someone else gets you out of the line of fire.
- *Shame.* Beating up on yourself is another way of denying personal responsibility for doing something different.
- *Justify.* Coming up with a good rationalization equips you to explain to others why it was okay to fail.

Whichever route is chosen, the carp again concludes, ''There's just no way to win.''

The Shark Scenario: Believing that he has to win, a shark will confront the prospect of the Big ''P'' with a flurry of activity. Not a necessarily well-thought-out, well-planned skein of action— just activity. Until now, the thought of failing has never troubled the shark mind. Thoughts of failure are for those who lack intestinal fortitude—for carps!

The shark thinks: ''When a winner commits, there is no

turning aside, even momentarily. Whatever it takes, those are your dues for coming out on top. Forget any thoughts of anything but a win, no matter who gets bounced around. *When the going gets tough, the tough get going!''*

Thus when the mailing fails, the shark gets even more narrowly focused on "the kill." Rather than doing something different, the shark does "more of the same harder" and thus just pushes himself farther down the back side of the wave.

There is a reputation to preserve. Well, actually not so much a reputation at this point, but a self-fabricated image that he has encouraged among family, friends, and colleagues. That talk about a million dollars in sales this year, two million next year, and five million by the end of year three, that boasting and high-five fervor and adrenaline-flavored jiving are now on the line. The shark's self-talk goes this way: "It's time to put it on the line, time to find out what kind of stuff I'm really made of, time to take some *real* risks, time to show some folks, time to do what I do best, time really to pull out all the stops."

So thinking, the shark heads in the same fatal direction as the carp, toward small "life," toward preservation, toward the very posture that, in a rapidly changing environment, markedly diminishes one's chances for survival.

Under pressure, sharks also head toward preservation— toward "small life."

How can we say the shark is also headed toward preservation in the face of all that frantic activity, that steely determination to win at all costs, that willingness to go against the steepest odds?

Because these qualities are among the very qualities that, fueled by addictive, "must win" neurochemicals, keep people from learning. When you aren't learning, you are arguing for your limits. When you argue for your limits, you get to keep them. When you keep your limits, you preserve the status quo. And in times of rapid change, preserving the status quo is usually not a viable option. But if learning is to be our goal, how do we go about learning from a failed promotional effort involving thirty thousand brochures promoting a software package for small contractors? For insights here, we turn in earnest to how the dolphin views change and failure, for the two are intimately and inextricably linked.

The Dolphin Scenario: So the mailing failed. Something's wrong.

Disappointed?

You bet.

Gonna quit?

Too early to tell. Don't know yet what went wrong.

What are you going to do now?

First I'm going to see if I can figure out why I didn't get it right the first time. Then I'm going to see what kind of choices I can create.

It really looks like you messed up good.

It does, doesn't it.

Bet all those people who told you this program'll go great guns in the marketplace were just pulling your leg?

That has to be a possibility.

You didn't do any test-marketing, did you?

Nope.

That's pretty dumb, isn't it?

Sure looks like you have a point.

You could have at least tried a small mailing first?

Could have. Appreciate the suggestion. I'll probably do that next time.

You're terribly undercapitalized, you know.

Tell me about it.

Really in a hole now, aren't you?

For sure, something's got to give.

Already lost your shirt. Now you're going to lose your house and probably your wife and kids, eh?

Oh, probably not.

Not much of a way to start a promising business, is it?

It certainly gives one pause.

I bet it's the mailing house's fault. They sold you a bad list.

The list looked good to me, but it's something I'm going to take another look at.

You're probably awfully hacked at that brochure designer.

I liked the brochure. But since something's wrong, I'll look at that, too.

You don't have a prayer. How about I buy your computer program—pay you a couple of thousand dollars—and you can at least pay off some of your debts?

Thanks, but it's a little early to think about bailing out.

Doesn't look to me like you've got much choice.

I can appreciate that it might look that way.

But be honest: Just what choice have you got?

Well, I'm not sure this is going to mean anything to you, but I've got a choice of giving up a lot and hunkering down or giving up a little and pushing the envelope. Maybe you could say I've got a choice of staying a caterpillar or trying it as a butterfly.

I don't get it.

It's not important.

But what's a butterfly got to do with computers?

Nothing, really. It's just a metaphor.

Metaphor?

Yeah, a metaphor to remind me that inside every butterfly there's a caterpillar that succeeded in letting go.

Butterflies? Caterpillars? You sound to me like you are one more confused fellow.

How right you are! That's where I'm at right now—the confusion part of the change and discovery process.

Then what?

We'll see in the next chapter as we examine how a dolphin self-directs the learning and change process to "escape" from conditions and a mind-set that aren't producing the needed results to ones that create the opportunity to succeed.

In this case, the entrepreneur decided to write a press release himself and placed it on an electronic "bulletin board." This resulted in a story in a computer trade journal that later lead to the sale of his system to a major software marketer.

DOLPHIN WORK

Exercise No. 1

The very act of reading *Strategy of the Dolphin* has likely triggered ideas about areas of your life, career, and business involvement that you'd like to change.

Now is as good a time as any to identify the most important one. On a separate sheet of paper record what it is.

Now take time to respond in writing to the following questions:

1. Specifically, what is the result/outcome I need from making this change?
2. What is the risk of not making this change?
3. What is the worst that could happen if I attempt this change and fail?
4. Am I willing to accept that?
5. What is the best that could happen if I succeed?
6. Am I willing to accept *that*?
7. Why haven't I taken this risk before, and how did not taking it serve me?
8. Why have more choice now?

Exercise No. 2

To open up wider choice on the issue you defined for yourself or any other issue important to you, determine to spend the time required to complete this exercise in futuring:

During the next week, be alert to information that touches on your priority issue, need, or desire. Take some time to pursue new information in libraries, talking with friends and colleagues, reading media materials at home and the office, and using any other available source that will provide new input on technological, social, environmental, or economic shifts or influences that are probable in the future.

At the end of your week, on a separate sheet of paper, briefly list the findings that seem most important to you.

Now jot down any similarities you see (these may be the most valuable results of your research):

In a place that offers privacy and calm, take some time to review your research results and think about your priority areas of concern. Listen to your intuition. Take your feelings seriously. Allow your mind to make movies of how the future will be.

After a while, make yourself some additional notes. What did your intuition—your "gut feelings"—tell you?

Now respond to the following guidelines:

"These are things both my reason *and* my intuition agree will probably happen."

"These are things both my reason *and* my intuition agree will probably not happen."

"These are things about which my reason *and* my intuition disagree."

The items where your reason and intuition agree are most likely good information from the future.

Where there is disagreement between your reason and intuition, it is appropriate to gather more information.

The process of developing an openness to the future requires forebrain thinking on *both* the rational and intuitive levels.

(Thanks to futurist David Loye for the basic idea for this exercise.)

7

ORCHESTRATING PERTURBATION: HOW DOLPHINS "PUSH THE ENVELOPE"

*I*n the sense that he has spent part of his adult life prowling through the "Breakthrough" Zone at the edge of space, aviator Chuck Yeager thinks like a dolphin. He and his high-flying colleagues—some still living, some long since claimed by accidents of God and audacity—pierced the skies over the Mohave Desert in the late 1940s, going where humans had never gone, doing what humans had never done. In their attempts to break "Mach 1," the speed of sound, in exotic machines like the Bell X-1 experimental aircraft, Yeager and his colleagues provided a prototype experience for what it's like to go against the unknown and a memorable way of referring to such episodes. Today, when we crowd against our limits in any kind of challenge, adventure, or exploit, it is not uncommon to hear ourselves speak of "pushing the envelope."

For Yeager, pushing the envelope meant seeking to exceed the speed of sound. More was involved than just flying faster than Mach 1—approximately 700 miles per hour. Pushing the envelope in the high skies at high speeds posed a dangerous, idiosyncratic set of control problems. Crack fliers that they were, the X-1 pilots quickly learned to their fascination and occasional panic that pushing the envelope violated instincts honed by years at the

You accept risk as part of every new challenge; it comes with the territory. So you learn all you can about the ship and its systems, practice flying it on ground runs and glide flights, plan for any possible contingency, until the odds against you seem more friendly. You like the X-1; she's a sound airplane, but she's also an experimental machine, and you're a researcher on an experimental flight. You know you can be hammered by something unexpected, but you count on your experience, concentration, and instincts to pull you through. And luck. Without luck.... CHUCK YEAGER, *YEAGER: AN AUTOBIOGRAPHY*

204

controls. Near the speed of sound, the stalwart craft's controls did not respond predictably. To keep the X-1 from tumbling out of control, a new world of flight had to be mapped, new responses developed, and new routines mastered.

"Pushing the envelope" originated with the aviation pioneers pursuing Mach 1.

Pushing the envelope is a dolphin's world. It is a set of skills and intuitions that offers something valuable to families, organizations, and societies contending for the first time with the rigors of rapid information exchange on a global scale. Routinely and consistently challenging your limits—the limits of your own thinking, acting, and feeling, limits posed by your own brain—requires a strategic kind of reversal in the way humans ordinarily go about the process of personal change. Drawing metaphorically on Chuck Yeager's experiences with Mach 1, we can say that pushing the envelope requires that *we* exert control over the environment outside the brain, manipulating it so it will force the controls *inside* the brain to shift. Orchestrating such circumstances repeatedly in the interest of doing something vitally new and different often goes against the mind's natural instincts, against most advice from others, against the clock, and against other competing forces. Pushing the envelope compels the dolphin to create a new understanding of how to go about changing one's mind. To appreciate the dolphin's approach, let's examine her view of "the pool" as depicted in Figure 7.1.

A strategic kind of reversal in the way humans go about changing.

R ecall once more our fledgling entrepreneur whom we left being rather intensely questioned at the end of the previous chapter. He had done something different—introduce a new product to market—and the initial response had been discouraging. What now?

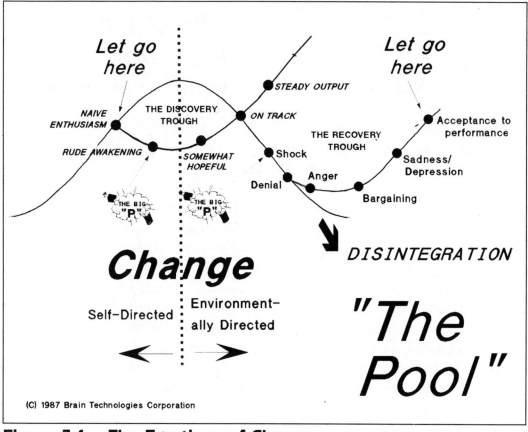

Figure 7.1. The Emotions of Change

Traditionally in such circumstances, human consciousness has often responded by waiting until the situation is grim and perhaps hopeless and then traveling what we call the Recovery Trough, which you again see pictured in Figure 7.1. The salient features of this painful route for reacting to the unexpected and the unknown are these:

- **The environment is in control.** There is no changing before the times. You are in reaction. You are waiting until something happens and only then do you respond, and that response is more or less automatic, a preprogrammed routine of debilitating emotions. When it kicks in, this "survival kit" for consciousness affords little room for pro-active strategies—at least not until it has consumed substantial energy.

- **You may ignore several rounds of warning signs.** Unrecognized by you, the problem may have been worsening for some time. Because you lack purpose and vision, any forewarned sense of danger or concern and any resilient, learn-as-you-go approach for moving forward on the problem, your mind is exceedingly vulnerable to the Boomerang Effect illustrated in Figure 7.2. The longer you ignore the problem, the lower you plunge on the wave, and the greater the pressures to be worked through when reality and recognition hits. Because of the Boomerang Effect, your first reaction is likely to be one of opposites—that is, you are likely to respond contrarily to what

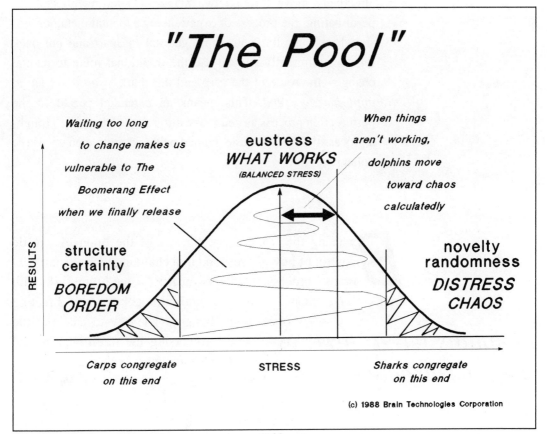

Figure 7.2. The Boomerang Effect

you have been doing, overreacting at that. This kind of response almost never proves satisfactory. Eventually in a rapid-change world *you* are going to have to change if you intend to remain a viable participant, and because of the route to change you have selected, you may be at the mercy of boomerang forces for an extended period, bouncing back and forth between order and chaos.

- **Not until the very end of the Recovery Trough do you "let go," freeing yourself or your organization to try something new, to look for new solutions and opportunities.** Remember Ilya Prigogine's process of releasing to a higher order of complexity? To emerge from this process successfully, capable of catching the new wave and riding in "the flow," you must effectively move through two stages: (1) letting go and (2) perturbating, the process of experiencing a mental metamorphosis where, literally, your mind gets taken apart and put back together differently. If you use the traditional route to mental change—the route of the carp and the shark—you don't let go *until the very end.* This means an extended period in the perturbation process as you move through the Recovery Trough, a process that guarantees extended pain and protracted unease or unhappiness.

*B*y using the frontal lobe powers of the brain to wrestle control of how we respond to a changing world from "old brain" processing centers, at least some brains—dolphin brains—have created a new mental protocol for self-directing one's own changes. The key to catching the new wave is reversing the traditional human response to an encounter with the unknown.

Look at Figure 7.1 again. Notice the reversal in the change process when you are changing as dolphins change, ahead of the times. Unlike carps and sharks, dolphins let go

Dolphins let go first, then perturbate— just the reverse of carps and sharks.

first, *then* perturbate. This way, the emotional dynamics of change are stood powerfully on their head. Instead of tendering a debilitating blockage with extended pain, emotions are freed to serve as directional indicators, as measures of elegance and effectiveness, as barometers of purpose. There is still pain, but it is swift, it is predictable, and, above all, it is meaningful and purposeful because it is you, internally, and not the environment, externally, who have determined that things must change. Self-initiating your own changes makes a world of difference.

To travel the dolphin's self-directed route to change, a participant begins by:

> When you finish a creative project, something that has consumed you for some time, it's like the end of a love affair. SUZANNE EICH-HORN

- *Being open to information arriving from the future and identifying the need to change.* Signs from the future may first arrive on the movie screen of your own consciousness or on someone else's screen. Dolphins aren't particular where future-run movies are shown; they just don't want to miss the opening. For this reason, you will want discipline your mind to scan both internally and externally.
- *Confronting the fears of letting go.* A step-by-step process for achieving this was suggested in the previous chapter (in fact, the entire chapter deals with such fears and such processing). To recap, our fears of letting go are usually rooted in these anxieties:

    —A fear that if you change you will be abandoned by those closest to you, a kind of *separation anxiety.*

    —A fear that if you try something new, you may fail, a kind of *performance anxiety.*

    —A fear that if you change your way of viewing the world, you will die, an *existential anxiety.*

For the carp, the shark, and to some extent the pseudo-enlightened carp, these fears are experienced almost totally at the unconscious level, a resistance so tenacious that it requires the lengthy pummeling of the Recovery Trough before an individual can let go. The existential fear that you will die—that you will disappear if you let go, if you change—calls to mind comments by grief expert Elisabeth Kübler-Ross in Kyoto, Japan, at the Ninth Conference of the International Transpersonal Association:

> I did not know [when I started my work with the terminally ill] what the meaning of a butterfly was. I was very touched by one poem, which said that man does not understand butterfly and butterfly does not understand man. That is where I was in 1945. In the next twenty-five years, man will understand butterfly and butterfly will understand man.

> We use the symbol of the butterfly when we work with dying children and they ask us what happens when they die. We do not tell them that you go to sleep. We do not tell them that you go to heaven. We use [a] universal language and tell them that you are not really what you seem to be. Your body is like a cocoon and when this cocoon gets damaged beyond repair, what happens is that it simply releases the butterfly that is much more beautiful than a cocoon.

Kübler-Ross has an intriguing name for life's perturbative moments: *windstorms*. She describes a windstorm as "one of the things that you will remember at the moment of your death." She says:

> There will be only two things that will be important at the moment of your death that you will think about. They are the beautiful moments and the windstorms. . . . [Windstorms] are meant to prepare you for life.

There is still much to be learned about the circumstances circumscribing death. The brain/mind studies that inspire *Strategy of the Dolphin* suggest strongly that what an individual can expect to experience in death will be determined by what kind of "window" that person prepared in life. And that is perhaps what Kübler-Ross is saying. If so, then dolphins can expect to relive

We have learned that most of the work of the brain is done completely unconsciously, and we have come to have a healthy respect for the quality and the complexity of the computing/control functions that are carried out this way. Even in what we consider to be our conscious mental activity, we are actually aware of only a part of what is going on in the brain. There must be intricate switching and scanning processes under way that move related thoughts successively into our consciousness; we are aware of the thoughts, but not of how they get there.   DEAN WOOLDRIDGE, *THE MACHINERY OF THE BRAIN* many windstorms because they will have generated many themselves. Because they understand the value of windstorms and what they can make happen, dolphins move through their fears of change very quickly, letting go. Then they can turn their energies, intuitive facilities, and abilities to make new things concrete to perturbating, the second and no less critical stage to be encountered in self-directing one's own changes.

Dolphins understand the value of windstorms—and getting over their fears quickly.

To understand the process of triggering one's own change-releasing, butterfly-freeing perturbations, we need again to view "the pool" from a dolphin's perspective, as we now do in observing Figure 7.3, a map to the brain made possible by two extraordinary surgeries:

*T*wice during the twentieth century, surgeons have cleaved living human brains into dual portions in procedures not entirely unlike cleaving a cantaloupe. In the earliest surgery, they severed the front portion of the brain in an attempt to bring relief to persons with severe psychosis. Later, in an effort to aid victims of *grand mal* seizures, they meaningfully separated the hemispheres of the brain. These drastic actions have enabled your authors to construct a guide to brain functioning useful in a variety of workaday enterprises—a guide we call The BrainMap. You see it pictured in Figure 7.3.

More than any other source of knowledge, the findings that underlie The BrainMap equip us to plot the origins of the carp and shark strategies biologically, although we do so with some caution.

The more we study the results of observing and testing "split brain" subjects, the more we realize that some of the earlier conclusions about what these results mean were erroneous: It is not so much separate brains-within-a-brain that these unparalleled

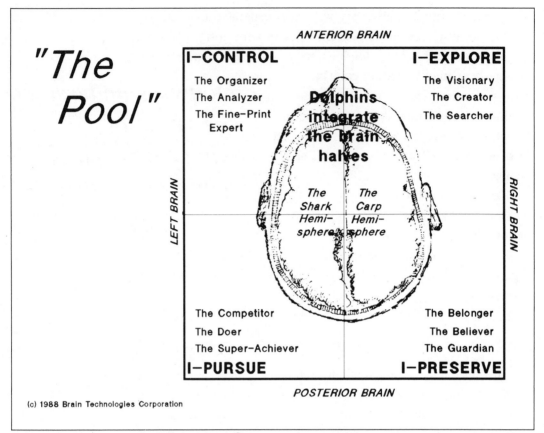

Figure 7.3.   The BrainMap®

Right brain, left brain: carp hemisphere, shark hemisphere.

surgeries have revealed but separate windows for observing a single brain of a thousand tricks, faces, and manifestations. When our window is the right brain—the right hemisphere—we see many of the symptoms of the carp. And when our window is the left brain, we see strong symptoms of the shark. Further valuable distinctions are possible when findings of the hemispheric commissurotomy—the left brain/right brain surgeries—are paired with findings of the prefrontal lobotomy or front brain/back brain surgeries. We have used this information to create the quadrants of The BrainMap® Self-Assessment Inventory: I-CONTROL, I-PURSUE, I-PRESERVE, and I-EXPLORE.

Typically, the worlds of professional training, sales and marketing, and management education have used The BrainMap model to aid with such needs as encouraging teamwork, building interpersonal communications skills, assessing career goals, and identifying information processing style.

For these purposes, all of which involve alerting individuals and groups to the current "face" individuals and their organizations place on reality, The BrainMap typically works well. But if this is the only use to which it is placed, then the deeper gains of this charting of brain functioning have been neglected. Carps miss this truth because of their hypnosis—their filters and their fears. Sharks miss it because of their addiction to chaos and crisis; they swim right past it. In contrast, dolphins swim directly into the knowledge that catching the new wave nearly always requires putting parts of the brain temporarily at war with themselves. Prior to the availability of the split-brain information, this process was just something that some persons—dolphins—did. With The BrainMap model, what was mostly art before can now be accompanied by a measure of technique. Such an advance always opens up what was heretofore privileged territory to a larger population. Here is how the dolphin employs and deploys the power of brain-mapping in the interest of, literally, brain-zapping:

You start with a "signature" of how your brain has currently organized its resources.

Figure 7.4 is the result of a decade's worth of use of The BrainMap. More than any others, these eleven profiles have emerged when users of The BrainMap instrument score their results. Dolphins score all over the map, since "dolphinhood" is a function more of brain agileness and flexibility than brain dominance. Thus when a dolphin takes The BrainMap instrument, she may find any of these "signatures" emerging, a result of the blend of brain functions she has used to ride the wave from which she is now disconnecting.

A majority of The BrainMap's users learn that they are

But shouldn't the simple have already potentially encompassed the complex? Where were the seeds of complexity during the first minutes of the universe?...

We stand amazed before this frenzy of organization. Matter seems able to draw advantage from even the most adverse circumstances....

The organization of the universe demands that matter abandon itself to the games of chance. HUBERT REEVES, *ATOMS OF SILENCE*

"Harmónia" is an atunement of opposites, a unification of the many, a reconciliation of dissentients.... THEON OF SMYRNA

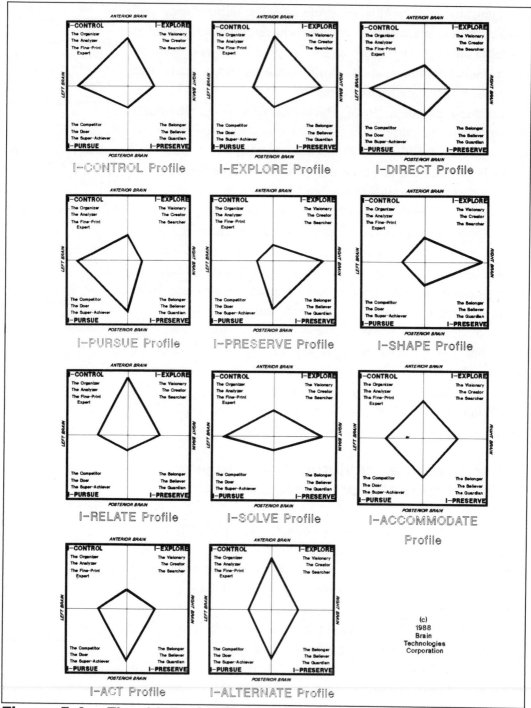

Figure 7.4. The 11 BrainMap Profiles

reflecting dominant brain functioning choices that are described by the model's quadrants: I-CONTROL, I-PURSUE, I-PRESERVE, and I-EXPLORE.

As pictured in Figure 7.3, the shark's hemisphere contributes two primary "systems" for vouchsafing an individual's world-view. The common denominator for the two is an ability to "storyboard" in the midst of disorder, charting and producing outcomes that are reasonably and logically anchored in current circumstances:

The I-CONTROL system is distinguished by

- a passion for facts and other information
- exacting standards for yourself and others
- an allegiance to trying harder, being better, getting smarter
- an insistence on order and systematic approaches

That is, I-CONTROL-oriented persons and groups prize their *knowledge*—their mastery of information—and build strong categories to pigeonhole the "facts" as they see them. They take great pride in this structure of knowing and defend it tenaciously. "I understand," says the individual; "therefore, I control."

The I-PURSUE system is distinguished by

- a sense of aliveness and self-worth that is tied to the freedom to react in correspondence to breaking events and prevailing urges
- an attraction to tools that make things happen
- a randomness that brings mobility
- competitiveness and immediate consequences

That is, I-PURSUE-oriented persons and groups have strong, immediate desires and find the chase is at least as real and rewarding as the capture. "I want," says the individual; "therefore, I act."

W hen taking its cues from the carp hemisphere, this holistic brain of ours produces two systems capable of seeing the world in "cartoon" fashion—at attaching meaning and significance to people, events, and situations on the basis of brief, swift insights and assessment of what is often a paucity of information:

The I-PRESERVE system is distinguished by

- seeing things in black and white, with a minimum of grays in between
- mental and emotional commitment to conserving what you believe in, caring for it and establishing strong bonds to it
- folding today's realities quickly back into a vision of what is right, moral, ethical, true, and time-proven
- spontaneity in situations involving people you care for

That is, I-PRESERVE-oriented persons and groups volunteer to serve as the guardians of tradition, cultures, values, and mores. "I respect," says this individual; "therefore, I defend."

The I-EXPLORE system is distinguished by

- dealing in possibilities, not in sureties
- being ahead of the times and often having to wait for others to catch up
- responding to variety—insisting on it, in fact
- seeing self as visionary and idea-oriented, with the ability to entertain novelty

That is, I-EXPLORE-oriented persons and groups relish putting together new perspectives for viewing, arranging, and explaining things. "I envision," says this individual; "therefore, I expect."

Referring again to Figure 7.4, we see that there are seven additional profiles. In the late 1970s, when researchers at Brain Technologies first began to test The BrainMap, there was no mention of profiles such as I-RELATE, I-ALTERNATE, I-SHAPE, and I-DIRECT in our interpretations of The BrainMap. Frankly, we had no idea they existed. But as the quantity of our research subjects grew, it became apparent that small yet significant numbers of brains conceptualize their worlds using these special-case profiles:

I-ALTERNATE

"I saturate; therefore, I shift."

This profile indicates intense mood and interest swings between highly "intellectual" periods and times of spontaneous pleasure-seeking as you alternately saturate first in one "state of mind" and later in the other.

I-SOLVE

"I puzzle; therefore, I resolve."

A BrainMap user with this profile is strongly attracted to problem-solving for its own sake but may have little interest in the social or individual uses of its results.

I-RELATE

"I empathize; therefore, I connect."

A person with this BrainMap signature is comfortable with

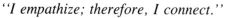

both technical and people aspects of high-complex tasks and situations.

I-ACT

"I sense; therefore, I proceed."

This profile describes a person who possesses an inbred sense of urgency and a preference for acting on "instinct."

I-DIRECT

"I persevere; therefore, I complete."

This profile suggests an individual with a compelling need to direct in order to accomplish tasks in an orderly, predictable, decisive way.

I-SHAPE

"I see; therefore, I adapt."

This is the BrainMap signature of a person with a lively interest in developing and promoting new ideas but only if they make sense in the context of one's current values or beliefs.

I-ACCOMMODATE

"I moderate; therefore, I reconcile."

If this is your standard BrainMap profile over an extended time span, you tend to be sensitive to the concerns and expectations of persons with other BrainMap profiles. (There is another possible interpretation for I-ACCOMMODATE, which will be discussed shortly.)

hen a dolphin is in "the flow" on the wave, his brain information processing signature serves primarily as knowledge to be used for fine-tuning. Whether the challenge is improving relationships, sales skills, presentation and public speaking effectiveness, use of time, or a myriad of other possibilities, the issue is being more competent wherever you are in the flow. But when the challenge is pushing the envelope, the use of information about your brain's current processing signature is very different. At this stage, fine-tuning is not the objective but rather perturbation. This time we *want* Humpty Dumpty to fall, and we have no intention of putting him back together again the way he was. Here is how dolphins proceed:

You push the envelope just enough to start the perturbation process.

[Bisociation is] an escape from boredom, stagnation, intellectual predicaments, and emotional frustration ... it is signalled by the spontaneous flash of insight which shows a familiar situation or event in a new light, and elicits a new response to it. The bisociative act connects previously unconnected matrices of experience; it makes us understand what it is ... "to be living on several planes at once." ARTHUR KOESTLER

It's called punctuated equilibrium. Think of it as a condition in which things work well and as planned for periods of time only to be followed by fruit-basket-turnover and turmoil after which, if the system survives, stability and equilibrium return once more.

It is Ilya Prigogine's genius that he has discovered and defined just such a process as the way by which all open systems of energy, including the human brain, change.

Prigogine has warned that:

- Change is not always positive. Especially if forced on you by the environment, perturbation can bring disintegration in place of transformation.
- Even if you avoid disintegration, the Boomerang Effect can unleash unhappy consequences. As we saw in Figure 7.2, the injection of extreme novelty into a situation that is overdue for change tends to create severe overreaction, thrusting the system toward the other pole. Even if the system—the brain, in this case—recovers and makes a shift, a lot of time is lost, energy

and resources are wasted, confusion is experienced, and pain is endured that could have been avoided.

It is just this devitalizing cycle that dolphins seek to elude. Significant is our discovery—call it our realization—of late that the invisible walls designating the compartments of open systems like the brain have the capacity to be "toughfrail" kinds of barriers.

When circumstances are such that they can do the job they were designed to do, these barriers to chaos are stalwart and resilient, performing estimably. But when it is time to perturbate, it is almost as if the brain of a dolphin suddenly commences the secretion of a psychic enzyme that converts those obdurate membranes into rubbery plastics capable of being molded into the next generation of possibility.

In working with groups where we routinely expect to find at least some dolphins, your authors have learned not to be surprised

The perturbating dolphin tests out I-ACCOMMODATE.

if The BrainMap identifies a dolphin who is perturbating. At first we didn't realize what we were seeing. In fact, The BrainMap signature that clues us to a possible perturbating brain mystified us considerably in the early going. It is the I-ACCOMMODATE profile, the "square" configuration connoting that there is little differentiation occurring among the four brain quadrants. Since our early confusion, we've developed great respect for the I-ACCOMMODATE signature. Now we realize that individuals who reside there permanently are often accomplished in dealing with the rest of us, at least in a reasonably routine workaday world. For the I-ACCOMMODATE-oriented person, the barriers and filters that may cause others of us to flee, rebel, attack, or show disinterest are not obstructions. The I-ACCOMMODATE style is often a very agile, productive, even creative mode of coping.

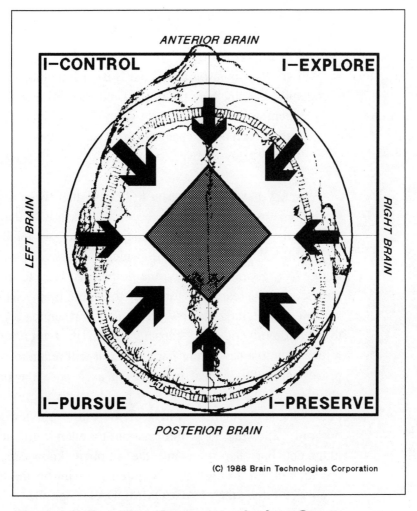

Figure 7.5. The Accommodation Stage

As we questioned dolphins who were testing out as I-ACCOMMODATE, however, we began to realize that at times something else was transpiring. The line of questioning often went more or less this way:

Us: "Does the I-ACCOMMODATE way of processing describe the way you have always been?"

Them: "Oh, no. I've always had very explicit thoughts on how things should be."

I had risen up to look into the jar, but now I was sunk in my chair, speechless. My eyes were fixed upon that jar as I tried to comprehend that these pieces of gunk bobbing up and down had caused a revolution, in physics and quite possibly changed the course of civilization. There it was.   STEVEN LEVY ON FINDING EINSTEIN'S BRAIN

Us: "You mean until recently one of the other BrainMap signatures would have fit you better?"

Them: "That's right."

Us: "This is just a guess, but is it possible that you are in the midst of something pretty fundamental right now?"

Them: "Like what?"

Us: "Like a major change in your values and worldview?"

Them: "How did you know?"

We now have every reason to believe that when a dolphin's brain prepares to perturbate, it becomes awash with that putative toughfrail "enzyme" and collapses into a temporary I-ACCOMMODATE condition, which we have portrayed in Figure 7.5. From this status, the dolphin is freed to try a lot of things quickly, searching for clues to a new brain configuration suitable for catching the new wave. This is when the brain begins to increase in cognitive capacity. Even if it recrystallizes or refocuses into a new BrainMap profile, it will retain the cognitive processing ability it had before even as it adds the processing abilities demonstrated by the new profile. This is also where the processing and cognitive filters of the old worldview collapse, not only allowing new information to enter without bias or judgment but also allowing the implicit knowledge of the previous profile to emerge as explicit knowing in the new. The likelihood that the I-ACCOMMODATE profile will be a permanent home for the dolphin is not a strong prospect. But for the moment, it *is* home, and the search for a new elegance can go forward.

Guided by The BrainMap, here are ways that a dolphin triggers the perturbative I-ACCOMMODATE mode:

By deliberately altering something you valued in the old mode.

If you were I-CONTROL before, give up some of your personal controls.

If you were I-PRESERVE, resign membership in some of your groups.

If you were I-EXPLORE, get intensely focused on something that is happening now, not in the future.

If you were I-PURSUE, relax. Be empty.

If you were I-DIRECT, put yourself in someone else's hands and let him shape you for a time.

If you were I-SHAPE, put yourself in someone else's hands and let him direct you for a time.

If you were I-RELATE, do something spontaneous and crazy.

If you were I-ACT, sign up for something with deadlines that you can't get out of.

If you were I-ALTERNATE, look for a long-range problem to solve.

If you were I-SOLVE, go tell it on the mountain.

If you were I-ACCOMMODATE, tell somebody else to fix it for a change.

By sampling activities in other profiles.

I-CONTROLLERS write books, research their genealogies, program computers, study, judge, teach, develop detailed plans.

I-PURSUERS run for office, are competitive in sports, hunt, track, manage things, act, dance, engage in endurance activities, give extemporaneous speeches.

I-PRESERVERS help people, volunteer, visit old haunts, keep personal journals and scrapbooks, join, laugh, take strong positions, and have strong feelings.

I-EXPLORERS paint, photograph, write poetry and science fiction, bike, sail, hike, jog, go to movies, seek out strange friends, try new techniques, move somewhere different, and follow their hunches.

By studying and emulating the strengths of others.

I-CONTROLLERS are good at:

- preferring verbal as opposed to visual methods of inquiry
- naming and labeling things
- computerizing
- marshaling methods that are strongly sequential and "digital"
- defusing emotions and providing time, materials, tools, and space for extended reflection, analysis, and model-building

I-PURSUERS are good at:

- injecting new stimuli at random and noting the results
- combining various ideas, approaches, components, or processes randomly and reacting spontaneously to the consequences
- taking action and basing the next round of action on reaction to the first round
- checking their fears and acting rapidly on reorganizing their awareness to eliminate the causes of those fears

I-PRESERVERS are good at:

- benefiting from games and other playful activities
- playing out their feelings on a topic or concern
- using memory
- being loyal and supportive of people they approve
- preserving past values, traditions, and culture
- establishing lasting relationships and ties
- finding and acting on the true power of beliefs

I-EXPLORERS are good at:

- producing breakthrough insights and ideas
- reframing

- setting a mood
- seeing relationships that are not obvious
- probing a wide range of possibilities
- trying new things
- quickening "exit stress" through the generation of choice

In the flow, the dolphin's goal is always "eustress"—positive stress, or stress that although it may be momentarily uncomfortable is capable of producing a positive outcome because it is self-generated and in alignment with an unswerving purpose.

But when the dolphin identifies a need to change, she generates "exit stress" by putting her brain in new and different situations and yet retaining a sense of balance, purpose, and vision.

Guided by a model like The BrainMap, she can preserve this sense of balance and yet be open to exploring and new choice-making.

You relax to a higher order.

Our choice of a name for the I-ACCOMMODATE profile was not by happenstance. We borrowed the term from psychologist Erik Erikson, who used it to describe a similar state of mind in which the mental furniture was basically being rearranged.

He also has provided us with a name for the brain's state of affairs when it is in the flow, enjoying the fruits of having perturbated successfully, having relaxed to a higher order, having caught the new wave. Though Erikson didn't use the model and language of open systems in his ideas on mind and brain change, he was very much in tune and in touch with some of the key fundamentals of exit stress, perturbation, and transformation to a higher order.

When we return to the assimilation stage, we are again acting strongly from our biases.

He subscribed to a kind of punctuated equilibrium theory of mind, and he called the relatively tranquil

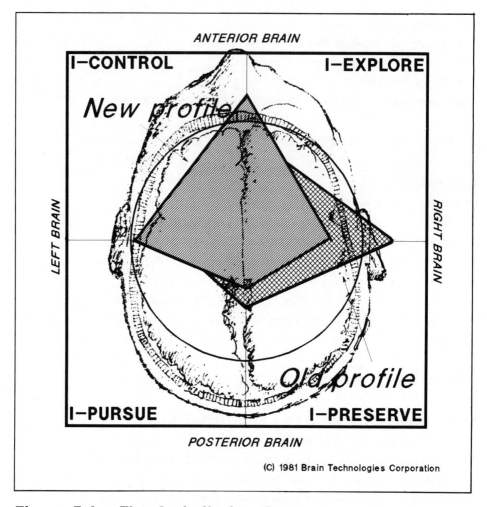

ANTERIOR BRAIN

I–CONTROL   I–EXPLORE

New profile

LEFT BRAIN

RIGHT BRAIN

Old profile

I–PURSUE   I–PRESERVE

POSTERIOR BRAIN

(C) 1981 Brain Technologies Corporation

Figure 7.6.   The Assimilation Stage

The mind is not a psychological entity but a sociological entity, being composed of many sub-mental systems. What can be done surgically and through hemisphere anesthetization are only exaggerated instances of a more general phenomenon. The uniqueness of man, in this regard, is his ability to verbalize and, in so doing, create a personal sense of conscious reality

stage—the flow stage—that follows perturbation by the name "assimilation." In the assimilation stage, there is absorption and incorporation of information along the lines of an obvious bias or focus.

Essentially, this is what The BrainMap does: It measures bias. In moving into the I-ACCOMMODATE mode, the dolphin's brain momentarily relaxes the viselike clutch of its biases or judgments. It creates confusion for itself as a way of opening up new choices, of discovering what works, of achieving new results, and of gaining new cognitive powers. Then, as Figure 7.6

suggests, there comes a time when it again makes sense to attach, to take up new focuses and deploy the newly won capabilities and configurations of the brain in the navigation of a new wave.

out of the multiple systems present. MICHAEL GAZZANIGA, *THE INTEGRATED MIND*

Some perturbations loom larger in our memories; others register hardly at all, so ordinary do they seem in the overall gyrations of our mental and emotional life.

As the dolphin progresses, perturbations large and small occur with growing frequency as "the system" that is the brain develops and refines its capacity and familiarity with self-change. In *Megabrain,* Michael Hutchison styled this quality of increasingly self-induced metamorphosislike activity as *autocatalytic* (meaning literally a "self-inducing and self-governing agent"). In time, the perturbations in the brain of a dolphin grow increasingly autocatalytic, meaning that less and less is it necessary for the dolphin to establish external conditions to coerce the brain into change. Assaying the need and seizing the moment, the dolphin brain increasingly perturbates on its own, spontaneously.

Each shift to a higher order brings new powers for dealing with complexity.

The consequences of continuous enrichment of a person's choice-creating and choice-making internal environment are suggested in Figure 7.7. Over time, a dolphin develops the capacity to operate efficiently and effectively in a wider and wider range, cultivating competence amid an increasing variety of worldviews and styles for coping and breaking through. As Figure 7.7 portrays, such a marshaling of skills and sensitivities involves the dolphin's balance of mastery on the one hand and challenge on the other.

Those two terms—mastery and challenge—emerged in the 1970s as buzzwords for an achievement-oriented genre of self-improvement called the "peak performance" movement. Numerous sharks and pseudo-enlightened carps rushed to try the positive mental attitude exercises, visualization strategies, calmness-inducing protocols, and stress-transforming practices and pronounced them powerful and transforming. Dolphins, however,

You cannot strengthen the weak by weakening the strong. You cannot build character by taking away man's initiative. You cannot help men permanently by doing for them what they could and should do for themselves. ABRAHAM LINCOLN

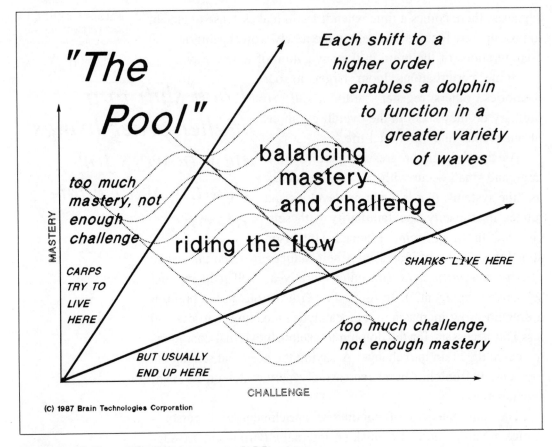

Figure 7.7. Challenge and Mastery

immediately recognized the deficiencies and dangers of the peak performance approach. Most glaringly absent in this philosophy, warmly embraced as it has been by corporate figures, publishers, and sports personalities, are these elements:

- **An understanding of perturbation.** Peak performers do not appreciate the raw power and strategic necessity of "mistakes." In the peak performance lexicon, a mistake is something to be accepted graciously, to be released and passed by as quickly as possible. For the dolphin, mistakes are tools to perturbate by.
- **Openness to the future.** Concentrating on the future, warn the advocates of peak performance, can open the gates of anxiety,

fear, and nervousness. Thus they counsel staying centered on the present to enhance calmness, relaxation, and an absence of pressure. No dolphin is about to succumb to such a strategy, knowing that in rapid-change times taking one's eye off the future is tantamount to flying blind and soon to flying blinded.

- **Openness to the past.** Just as they condemn orientation toward the future, so the peak performers frown on backward glances. A focus to the rear, they argue, invites the specter of guilt, anger, and frustration. Dolphins beg to differ, perceiving that a wealth of valuable experience is housed in the past.

- **A real sense of the wave.** Peak performers demonstrate a disconcerting innocence about the nature of reality. They recognize only the lure of abundance and seek to blot out the realness of scarcity. Dolphins understand that when the wave falters and plunges, no amount of "creating and utilizing positive images," no amount of "maintaining positive energy flow," and no amount of "achieving peak performance" will alter the actuality that a physical brain must now relax to a higher order or grow increasingly vulnerable. Dolphins have skills for transforming; peak performers, in considerable part because they lack a basic comfort and familiarity with the natural cycle of growth, are crippled by their inability to accept themselves performing constructively anywhere but at the peak.

We dwell at some length on the "peak performance" issue because it represents the heart of the failure to now of the consciousness movement to offer anything approaching genuine hardiness for coping powerfully and elegantly with change.

Because of its attraction to existential psychology, the movement—including the peak performers—has understood the importance of being committed to what you are doing, of taking responsibility for your own actions, of developing confidence in yourself and your inner resources. Much has been made of the peak performer's propensity for the three "Cs" of commitment, confidence, and control.

One "C," however, is missing; the most important "C" word

It has long been known that science is only one of the methods of studying the world around us. Another—complementary—method is realized in art. The joint existence of art and science is in itself a good illustration of the complementarity principle. You can devote yourself completely to science or live exclusively in your art. Both points of view are equally valid, but, taken separately, are incomplete. The backbone of science is logic and experiment. The basis of art is intuition and insight. But the art of ballet requires mathematical accuracy and, as Pushkin wrote, "Inspiration in geometry is just as necessary as in poetry." They complement rather than contradict each other. True science is akin to art in the same way as real art always includes elements of science. They reflect different, complementary aspects of human experience and give us a complete idea of the world only when taken together. Unfortunately, we do not know the "uncertainty relation" for the conjugate pair of concepts "science and art." Hence we cannot assess the degree of damage we undergo from a one-sided perception of life.   LEONID PONOMAREV, *IN QUEST OF THE QUANTUM*

Managing change and changing constitute two different worlds.

of all: *change*. Without the dolphin's understanding of the process of change, the peak performer is at best a shark seeking to convince others that she is "on porpoise" or a pseudo-enlightened carp benefiting from the happy circumstances of catching the wave prior to the peak with enough innate skills to ensure, at least for the moment, the ride of his life.

Balancing mastery and challenge using all the tricks—visualization, relaxation, self-talk, exercise, deep breathing, the works—of the peak performer's trade is a great way to convince ourselves and others that we are adept at "managing change."

But managing change and changing constitute two different worlds.

There is only the barest resemblance between what the shark and pseudo-enlightened carp (it really isn't an issue for the pure carp, who sees no prospect of winning) mean when they speak of balancing mastery and challenge and what the dolphin does. And what does the dolphin do?

Once more, quickly—he:

- monitors the future steadily
- learns constantly from the past
- searches for the appropriate response
- understands the dynamics of risk and stress
- anticipates lag
- lets go up front
- is open to purpose both as compass and barometer
- clearly articulates her vision
- self-corrects
- self-directs
- self-perturbates
- learns early
- learns quickly
- learns lastingly
- tells the truth with power to herself and to others
- uses mistakes to test the winds and the waters

- knows where he is
- knows where he is aiming
- knows where he is on the curve
- uses the power of flow
- uses the power of novelty
- uses the power of order
- decouples ego from failure and success
- avoids blame
- avoids shame
- avoids the need for self-justification
- avoids drama
- takes responsibility
- creates choice
- acts to expand the pool
- changes the meaning of events
- looks for alternatives
- does more with less
- does something different
- favors elegant solutions
- stands the heat if it matters
- gets out of the pool if it doesn't matter
- appreciates that not everyone can be a dolphin
- appreciates that not everyone wants to be a dolphin
- appreciates the good qualities of a carp
- appreciates when it makes sense to think like a shark
- believes in both scarcity and abundance
- believes in appropriate retaliation
- believes in immediate forgiveness
- believes we can all win most of the time
- knows how to use the power of brain parts
- knows how to use the whole brain
- accepts that there are some things he has no control over
- is open to surprise
- accepts responsibility for experiences and feelings
- can admit failure
- avoids stupidity

- goes for breakthrough
- understands that there is more to consciousness than dolphin consciousness
- appreciates caterpillars
- admires butterflies
- pushes the envelope

DOLPHIN WORK

A good general rule for a dolphin is that approximately 80 percent of our limits are self-imposed. To create more choice, we must change beliefs that limit us. Here is an exercise to help you identify things that have changed for you, and things that can.

Think of your childhood and teenage years and on a separate sheet of paper complete both parts of each of the following statements:

"I used to believe I couldn't . . . but now I believe that. . . ."

"I used to think I was . . . but now I know that I am. . . ."

"I used to think that I always should . . . but now I know that it's okay to. . . ."

"My greatest fear used to be . . . but now I feel. . . ."

In the second part of this exercise, think of your life in the future and complete the following on your sheet of paper:

In the future I will not be able to:

In the future I will be able to:

Looking back at both sets of information, what kind of trend do you see?

Are you becoming more or less limited?

How does your future compare with your past?

If you were to rewrite your beliefs to give yourself more choice, what would your new beliefs be?

Make notes for yourself on your sheet of paper.

8

THE DOLPHIN'S "AUTOCATALYTIC" WORLD: CAN WE SHIFT IN TIME?

*N*o, John Locke, fine thinker that you were, you called this one wrong: The human brain isn't a *tabula rasa*—a "blank slate." Unprecedented experiments such as those conducted in the 1950s and 1960s by Dr. Stanislav Grof, the Czech-born psychiatrist who legally used psychedelics like LDS-25 to help his clients probe "the historical content of the DNA," make us wonder: Just exactly what kind of information *is* stored in the brain tissue of a newborn? (Remembering chaos theory, it now appears likely that DNA is "fractally" encoded and may even contain archetypal kinds of templates acting as the "strange attractors" that help shape values and beliefs.)

At this point we know of no commanding evidence to challenge the idea that every healthy human brain is born a potential dolphin. That brain must be nourished well and have access to a stimulating environment and, from some source, modeling for tomorrow. But it can be argued—we'll argue it—that even those persons with substantially less than genius-level intelligence have a shot at dolphinhood. Our point is this: You can take an infant from the Yi and raise it lovingly and intelligently in the "First World," and the potential is there to grow to adulthood

Were we gifted with the vision of the whole Universe of life, we would not see it as a desert sparsely populated with identical plants which can survive only in rare specialized niches. Instead, we would envision something closer to a botanical garden, with countless species, each thriving in its own setting. GERALD FEINBERG AND ROBERT SHAPIRO, *LIFE BEYOND EARTH*

234

a brain capable of dealing fluidly with novelty *and* structure. That's the good news.

For the discerning leader in business and other kinds of organizations a more sobering thought is the realization that developments in technology have swiftly outstripped the brain's ability to keep pace. Epic waves of change, such as the Information Wave, ride in on the flood tides of laboratory discoveries and R&D innovations, and we suddenly see that the evolution of our technology has advanced beyond the evolution of our ability to cope.

It is a case of the few affecting the many. A relatively few brains capable of handling challenges and issues of high complexity are creating a technological push that is altering and changing the world for us all.

In one sense, we can say that this has been going on for six thousand years—beginning with the accelerating maturation of human consciousness. But it is more accurately a distinct phenomenon of the second millennium after Christ, and in particular a twentieth-century phenomenon. You might say that the human race has run a dare, if a largely unpremeditated or unconscious one, and to now has managed to escape most of the elemental consequences. What we have pulled off thus far is a protacted period in which mind and the environment have coevolved. It has been a bootstrap affair. A little progress technologically, a little progress in the mind's ability to handle complexity. A breakthrough in communicating learning, a breakthrough to a new level of thinking about thinking. There has been less time each time for large numbers of humans to prepare collectively to handle the new worldview and its new capabilities—but to now *enough* time.

Suddenly a very different set of possibilities confronts today's leader and manager, and it is a set for which the worldviews of the carp, the shark, and the pseudo-enlightened carp are ill-equipped. The evidence, we'd argue, is already pervasive. A situation very

We live in terror because persuasion is no longer possible ... because [man] can no longer tap that part of his nature, as real as the historical part, which he recaptures in contemplating the beauty of nature and of human faces. ... We suffocate among people who think they are absolutely right, whether in their machines or their ideas. And for all those who can live only in an atmosphere of human dialogue ... this silence is the end of the world. ALBERT CAMUS, *NEITHER VICTIMS NOR EXECUTIONERS*

Today's business environment is experiencing frantic searches for a safe niche.

similar to that depicted in Figure 8.1 now appears to be unfolding
before our startled eyes, one that threatens to leave billions in an
exploding population entrapped in dysfunctional societies and
organizations. Already, in reaction, today's business environment
is a frantic scene as players search for a safe niche, one where
there is some functional, defensible link between mastery and
challenge, between proficiency and what is required to survive.
Can we not see the instructive irony when in the space of half a
decade management's favorite guru, Tom Peters, goes from a
search for excellence to thriving on chaos? He's partly right. The
chaos we have. The excellence in management has largely eluded
us. . . .

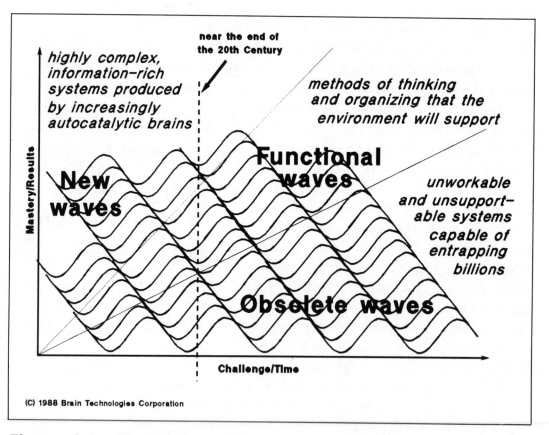

Figure. 8.1.   The Global Consequences of Accelerating Change

A s its name implies, Cummins Engine Company of Co-
lumbus, Indiana, builds engines—diesels. More than
most corporations, Cummins has also taken great pride
over the years in building character: in its managers and employees, in its home community, in the business culture at large. When
modelers of how corporate America "ought to be" went looking
for prototypes of socially responsible and enlightened companies,
they nearly always included Cummins Engine.

Customarily, the company has also been considered to be well
managed. Monitoring markets that thrust its engines into all
corners of the globe, Cummins usually could
be counted on to respond—once again— *No major break-*
reliably and responsibly. In 1984, for example, *through in manage-*
the company's forecasts projected sluggish
demand for truck engines, and Cummins acted *ment has occurred*
quickly, cutting costs, slashing inventories,
and closing one engine components plant—in *yet.*
Walesboro, Indiana—altogether.

Within three months, however, it was obvious that Cummins'
call on the market had been wrong. Whereas the company's
internal forecasts had projected production of only two hundred
engines per day in early 1987, production lines were turning out
three hundred. Demand accelerated even more, and the situation
grew worse. Finally convinced that they were looking at a boom
of some duration, Cummins executives began summoning laid-off
workers. Ironically, as these workers entered the plant, they often
met Cummins' most highly skilled employees leaving for the final
time, having responded to the company's early retirement plan.

T he company's once-praised "just in time" inventory
system created major problems. With the dollar dropping,
Cummins once again looked to domestic suppliers—up to
20 percent of its components were being produced offshore—but
the company's overseas purchases and conservative inventory

policies in the early 1980s had caused a surge of plant closings and consolidation among domestic components manufacturers. Domestic suppliers needed time to gear up, and burned before, they weren't about to overstaff and overinvest recklessly. One Michigan foundry operator told *The Wall Street Journal* he was unlikely to expand rapidly, at least anytime soon. But what if Cummins needed the parts? It would have to look offshore, where the value of the dollar was now less than half of what it had been just a few months earlier.

*T*he lessons at Cummins, one of the best, are amplified when we look at the thousands of companies and other organizations whose abilities to manage effectively in a swiftly changing world are only so-so. At the moment, the most realistic assessment is that the "cream" of the major players—the Hewlett-Packards, the 3Ms, the IBMs—deploy breakthrough strategies such as the strategy of the dolphin only sporadically, in small pockets of dolphin thinking. While the organizational mind has found ways to break through repeatedly in such technical areas as communications, data processing, components fabrication, computer-aided design, robotics, and even marketing levels, as yet *it has made no such widescale breakthrough in management*! Not in commercial organizations, not in political organizations, not in governmental organizations, not in any organization of substantial size. There as yet has been no widely shared and implemented embrace as an "organizational paradigm" of the notion of human thinking capabilities leading to frequent breakthrough solutions, to genuinely elegant use of resources, to a sustainable philosophy of global abundance, and to the persistent and sustainable use of power intelligently and humanely. And so the evidence of humankind's severest limitation—its hard-wired stupidity and inability to learn—is accumulating as fast as ever.

Consider these examples, available to anyone who pays any attention to current events:

- Western Europe lacks enough runways, airports, airspace, or air-traffic controllers to handle existing aviation demand, and traffic is expanding at about 10 percent annually. Yet little is being done to increase capacity.

- According to research at the Medical College of Wisconsin, women who smoke are at greater risk for gynecological abnormalities, such as early menopause, and are more likely to have facial hair—not to mention lung cancer—than women who do not. Yet teenage girls are the tobacco companies' biggest growth market. Eighteen percent of college women smoke daily compared to 10 percent of college men.

- In the immediate days after the stock market's Black Monday in October 1987, congressional staffers for committees such as the House Energy and Commerce Committee were prepared for an overhaul of the financial markets resembling those of the 1930s. But when their phones didn't ring and their mailboxes stayed empty, they knew little would be done. Talk of dealing with inadequacies in the market's mechanisms quickly faded.

- Long after the Rural Electrification Administration has completed its New Deal-assigned task of bringing electricity to the countryside, this powerful lobby continues to drain tens of millions from the federal treasury annually by loaning the taxpayers' money to its co-op members at 2 percent and 5 percent. Thus far, the REA has provided its co-op members with *$51 billion* to electrify virtually every square inch of nonurban America. Not even Ronald Reagan at his most popular moment could persuade Congress to touch this sacrosanct anachronism.

- The white beluga whales in the St. Lawrence River numbered around five thousand at the turn of the century. Today they number about 450. They are dying of blood poisoning, bronchial pneumonia, hepatitis, perforated gastric ulcers, pulmonary abscesses, and bladder cancer. Researchers have identified very high levels of more than thirty hazardous chemicals in the river, including DDT, polychlorinated biphenyls, the pesticide Mirex, metals such as mercury and cadmium, and polycyclic aromatic hydrocarbons similar to those found in cigarettes.

- The Mexican Association of Studies for the Defense of the Consumer estimates that as many as 90 percent of the country's tortilla shops—and Mexico City alone has about fifty-five thousand—shortchange their customers, giving them fewer tortillas than they pay for. A study of packaged snack cookies and crackers showed that they consistently weighed one half the amount listed on the label. The association's director, Arturo Lomeli, says Mexicans are so used to being cheated, they don't complain much.

- Major corporations have so inefficiently overloaded their computer software programs that corporate programmers are spending about 80 percent of their time doing patchwork. "A maintenance nightmare" is what one accounting executive called programs that over a ten- or twenty-year period have become so unwieldy that by the time a programmer identifies a glitch, she may be able to write only five or ten lines of computer code a day.

- Washington foreign policy luminaries issue a study assembled by the auspicious-sounding Commission on Integrated Long-term Strategy that calls for spending billions on high-tech "smart weapons." At about the same time, Yale professor Paul Kennedy writes in *The Rise and Fall of the Great Powers* that the United States is already in decline because, like great nations and empires previously, it is mindlessly spending itself into bankruptcy trying to defend its world position with things like high-tech "smart weapons."

- When they travel outside the Soviet Union, the country's economists gather all the information they can in places such as Vienna, Bonn, and London, since outsiders usually know more about the Soviet's "big picture" than insiders do. For years, the Soviets have padded their economic progress by disguising inflation as growth. Even the Soviets are beginning to admit to this kind of mismanagement: producing twice as much steel as the United States but leaving much of it to rust in warehouses; producing 4.5 times as many tractors as the United States but since the country has less tillable land, selling the machines to collective farms that don't need them; producing 3.2 pairs of shoes per citizen annually, many of which remain unsold because of their poor quality.

- International bankers continue to sweat out the outcome of the global debt crisis, which is intensifying. The World Bank estimates that the external debts of developing countries will rise to $1.25 trillion during 1988, up from $1.12 trillion in 1986. The bankers who made these often questionable loans are seeking to shift as much of the responsibility as they can to governments and their taxpayers.

- Africa is experiencing an outbreak of cults. In Guinea-Bissau, on the Atlantic coast, the Yank Yank (for ''Shadow of God'') cult has swayed tens of thousands of young women to abandon their husbands and all but their breast-feeding children and withdraw to forests and mangrove swamps. There they often chew roots and leaves, falling into trances.

Extraordinary, isn't it? That in a world capable of heart transplants, the Voyager explorations of space, the personal computer, the American supermarket, computerized tomography "CAT" scanners for picturing the living brain, the laser printer, and technology capable of finding the *Titanic,* we confront such a burlesque of the human enterprise so universally and so maddeningly predictable. Most students of human behavior have pointedly ignored the study of *anti*-intelligence, but not all. Dr. James F. Welles writes in his devastatingly targeted *Understanding Stupiddity: An Analysis of the Premaladaptive Beliefs and Behavior of Institutions and Organizations:*

While much is made of the human brain's ability to associate various cognitions (ideas) in meaningful and relevant cause/effect relationships, the amount of stupidity in the world suggests that the brain might also prevent or inhibit such functional associations while it promotes irrelevant connections.

[The] current emphasis on brainpower rather than brawn irrevocably led to the decline and fall of the management era. Industrial Age corporate practices, geared to the manufacture of physical products, are glaringly ill equipped to promote creativity in the more rarefied realm of intangible ideas. It is institutionalized innovation that distinguishes companies that excel from those that stagnate or merely muddle through. Gold-collar managers must be aware that producing, processing, packaging, and delivering knowledge requires a drastically different approach. They must accept the often unpalatable fact that the old rules, and the logic that engendered them, inevitably cripple the prospects for Information Age success.   ROBERT E. KELLEY, *THE GOLD-COLLAR WORKER*

The child's brain begins by treating all possibilities as being equally probable. Learning couples certain stimuli with certain reactions. No Behaviorist's model of functional rewards, however, could possibly account for the diversity of the world's religions nor the battle that science has waged against both ignorance and agnosticism.

In this cognitive context, it appears that stupidity is a very normal way for the human mind to deal directly with information coming from the physical environment and rewards from the social environment. This is basically a schizophrenic reaction which permits us to cope with distinct but interacting features of the human condition. For each of us, the invention and development of our special strategies are functions of an emotional commitment to a particular life style defined by our culture and shaped by our experiences.[1]

Against such a backdrop, it makes sense to ask what is perhaps the central question for all humanity as the twentieth century closes: Can our experiences shape enough of us in time to avoid a truly painful epoch on the planet, one this time affecting billions, not millions? It is a question that really should be on the minds of serious business leaders because it is a question pivotal to their understanding of how best to plan for even the moderately short term.

Some critics—we call them "eschatologists of the third kind" as opposed to "futurists"—have proposed that we slow things down as a way of keeping up. Through a tunnel narrowly, it is an idea with seeming commonsensical appeal. Why rush into the future if you aren't ready? The answer is that lifting our foot off the accelerator is a choice no longer available. It probably hasn't been since the 1960s. This was the decade that truly spawned the worldview of the pseudo-enlightened carp. The idea of establishing a spiritual utopia—the idea, as Timothy Leary couched it, of "tuning in, turning on, and dropping out"—was one of the more bizarre reactions to this awesome fact: For the first time in human history, it was possible for the human race to say, "I believe in potential scarcity *and* in potential abundance." Prior to that, it was a sane thing to say only, as most of the world still does, "I believe in scarcity." Today, thanks to our technological push, the planet has the capacity to feed all its denizens, and house them, and offer a relatively decent life. The ideal falls much short, of course. But *now* it is possible; before, it wasn't.

In about 1965, humans for the first time could believe intelligently in both abundance and scarcity.

A hungry Chesapeake Bay blue crab is lured by a chunk of dead fish into a trap that ultimately results in its being boiled alive. The promise of glorious growth lures itchy investors and managers into equally lethal traps. Is there any intrinsic difference between a hungry crab and an overreaching human being? There ought to be, for unlike crabs, human beings supposedly are able to learn from history. Yet in spite of what should be a decisive advantage, millions of supposedly sophisticated people crawl crablike into growth traps every year. P. T. Barnum was wrong. A rate of one sucker born every minute wouldn't even come close to maintaining the current population of suckerdom.   G. RAY FUNK-HOUSER AND ROBERT R. ROTHBERG, *THE PURSUIT OF GROWTH*

Buckminster Fuller said the turning point arrived about 1965. That seems as good a date as any. We would suggest that since the mid-1960s, the "brain of the culture" has been largely unconsciously self-directing its own changes. We can't turn back the clock or slow down the rate of advance because, as is nearly always the case with open systems, the advance has taken on a life of its own. To use one of our favorite words, the process of change has become autocatalytic. It is reproducing itself. The waves are coming faster now, and with the arrival of each, the "fractal technologies" of mind identified by the late Clare Graves and others imply that the brain must synthesize and shift into at least two major new worldviews. You'll remember that in Chapter 4, we tied the emergence of the Involver and Choice-Seeker worldviews to the appearance of the Information Wave. In Chapter 2 it was observed that Wave 4 seems to be taking shape rapidly and that the patterns of acceleration we are seeing lead to the suspicion that still other, as yet unmeasured and undefined waves lie just over the horizon.

If so, then we humans, whether businesspeople, politicians, academicians, or whomever, are living in a time when our technological push is shoving us toward a hyperacceleration point in the generation of change. And our brains, plainly stated, aren't keeping up with the pace. What is a dolphin, and everyone else, to expect, and what is a dolphin to do?

Pondering our studies of dolphin thinking, we can point to these ideas as central to how a dolphin's brain views the changes needed, particularly in organizations and in cultures/societies usually considered advanced at a time when change is accelerating and the outcome is far from clear:

Creativity must be pursued for the purpose of "eating entropy."

In the winter, at Woods Hole, the sea gulls are my main company. These gulls, the "herring gulls," have a red patch on their beaks. This red patch has an important meaning, for the gull feeds its babies by going out fishing and swallowing the fish it has caught. Then, on coming home, the hungry baby gulls knock at the red spot. This elicits a reflex of regurgitation in Mama, and the baby takes the fish from her gullet. All this may sound very simple, but it involves a whole series of most complicated chain reactions with a horribly complex underlying nervous mechanism. How could such a system develop? The red spot would make no sense without the complex nervous mechanism of the knocking baby and that of the regurgitating mother. All this had to be developed simultaneously, which, as a random mutation, has a probability of zero. I amunable to approach this problem without supposing an innate "drive" in living matter to perfect itself. ALBERT SZENT-GYOERGYI

Entropy—the loss of animation—results from stupidity. (Remember that we are using "stupidity" in a very precise, even technical way. We define it as the inability of the brain or any other part of nature to accept useful information, learn from it, and act intelligently on it.)

In "strategy of the dolphin" terms, stupidity *always* evolves eventually into a lose/lose outcome. Therefore, entropy and stupidity are barriers to the emergence of the critical life force that "drives" every worthwhile enterprise and whose measure determines its destiny, its chances for survival.

Because of their mental flexibility and emotional "trans*stability*," dolphins enable the organization to "eat entropy" by being creative. Unlike sharks, dolphins don't think up new things for the purpose of "solving problems" as much as they think up new ways to eliminate entropy.

Though it may seem like a thin difference, it really is a crucial one. Solving problems as opposed to eating entropy is the difference between a Newtonian view and a quantum view. It is the difference between a Band-Aid and a cure. It's the distinction between an occasional brainstorming session or a frantic find-the-answer "fire drill" and a state of mind that is geared to constant vigilance at cutting edges.

Archimedes shouted "Eureka!" in the bathtub not because things suddenly fell into place but because some undesirable things suddenly fell *away*. The entropy that was retarding his purpose was unexpectedly "eaten," and an expanded measure of this powerful life force we are addressing rushed into his awareness. Such an occurrence is exhilarating. It is empowering. It buys us time. And it widens our horizons, enabling us to process at a higher level of complexity.

Entropy retards the emergence of an organization's life force.

There are more things in heaven and earth, Horatio, than are dreamt of in your philosophy.
SHAKESPEARE

The process of creativity can be befuddling to a carp or a shark. Looking at the creation of a new wave, they often can see only an impediment. As we saw in Chapter 6, the perturbative, or wave-creating process, takes time. It nearly always creates lag. The deadly mistake often made by carps and sharks is viewing lag as just more entropy, more waste, more delay.

Valuable, oh, so very valuable, is the leader, manager, or employee who can distinguish between a *syntropic* event and an entropic one.

It's time to challenge organizational stupidity—the failure to learn from our organizational mistakes.

Within large organizations, there is too often a tendency to rescue or hide failing business units rather than reform or disband them, and organizational stupidity is the result. There is no learning. And often the mistake is repeated. The pockets of failure in the organization keep failing—that is, keep doing more of the same harder. It's a tragedy all around, since the participants can never win, and the entropic factor for the overall entity keeps going up. Meanwhile, the organization gets farther and farther "off purpose" (which is why delayed learning experiences are so painful; the more you are "off purpose," or off track, the greater the distress caused by the "long road back" to viability).

Dolphins pounce on a failure as a potential gateway to breakthrough.

Managers who are mucking up need to be told, "Hey, fella, this isn't cutting it. We're going to give you time to figure out what's wrong, and we'll give you all the resources, support, and guidance you need to get things fixed. And if that doesn't do it, you're out of here."

Dolphins pounce on a failure as having the potential for breakthrough, whereas carps grovel in it, sharks play games with it or deny it, and pseudo-enlightened carps just accept it as an illusion and never learn from it.

Let's be willing to stand the pain it takes to break up our illusions.

Each age is characterized by its own astronomical myriads of new, special-case experiences and problems to be stored in freshly born optimum capacity human brains— which storages in turn may disclose to human minds the presence of heretofore undiscovered, unsuspectedly existent eternal generalized principles. BUCKMINSTER FULLER

We once heard of a therapist who thought it was easy to write quality poetry.

He asked a client who was a writer to critique *his* writing.

As kindly as he could, the client told him the truth. His poetry had a long way to go.

His reaction was an angry one. In fact, he exploded at the patient's audacity in speaking frankly of the problems in his efforts. He learned nothing. He kept his illusions.

In today's management culture, we are beset with illusions. And we tend to keep them because we don't do a very good job of assessing where we are compared to where we want to be. In the American management culture particularly, we don't introspect well. We fail to take a good look at ourselves and identify what is happening and what needs to happen. Thus we create illusions about our results and performance that keep us from doing something different.

Dolphins can self-correct because they are introspecting constantly. They are good self-navigators. You might say that there is one box in their minds that tells them where they are and another box that tells them where they are headed. A third—and a critical—box corrects for the difference. Where carps, sharks, and pseudo-enlightened carps get into trouble is by snipping the wires among the three boxes. As Figure 8.2 illustrates, carps cut the connections among all three boxes and thus have little sense at any given time of their status, needs, or condition; they don't know where they are or where they are going, and they have destroyed their power to correct. Sharks can create a short-term vision and are willing to take action but tend to eliminate the box that tells them where they are. PECs usually disconnect the box for correction and often the box tells them where they are. They have a glowing, global, humanitarian vision, but they lack the ability to know where they are and how to correct if they are off course.

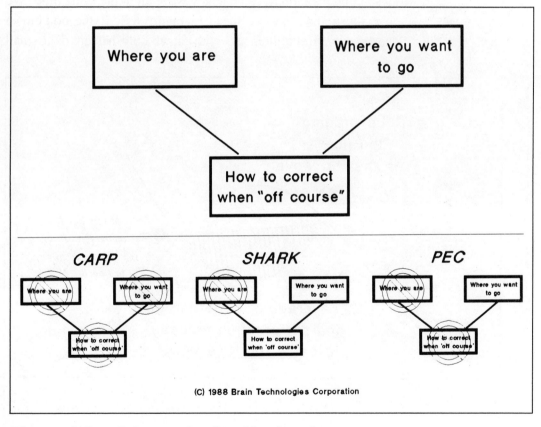

Figure 8.2. Schematics for Navigating

We need to learn to leverage the wave twice.

The wave, of course, is our bell-curve-shaped path along which any effort or enterprise powers itself within the limits imposed by the correctness of its course, the balance between its levels of challenge and mastery, and the degree to which its appropriation of life force is being dispelled by entropy.

One important way that dolphins often leverage the wave is by avoiding an "all or nothing" outlook.

If handled adroitly, the cost of doing something different can be "averaged" by both continuing to utilize the flow and cutting loose in preparation to catch a new wave all at the same time. We have illustrated what we mean in Figure 8.3. If the dolphin in question is an entrepreneur, with either only herself or a small

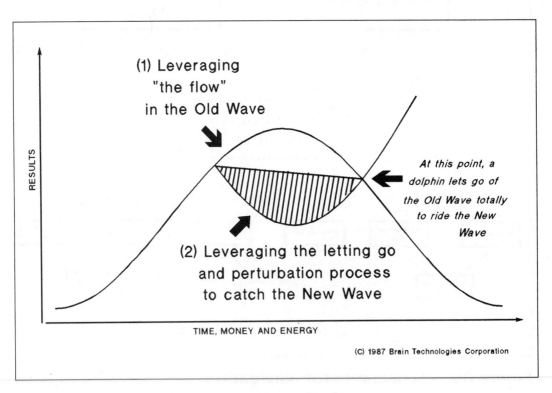

Figure 8.3. Leveraging the Wave Twice

number of employees, she may handle this process almost completely within her own head.

At one moment she is bypassing a lot of the risk and drama of lag—of preparing to do something different—by continuing to market her old products and services to her traditional markets in her traditional manner. At the same time, she minimizes emotional pain by channeling support and resources and providing an understanding of the process to those making the change. Yet, since the wave is still empowered, she is also continuing to benefit from "the flow."

However, at the next moment she may be deeply involved in the task of phasing out of the old wave and phasing in the new. Here she encounters the emotional drama and costs of lag, but because she has in effect leveraged the wave twice, she has cut her costs in half.

Our dolphin thinker also enhances her performance on the wave by abstaining from a common misunderstanding of the way things change.

Characteristically, the shark thinker assumes that "changing just before the times" is the only lag to be avoided. Figure 8.4 demonstrates differently, however. Interestingly enough, even "changing with the times" creates more lag than "changing just before the times." In fact, in "changing with the times," you will experience several magnitudes' more lag than if you change just ahead of the times. Nor is "changing way ahead of the times" any improvement. Changing too soon is usually a shoo-in guarantee that you'll enjoy virtually no gain in results. (Ask Leonardo da Vinci, whose futuristic drawings of such objects as helicopters were *five hundred years* ahead of the times.)

Changing just before the times is usually optimal.

The next major breakthroughs must come in "brain technologies."

In these times of rapid change, nearly everyone is going to need to become an information worker. Perhaps an apt term for

If the only laws that you find are those which you have just finished observing, then you can never make any predictions. Of course, this means that science is uncertain—the moment that you make a proposition about a region of experience that you have not directly seen, then you must be uncertain. But we always must make statements about the regions that we have not seen, or the whole business is no use.

I can live with doubt and uncertainty. I think it's much more interesting to live not knowing than to have answers which might be wrong. RICHARD FEYNMAN

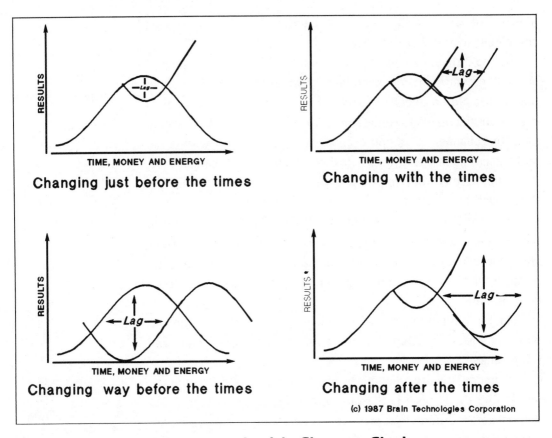

Figure 8.4. **Lag Connected with Change Choices**

describing this is "higher-yet technology." As our colleague Ken Adams has reminded us, "High technology is like money at a poker game. It will get you into the game, but it doesn't mean you'll win."

We also like the thrust of Robert E. Kelley's assessments in *The Gold-Collar Worker: Harnessing the Brainpower of the New Work Force:*

> Before long, organizations will confront two unsettling situations that signal the impending end of the management era. Gold-collar workers [comparable in part though not in whole to our dolphins], most of whom know their jobs better than their managers do, will compose the majority of the work force, and

a new generation of computers, whose artificial intelligence surpasses the natural intelligence of managers, will be widely available. Managers, as a result, either will become modern-day Luddites resisting the inroads of progress, or they will adapt to the new age by learning to use the smart people and smart machines over which they exert increasingly less control.[2]

If we disagree on any point with Kelley, it is that adapting won't be enough. The future in view holds the prospect of a time when only raw creation of wholly different ways for running businesses and organizations will suffice. The idea of people "plateauing"—getting trapped in a kind of inert career limbo—is really a myth. What has been classified as a plateau is actually a disintegration. Change occurs so rapidly today that the stage for plateauing has virtually disappeared. Either you are changing syntropically or entropically. You are growing or dying. You are getting results or you are slipping.

Endangered, too, is the opportunity for enjoying flow on a single-stage wave. Those waves of change are stacking up. No sooner have you grown comfortable with your level of mastery vis-à-vis the dynamics of one wave of change than here comes another. And another. And another. In the future, we are going to operate more and more *in flux* and less and less in flow until flux itself becomes a flow state.

At that point, rapid, global dissemination of change will likely create chaos on an unprecedented scale. Such an extraordinary development would prepare the entire planet for perturbation and represent a widescale opportunity for escaping to a higher order of processing and complexity. In anticipation of this possibility, dolphins will be increasingly attracted to our new insights into such a fascinating hodgepodge of fields as information theory, quantum physics, neurophysiology, and general systems theory to buttress their realization that "old brain" processing simply isn't adequate in the kind of advanced change environment that is emerging.

Because nature has already generated sufficient choice to offer

It follows that the more specialized society becomes, the less attention does it pay to the discoveries of the mind, which are intuitively beamed toward the brain, there to be received only if the switches are "on." Specialization tends to shut off the wide-band tuning searches and thus to preclude further discovery of the all-powerful generalized principles.   BUCKMINSTER FULLER, *SYNERGETICS*

us a "way out of the flybottle," it really isn't a dilemma, but it certainly involves a dichotomy. Controversial though it has been at times, The BrainMap® model of brain functioning developed by Brain Technologies Corporation and the studies on which it is based are proving exceedingly fertile and illuminative in understanding human limitations during rapid-change times.

What we now realize is that no matter whether the individual's, the organization's, or the culture's emphasis is skewed toward the carp hemisphere or the shark hemisphere, if the vital integrative powers of the frontal lobes are absent, the operational "envelope" for the mind in question stretches only so far.

If you remember your high school physics, you'll understand what we mean when we say that the brain has an inexplicable

Eventually flux itself will become a flow state.

"viscosity" problem. One side of the brain can be said to hold water; the other, oil. The two, of course, don't combine easily. Just how resistant the brain is to commingling them at all in certain of its processing configurations is demonstrated in Figure 8.5.

Individuals who score as I-PURSUERS on The BrainMap—in the lower left hemisphere—produce a strong "nowness" in accomplishing a task. Time and space may "go on" for the rest of us, looking on, but from the outside, these qualities appear suspended much of the time for I-PURSUERS. (One of our colleagues compares it to watching a cat stalk a bird.) In a word or two, the goal of I-PURSUERS is to "get it."

The "old brain" I-PRESERVE response in the carp hemisphere—the right brain—is "keeping it." Persons who test out and who live their lives out here fashion strong relationships and traditional modes of operation. (This is truly where you get plugged into doing more of the same harder.)

Our political, religious, business and educational institutions tend to perpetuate people having blinders on—the narrowing of minds rather than the broadening of them.
PAUL MACCREADY

As we activate more and more of the frontal lobe processing qualities, we alter somewhat the nature of the results in both hemispheres. Frontally in the shark hemisphere, we see I-CONTROL qualities materialize. For those of us showing a dominance in processing preferences there, the issue becomes,

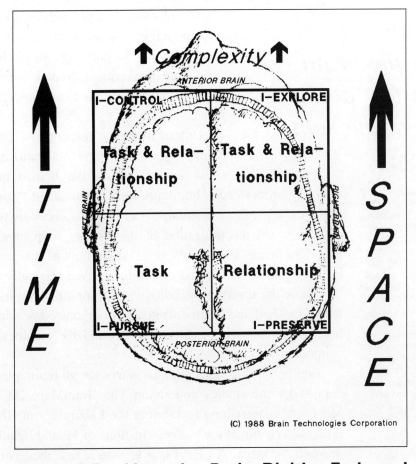

Figure 8.5. **How the Brain Divides Task and Relationship**

"What do I *do* with it?" And frontally in the carp hemisphere—
the I-EXPLORE tissue—the central processing question is, "Where do I go from here?" In both of these cases, there is mixing of task and relationship but with very different outcomes.

What emerged from our theoretical musings is a concept that contains the ability to expand our understanding of why carps and sharks resist the mixing of oil and water—task and relationship—in such unbridled fashion and thus set themselves up for such excruciating pain.

If the power of the frontal lobes is diminished, so is the mind's ability to stretch.

Typically, under stress the brain retreats to "doing more of the same harder."

You and I would never sit by and watch our own business enterprise slide into disaster. We would act. Even the slightest possibility that our company might fail within a few years would prompt us to reassess basic assumptions, discard potentially disastrous policies, and look for workable alternatives. As business people, we learn to understand that we benefit by recognizing a mistaken commitment and changing direction. Mistakes are forgivable. What is unforgivable—for countries as well as corporations—is continuing on a losing course, especially when that course could prove suicidal.   HAROLD WILLENS, *THE TRIMTAB FACTOR*

When change is rapid and doing something new and integrating the world at new levels of complexity are the prescriptions of choice, the brain *sans* the critical frontal lobe element appears *always* to retreat to a simpler, narrower focus.

Unless what we have on our hands is a dolphin generating and "actualizing" self-stress or exit stress, the human brain still typically shifts to back-brain modes as it retreats to "doing more of the same harder." In groups, if a crisis hits, there are two likely outcomes: (1) the utilization of the whole group mind, which generally results in synergy, or (2) the retreat of the group to its lowest common denominator. Painfully, even tragically at times, it is more the second possibility than the first that we most often witness. Then the neurochemicals of organized stupidity take over, producing the insanity of mobs and the inanities of "the commons."

Figure 8.6 illustrates that this is true for all brain quadrants as defined by the studies underlying The BrainMap: Dr. Paul D. MacLean's career-long research at the Laboratory of Brain Evolution and Health of the National Institute of Mental Health; Soviet neurophysiologist A. R. Luria's work; and the inquiries of Michael Gazzaniga, Jere Levy, Roger Sperry, and the other ever-increasing investigators of the "split brain" phenomenon.

The back up, or stress, modes for the I-PURSUE and I-PRESERVE systems now appear to be each other. There is no "forward" movement toward integration of task and relationship, toward the expansion of time and space.

For I-CONTROL and I-EXPLORE, the backup mode is downward to either I-PURSUE or I-PRESERVE.

In all cases, it is either/or. It is oil or water. It is either task or relationship.

Thus we arrive at one of the central insights of why dolphin-hood indicates such a momentous shift in the business and other forms of human consciousness. For the first time in a single brain,

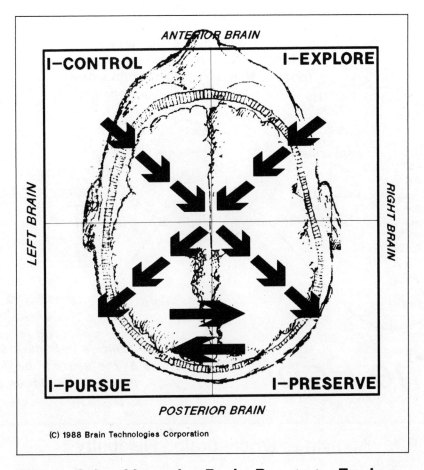

Figure 8.6.   How the Brain Reacts to Environmental Stress

we are integrating task *and* relationship under a future-focus vision of larger space-time, and the result is more than just an altered BrainMap profile. The result is an actual expansion of the space-time envelope in which the envelope in which the individual operates. So it isn't just Elliott Jaques' "time horizons" that are expanded in the dolphin. It is also the utilization of space.

Think, then, of an expanding space-time bubble occupied by a brain/mind capable of responding to the wave and to its position on the wave with increasing flexibility and functional selectivity. Such a concept is illustrated in Figure 8.7. For the "discovery"

Because everything we do and everything we are is in jeopardy, and because the peril is immediate and unremitting, every person is the right person to act and every moment is the right moment to begin, starting with the present moment. JONATHAN SCHELL, *THE FATE OF THE EARTH*

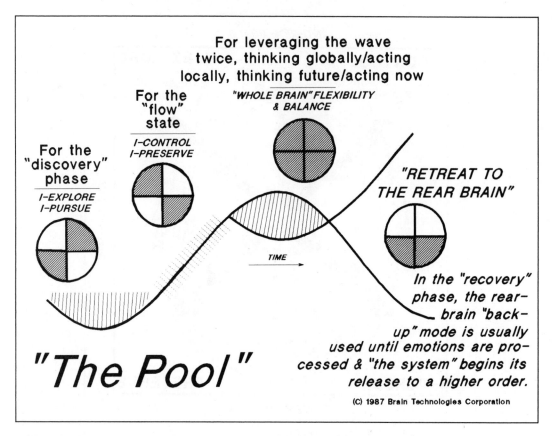

For leveraging the wave
twice, thinking globally/acting
locally, thinking future/acting now

"WHOLE BRAIN" FLEXIBILITY
& BALANCE

For the
"flow"
state

I-CONTROL
I-PRESERVE

For the
"discovery"
phase

I-EXPLORE
I-PURSUE

"RETREAT TO
THE REAR BRAIN"

TIME

In the "recovery"
phase, the rear-
brain "back-
up" mode is usually
used until emotions are pro-
cessed & "the system" begins its
release to a higher order.

"The Pool"

(C) 1987 Brain Technologies Corporation

Figure 8.7.   Applying "Whole Brain" Flexibility

phase—the initial start-up phase—of the wave, the brain's I-EXPLORE and I-PURSUE operating systems can provide the momentum and openness to variety and possibility needed to fuel the "git-go" process. Later, when you find yourself firmly and successfully ensconced in a productive new way of proceeding and producing, the calming winds of stability are to be preferred to the lusty gusts of experimentation, and for this "flow" state, the brain's I-CONTROL and I-PRESERVE operating systems are the modes of choice. Later even yet, when the time arrives to leverage the wave twice, the need arrives to function with "whole brain" flexibility and balance, moving from role to role, playing first one position and then another, changing hats and mental outlooks as rapidly and as frequently as a chameleon alters hues. Such cognitive virtuosity is simply not possible once the brain stumbles into the emotional quagmire of the "Recovery trough," where we frequently encounter the more manic qualities of the I-PURSUE system or the depressive qualities of I-PRESERVE.

An expanded space/time bubble will require increasing degrees of freedom, interconnections, and tolerance of instability of both the individual and the global brains. We can so assume because of the growing evidence that systems escaping to higher orders of complexity become more unstable, interconnected, and require greater degrees of freedom.

Thus as more and more of our people learn to learn, learn to relate, and learn to choose—as futurist Alvin Toffler so eloquently phrased it—a new kind of world becomes possible because a new kind of thinking has been actualized.

An integrated kind of thinking, all in the same brain.

A merger of task and relationship.

A whole brain kind of integration putting the front brain in concert with the back brain, the carp brain in league with the shark brain, the frontal left brain in cooperation with the lower right brain, and so forth. Not only, as Marshall McLuhan suggested, will we have to think globally and act locally, we must also think in the future and act now.

It is the quality of the brain's integration that is the key to dolphin thinking, and the key to achieving this synthesis is the forebrain. Again quoting Ken Adams: "The forebrain is the biocognitive mechanism for the living expression of relativity as it integrates space-time into a world-space."

*A*world-space. Will we make it? Will enough brains transform to dolphinhood and beyond swiftly enough to permit us to navigate an entire planet with reasonable safety through our accelerating waves of change? If at any time the symbiosis of brain and environment deployed thus far with at least as many pluses as minuses—if that collapses through the ultimate stupidity of nuclear war or some other hideously calamitous result, then regardless of the pseudo-enlightened carp's faith in a "happy trails" outcome, the entire species is capable of whistling right on past zero.

Barring that, however, we may find ourselves as possible participants in one of the universe's deliciously impersonal paradoxes. The current chaos and turmoil that our organizations and we, ourselves, as individuals confront may be just the cultural mind's way of perturbating itself. And the more mistakes we make, the faster it will happen.

All the more reason to begin to think more like a dolphin than like a shark or a carp, even a pseudo-enlightened one.

NOTES _____

INTRODUCTION

1. Anthony Rais, *Human Resource Planning,* Vol. 8, No. 4 (1985), pp. 201–7.

2. For this quote and several other ideas developed in this and other sections of this book, we are indebted to Dr. James F. Welles and *Understanding Stupiddity: An Analysis of the Premaladaptive Beliefs and Behavior of Institutions and Organizations* (Orient, N.Y.: Mount Pleasant Press, 1986).

Chapter 1

1. Stewart Emery, *Actualizations: You Don't Have to Rehearse to Be Yourself* (Garden City, N.Y.: Doubleday & Company, 1977), p. 66.

2. Anne Wilson Schaef and Diane Fassel, *The Addictive Organization* (New York: Harper & Row, 1988), pp. 75–76.

3. Emery, p. 70.

4. Douglas K. Ramsey, *The Corporate Warriors: Six Classic Cases in American Business* (Boston: Houghton Mifflin Company, 1987), p. xvii.

5. Robert Lawrence Kuhn, *Dealmaker: All the Negotiating Skills & Secrets You Need* (New York: John Wiley & Sons, 1988), p. 178.

6. Alfie Kohn, *No Contest: The Case Against Competition* (Boston: Houghton Mifflin Company, 1986), p. 190.

7. James P. Carse, *Finite and Infinite Games* (New York: The Free Press, 1986), p. 10.

8. Carse, p. 190.

9. Kohn, p. 67.

10. Robert Axelrod, *The Evolution of Cooperation* (New York: Basic Books, 1984), p. 100.

11. Martin Patchen, "Strategies for Eliciting Cooperation from an Adversary," *Journal of Conflict Resolution,* Vol. 31, No. 1 (1987), pp. 164–85.

12. The above three entries are the titles of Chapters 5–7 of Robert **259**

J. Ringer's *Winning Through Intimidation* (New York: Fawcett, 1976), table of contents.

13. Kohn in *No Contest: The Case Against Competition* develops arguments why each of the previous four points fails to deliver the benefits often attributed to them.

Chapter 2

1. Sherry Turkle, *The Second Self: Computers and the Human Spirit* (New York: Simon & Schuster, 1984), p. 87.

2. Jeremy Rifkin, *Time Wars: The Primary Conflict in Human History* (New York: Henry Holt and Company, 1987), p. 15.

3. See *The Tomorrow Makers: A Brave New World of Living Brain Machines* (New York: Macmillan Publishing Company, 1986) by Grant Fjermedal.

4. Stanley M. Davis, *Future Perfect* (Reading, Mass.: Addison-Wesley Publishing Company, 1987), p. 25.

5. Michael Hutchison, *Megabrain* (New York: William Morrow & Company, 1986), p. 85.

6. Hutchison, p. 67.

Chapter 3

1. George Ainsworth-Land, ''The Dynamics of Creative Process— Key to the Enigmas of Physics,'' *Journal of Creative Behavior*, Vol. 15, No. 4 (1981), p. 241.

2. James W. Botkin, Mahdi Elmandja, and Mircea Malitza, *No Limits to Learning* (Elmsford, N.Y.: Pergamon Press, 1979), p. 10.

3. Botkin, pp. 11–12.

4. Paul Watzlawick, John H. Weakland, and Richard Fisch, *Change: Principles of Problem Formation and Problem Resolution* (New York: W. W. Norton & Company, 1974), pp. 90–91.

5. Matthew McKay, Martha Davis, and Patrick Fanning, *Thoughts & Feelings: The Art of Cognitive Stress Intervention* (Richmond, Calif.: New Harbinger Publications, 1981), p. 184.

6. McKay, Davis, and Fanning, p. 198.

7. Watzlawick, Weakland, and Fisch, p. 95.

8. Jay Haley, ed., *Advanced Techniques of Hypnosis and Therapy: Selected Papers of Milton H. Erickson* (New York: Grune & Stratton, 1967), p. 131.

Chapter 4

1. John Sculley, *Odyssey* (New York: Harper & Row, 1987), pp. 79–81.

2. Dr. George Edgin Pugh, *The Biological Origin of Human Values* (New York: Basic Books, 1977), pp. 151–52.

3. Harold Willens, *The Trimtab Factor: How Business Executives Can Help Solve the Nuclear Weapons Crisis* (New York: William Morrow & Company, 1984), p. 27.

4. Jean Houston, *The Search for the Beloved* (Los Angeles: Jeremy P. Tarcher, 1987), p. 133.

Chapter 5

1. Elliott Jaques, "The Development of Intellectual Capability: A Discussion of Stratified Systems Theory," *The Journal of Applied Behavioral Science*, Vol. 22, No. 4 (1986), p. 364.

2. A. R. Luria, *The Human Brain and Psychological Processes* (New York: Harper & Row, 1966), p. 531.

3. David Loye, *The Sphinx and the Rainbow: Brain, Mind, and Future Vision* (Boulder, Colo.: Shambhala, 1983), p. 58.

4. Jaques (ed.), *Levels of Abstraction in Logic and Human Action* (London: Heinemann, 1978), pp. 258–61.

5. Quoted by Lawrence LeShan, *The Medium, the Mystic, and the Physicist* (New York: Viking, 1974), p. 69.

6. Jaques, *Levels of Abstraction in Logic and Human Action*, p. 14.

7. Jaques, *Levels of Abstraction in Logic and Human Action*, pp. 253–61.

Chapter 6

1. Fjermedal, p. 201.

2. James Gleick, *Chaos: Making a New Science* (New York: Viking, 1987), p. 174.

3. This concept was developed by Marshall Thurber.

4. Carse, p. 18.

5. The idea for this term and the others similar to it that appear in Figure 6.7 was prompted by a drawing in *The Emotional Cycles of Change* (Atlanta: Recourses, Inc.).

6. The content of this graphic is based on an idea from Ken Wilber.

Chapter 8

1. Welles, p. 5.

2. Robert E. Kelley, *The Gold-Collar Worker* (Reading, Mass.: Addison-Wesley Publishing Company, 1985), pp. 182–83.

A DOLPHIN'S LIBRARY: SUGGESTED READINGS

Axelrod, Robert. *The Evolution of Cooperation*. New York: Basic Books, 1984.

A fine study of how cooperation evolves when communication is limited.

Barrow, John D., and Frank J. Tipler. *The Anthropic Cosmological Principle*. New York: Oxford University Press, 1986.

Articulates in weighty detail—including the mathematics and the physics—major teleological possibilities on the direction and meaning of the universe, humanity's place in it, and our role as information-gatherers.

Beattie, Melody. *Codependent No More*. New York: Harper & Row, 1987.

Offers a competent summary of the many, varied, codependent behaviors that are characteristic of most carps operating in addictive systems. Unfortunately, its solutions are still essentially carp solutions, since its author takes an Alcoholics Anonymous-like approach and reinforces in so many words the carp belief that a codependent is a victim in need of lifelong healing.

Botkin, James W., Mahdi Elmandjra, and Mircea Malitza. *No Limits to Learning: Bridging the Human Gap*. Elmsford, N.Y.: Pergamon Press, 1979.

Although some of the trends predicted in this report to the Club of Rome never materialized, *No Limits to Learning* builds a strong case for the value of lifelong learning.

Capra, Fritjof. *The Turning Point: Science, Society, and the Rising Culture*. New York: Simon & Schuster, 1982.

A brief overview of historical and cultural evolution with a pointed discussion of current problems and future waves and needs by this physicist-turned-philosopher.

Carse, James P. *Finite and Infinite Games.* New York: The Free Press, 1986.
Stresses in succinctly readable fashion the need for staying open to surprise by living flexibly.

Davis, Stanley M. *Future Perfect.* Reading, Mass.: Addison-Wesley Publishing Company, 1987.
A comfortable "read" for managers who are open to its message: In rapid-change times, you need to spend quality time creating your "perfect future" and focusing the effort needed to pull your "present" into it.

Dixon, Douglas. *After Man: A Zoology of the Future.* New York: St. Martin's Press, 1981.
A fascinating and imaginative hypothesis on the character of the evolution of life with humanity removed from the scene.

Emery, Stewart. *Actualizations: You Don't Have to Rehearse to Be Yourself.* Garden City, N.Y.: Doubleday & Company, 1977.
Puts the carp belief systems in a relentless spotlight and stresses the need for personal responsibility and correcting course.

Foster, Richard N. *Innovation: The Attacher's Advantage.* New York: Summit Books, 1986.
One crisp argument after another and one pithy example after another offering testimony to the value of changing before the times.

Frankl, Victor. *Man's Search for Meaning.* Boston: Beacon, 1962.
A classic by a survivor of the Holocaust who argues eloquently for knowing why you value being alive.

Fuller, R. Buckminster. *Synergetics: Explorations in the Geometry of Thinking.* New York: Collier Books, 1982.
A comprehensive view as only Bucky could envision and describe it of how nature uses synergy to do more with less.

Garfield, Charles. *Peak Performers: The New Heroes of American Business.* New York: William Morrow & Company, 1986.

Although overgeneralized, a good representation of the need to be "present"-centered with a balance of challenge and mastery when you are "in the flow."

Gleick, James. *Chaos: Making a New Science.* New York: Viking, 1988.

One of those superb postmodern works in which science writing approaches the threshold of classical literature. Traces the emerging science of chaos, looking first at the fundamental discoveries and the leading discoverers before moving on to the global implications of this startling new way of viewing reality.

Graves, Clare W. *The Graves Technology.* Denton, Tex.: National Values Center, 1988.

A collection of articles and transcripts of lectures by or about the creator of the fractal-like, scaling-oriented Graves "biopsychosocial" theory of human values and beliefs.

Hutchison, Michael. *Megabrain: New Tools and Techniques for Brain Growth and Mind Expansion.* New York: Beech Tree Books, 1986.

One of the first works to deal imaginatively with the implications of Nobel Prize-winner Ilya Prigogine's theory of dissipative structures for the human brain.

James, Muriel, and Dorothy Jongeward. *Born to Win.* New York: New American Library, 1971.

An "oldie but goodie" that offers a wonderful education in the Drama Triangle and the games that go with it.

Jaques, Elliott (ed.), with R. O. Gibson and D. J. Isaac. *Levels of Abstraction in Logic and Human Action.* London: Heinemann, 1978.

A mostly technical work that marries the research of Gibson and Isaac into discontinuity in psychological development with Jacques' studies of levels of abstraction in mental activity and bureaucratic stratification but one that contributes convincingly to the idea that changing society and the organization requires a change in the brain.

Kelley, Robert E. *The Gold-Collar Worker: Harnessing the Brainpower of the New Work Force.* Reading, Mass.: Addison-Wesley Publishing Company, 1985.

Like dolphins, Kelley's gold-collar workers are formidable in their insistence on resources, flexibility, meaningful work, and self-management.

Kohn, Alfie. *No Contest: The Case Against Competition*. Boston: Houghton Mifflin Company, 1986.
A well-researched, well-documented, and comprehensive argument that competition demonstrates none of the positive characteristics typically put at its credit and thus is maladaptive behavior.

Kuhn, Robert Lawrence. *Dealmaker: All the Negotiating Skills and Secrets You Need*. New York: John Wiley & Sons, 1988.
A short course in shark behavior.

Kuhn, Thomas S. *The Structure of Scientific Revolutions*, 2nd ed. Chicago: University of Chicago Press, 1970.
A landmark book identifying the nature of paradigm shifts.

Land, George T. Ainsworth. *Grow or Die*. New York: John Wiley & Sons, 1986.
A reissue of Land's original work anticipating the wide-scale application of theories of ''punctuated evolution'' to the development of all systems, including societies and organizations.

Laszlo, Ervin. *Evolution: The Grand Synthesis*. Boston: New Science Library, Shambhala, 1987.
Narrates what happens as you ascend the growth curve.

Levy, Amir, and Uri Merry. *Organizational Transformation: Approaches, Strategies, Theories*. New York: Praeger, 1986.
An excellent overview of ''OD'' theory and approaches prior to the ''strategy of the dolphin.''

Loye, David. *The Sphinx and the Rainbow*. Boulder, Colo.: Shambhala, 1983.
Explores and documents the role of the forebrain in thinking about and receiving information from the future.

Lynch, Dudley. *Your High-Performance Business Brain: An Operator's Manual*. Englewood Cliffs, N.J.: Prentice-Hall, 1985.
A sashay through two decades of brain research with an eye out for findings useful to the players in business.

Mandelbrot, Benoit B. *The Fractal Geometry of Nature.* New York: W. H. Freeman & Company, 1977.

Sometimes maddeningly obscure, this pioneering work on fractals, their implications, and their applications still can engender feelings of awe as the creator of the fractal concept takes you on a tour of nature's often exquisite jagged edges.

Prigogine, Ilya, and Isabelle Stenders. *Order Out of Chaos: Man's New Dialogue with Nature.* New York: Bantam Books, 1984.

A foundation kind of book for an era in which the human brain and human systems are coming to be viewed more and more as the "kissing kin" of dissipative structures throughout nature.

Ringer, Robert J. *Winning Through Intimidation.* New York: Fawcett, 1976.

One of the first and the best guides to shark-infesting business waters—and how to survive them.

Schaef, Anne Wilson, and Diane Fassel. *The Addictive Organization.* San Francisco: Harper & Row, 1988.

These authors, while they fail to pioneer in suggesting solutions, do a praiseworthy job of identifying the addictive nature and characteristics of shark behavior in organizations.

Stableford, Brian, and David Langford. *The Third Millennium: A History of the World: A.D. 2000–3000.* New York: Alfred A. Knopf, 1985.

A fantasy of future history and cultural evolution that starts the wheels of the imagination churning.

Toffler, Alvin. *The Third Wave.* New York: William Morrow & Company, 1980.

The definitive work on the first two great waves of change.

Watzlawick, Paul, John H. Weakland, and Richard Fisch. *Change: Principles of Problem Formation and Problem Resolution.* New York: W. W. Norton & Company, 1974.

A primer on what to do when the solution becomes the problem. And the answer is . . . tap the power of paradox.

————. *The Situation Is Hopeless but Not Serious: The Pursuit of Unhappiness.* New York: W. W. Norton & Company, 1983.

A funny, informative, and powerful use of paradoxical thinking to show how dysfunctional belief systems create dysfunctional outcomes through dysfunctional behavior.

Welles, James F. *Understanding Stupiddity: An Analysis of the Premaladaptive Beliefs and Behavior of Institutions and Organizations.* Orient, N.Y.: Mount Pleasant Press, 1986.
''The compleat guide'' to stupidity in its current form.

Willens, Harold. *The Trimtab Factor: How Business Executives Can Help Solve the Nuclear Weapons Crisis.* New York: William Morrow & Company, 1984.
Charts in easy-to-follow fashion show the self-defeating consequences of doing more of the same harder.

Wolf, Fred Alan. *Star Wave: Mind, Consciousness, and Quantum Physics.* New York: Macmillan Publishing Company, 1984.
A good, mind-expanding look that leaves you all the more suspicious of the Newtonian paradigm's contentions on the subject of mind at the same time you are tending to shrug off Wolf's suggested replacements as intriguing but probably wide of the mark.

DOLPHIN LEARNING MATERIALS

The "dolphin" approach to management is more than just a strategy. It is also a learning and training technology accessible through the use of a number of cutting-edge educational and orientational tools developed by Brain Technologies Corporation.

A companion self- and group-study guide, *DolphinThink™: Mastering the Skills You Need to Get Tough, Get Free, Get Focused and Get Going as a New Kind of Winner,* has been created by the authors of *Strategy of the Dolphin®.* This publication provides exercises, individual and group activities, and additional illustrations and written content to help you develop dolphin thinking in you and your organization.

The *m*Circle® Instrument is often referred to as "the dolphin instrument" because the idea for this self-administered and self-interpreted instrument resulted in part from research into the abilities of dolphins to respond creatively to a changing environment.

The BrainMap®, mentioned in Chapters 7 and 8, and The Couples BrainMap® provide you with clues to what is in the slice of the world your brain has been conditioned to recognize and suggest numerous options for triggering new choices and opportunities. They also are self-scored and self-interpreted.

MindMaker6® is another learning instrument that helps you chart your values and beliefs using the Great Attractor-generated model outlined in Chapter 4.

Instructional guides and audiovisual aids (including 35mm slide sets, overhead transparencies, and scripts) to assist in using each of these instruments in team and other management and employee training sessions are also available.

For more information on these materials and on the seminar, consulting, and executive presentation services of the authors of *Strategy of the Dolphin,* call (303) 493-9210 or write Brain Technologies Corporation, 2290 East Prospect Road, Suite Two, Fort Collins, CO 80525.

INDEX

A

Accommodation stage, the, 220–222, 226

Achiever worldview, 119–120, 121, 127, 133

Actualizations: You Don't Have to Rehearse to Be Yourself, 24

Adams, Kenneth L., 8, 115, 257

Addictive Organization, The, 25

Agricultural wave, 72–73. *See also* Waves of change

Aiken, Conrad, 177

Alcoholics Anonymous, 135–136

Ambiguity, 148–150, 154–157

Amerada Hess Corp., 31

Anthony, Susan B., 135

Apartheid, 50

Apollo moon flight, 142

Ardrey, Robert, 96, 107

Aristotle, 141, 165

Armstrong, Neil, 142

Aronson, Elliot, 32

Ashby, W. Ross, 102

Assimilation stage, the, 225–227

Autocatalysis, 227, 243–244

Axelrod, Robert, 54–58

B

Bach, Richard, 93

Balkin, David, 168

Bannister Effect, the, 101

Barrow, John D., 180

Bateson, Gregory, 121

Beck, Don, 7, 126

Beluga whales, 239

Bentley, Richard, 123

Bergson, Henri, 116

Bernanos, Georges, 170

Bertalanffy, Ludwig von, 17

Beyond Boredom and Anxiety, 81

Bifurcation point, the, 82, 173–175. *See also* Perturbation

G

H